DATE DUE

			PRINTED IN U.S.A.

ISSN 1040-5682

K

Authors & Artists for Young Adults

VOLUME 34

GALE GROUP

Detroit
New York
San Francisco
London
Boston
Woodbridge, CT

Thomas McMahon, *Editor*

Alan Hedblad, *Managing Editor*
Susan Trosky, *Literature Content Coordinator*

Victoria B. Cariappa, *Research Manager*
Tracie A. Richarson, *Project Coordinator*
Andrew Guy Malonis, Gary J. Oudersluys, Cheryl L. Warnock, *Research Specialists*
Tamara C. Nott, *Research Associates*
Tim Lehnerer, *Research Assistants*

Maria Franklin, *Permissions Manager*
Edna Hedblad, *Permissions Specialist*
Sarah Chesney, *Permissions Associate*

Mary Beth Trimper, *Production Director*
Stacy L. Melson, *Buyer*

Randy Bassett, *Image Database Supervisor*
Michael Logusz, *Graphic Artist*
Robert Duncan, *Imaging Specialist*
Pamela A. Reed, *Imaging Coordinator*
Dean Dauphinais, Robyn V. Young, *Senior Image Editors*
Kelly A. Quin, *Image Editor*

The paper used in this publication meets the minimum requirements of
American National Standard for Information Sciences—Permanence Paper
for Printed Library Materials, ANSI Z39.48-1984.

Library of Congress Catalog Card Number 89-641100
ISBN 0-7876-3234-1
ISSN 1040-5682

10 9 8 7 6 5 4 3 2 1

Printed in the United States of America

Authors and Artists for Young Adults

TEEN BOARD ADVISORS

A number of teen reading boards were consulted to help determine series' content. The teen board advisors for this volume include:

Terry Christner
Children's librarian, and advisor for young adult programming and young adult board at the Hutchinson Public Library in Kansas

Joan Eisenberg
Children's librarian and advisor to the "Bookies" reading group at the Cambridge Public Library in Massachusetts

Francisco Goldsmith
Senior librarian for Teen Services, and advisor to "Feedback," a teen advisory group, at the Berkeley Public Library in California

Jesse Warren
Children's and young adult library assistant, and young adult advisory board director at the Boulder Public Library in Colorado

Contents

Introduction

Authors and Artists for Young Adults is a reference series designed to serve the needs of middle school, junior high, and high school students interested in creative artists. Originally inspired by the need to bridge the gap between Gale's *Something about the Author,* created for children, and *Contemporary Authors,* intended for older students and adults, *Authors and Artists for Young Adults* has been expanded to cover not only an international scope of authors, but also a wide variety of other artists.

Although the emphasis of the series remains on the writer for young adults, we recognize that these readers have diverse interests covering a wide range of reading levels. The series therefore contains not only those creative artists who are of high interest to young adults, including cartoonists, photographers, music composers, bestselling authors of adult novels, media directors, producers, and performers, but also literary and artistic figures studied in academic curricula, such as influential novelists, playwrights, poets, and painters. The goal of *Authors and Artists for Young Adults* is to present this great diversity of creative artists in a format that is entertaining, informative, and understandable to the young adult reader.

Entry Format

Each volume of *Authors and Artists for Young Adults* will furnish in-depth coverage of twenty to twenty-five authors and artists. The typical entry consists of:

—A detailed biographical section that includes date of birth, marriage, children, education, and addresses.

—A comprehensive bibliography or filmography including publishers, producers, and years.

—Adaptations into other media forms.

—Works in progress.

—A distinctive essay featuring comments on an artist's life, career, artistic intentions, world views, and controversies.

—References for further reading.

—Extensive illustrations, photographs, movie stills, cartoons, book covers, and other relevant visual material.

A cumulative index to featured authors and artists appears in each volume.

Compilation Methods

The editors of *Authors and Artists for Young Adults* make every effort to secure information directly from the authors and artists through personal correspondence and interviews. Sketches on living authors and artists are sent to the biographee for review prior to publication. Any sketches not personally reviewed by biographees or their representatives are marked with an asterisk (*).

Highlights of Forthcoming Volumes

Among the authors and artists planned for future volumes are:

Mitch Albom	William Joyce	Man Ray
Avi	Jonathan Kellerman	Diego Rivera
Martha Brooks	Tracy Kidder	Spider Robinson
Eileen Charbonneau	Norma Klein	Louis Sachar
Christopher Paul Curtis	Janet Lunn	Charles Schulz
Nora Ephron	Albert Marrin	William Shakespeare
Paul Fleischman	George R. R. Martin	William Sleator
Jack Gantos	Lurlene McDaniel	Todd Strasser
Adele Griffin	Hayao Miyazaki	John Updike
Rosa Guy	Gordon Parks	Andrew Lloyd Webber
Sonya Hartnett	Randy Powell	John Woo
Kimberly Willis Holt	Anna Quindlen	Paul Zindel

Contact the Editor

We encourage our readers to examine the entire *AAYA* series. Please write and tell us if we can make AAYA even more helpful to you. Give your comments and suggestions to the editor:

BY MAIL: The Editor, *Authors and Artists for Young Adults,* 27500 Drake Rd., Farmington Hills, MI 48331-3535.

BY TELEPHONE: (800) 347-GALE

Authors & Artists for Young Adults

Kevin J. Anderson

als Research Society, Pittsburgh, PA, columnist, 1988—; International Society for Respiratory Protection, Salem, OR, copy editor, 1989—. *Member:* Science Fiction Writers of America, Horror Writers of America.

■ Awards, Honors

Nominated for best small press writer, Small Press Writers and Artists Organization, 1984; Dale Donaldson Memorial Award for lifetime service to the small press field, 1987; Bram Stoker Award nomination for best first novel, Horror Writers of America, 1988 for *Resurrection, Inc.*; "Writers of the Future" honorable mention citations, Bridge Publications, 1985, 1988, and 1989; nominee for Nebula award for Best Science Fiction Novel for *Assemblers of Infinity*, 1993; Locus magazine award for best science-fiction paperback novel of 1995 for *Climbing Olympus*.

■ Personal

Born March 27, 1962, in Racine, WI, son of Andrew James (a banker) and Dorothy Arloah (a homemaker; maiden name, Cooper) Anderson; married Mary Franco Nijhuis, November 17, 1983 (divorced June, 1987); married Rebecca Moesta (a technical editor), September 14, 1991; children: Jonathan Macgregor Cowan (stepson). *Education:* University of Wisconsin—Madison, B.S. (with honors), 1982. *Hobbies and other interests:* Hiking, camping, reading, astronomy.

■ Addresses

Home—Livermore, CA. *Office*—c/o Bantam Books Inc. 1540 Broadway, New York, NY 10036-4039. *Agent*—Richard Curtis, 171 East 74th St., New York, NY 10021.

■ Writings

NOVELS WITH DOUG BEASON

Lifeline, Bantam, 1991.
The Trinity Paradox, Bantam, 1991.
Assemblers of Infinity, Bantam, 1993.
Ill Wind, Forge, 1995.
Virtual Destruction, Ace Books, 1996.
Ignition, Forge, 1997.
Fallout, Ace Books, 1997.

■ Career

Lawrence Livermore National Laboratory, Livermore, CA, technical writer/editor, 1983—; Materi-

Lethal Exposure, Ace Books, 1998.

NOVELS WITH KRISTINE KATHRYN RUSCH

Afterimage, Roc Books, 1992.
Afterimage/Aftershock, Meisha Merlin, 1998.

Also co-author of *Aftershock,* Roc Books.

THE "X-FILES" SERIES

Ground Zero, HarperPrism, 1995.
Ruins, HarperPrism, 1996.
Antibodies, HarperPrism, 1997.

SCIENCE FICTION

Resurrection, Inc., Signet, 1988, reprinted in a tenth
   anniversary limited edition, Overlook Connection
   Press, 1998.
Climbing Olympus, Warner, 1994.
Blindfold, Warner, 1995.
(Editor) *War of the Worlds: Global Dispatches* (anthol-
   ogy), Bantam, 1996.

"GAMEARTH" SERIES

Gamearth, Signet, 1989.
Gameplay, Signet, 1989.
Game's End, Roc Books, 1990.

FOR YOUNG ADULTS

(With John Gregory Betancourt) *Born of Elven Blood,*
   Atheneum, 1995.
Bounty Hunters, Bantam, 1996.

"STAR WARS" SERIES

Darksaber, Bantam, 1995.
(With Rebecca Moesta) *Delusions of Grandeur,* Boule-
   vard, 1997.
(With Moesta) *Diversity Alliance,* Boulevard, 1997.
Dark Lords, D.I. Fine, 1997.
(With Moesta) *Jedi Bounty,* Boulevard, 1997.

STAR WARS: "JEDI ACADEMY TRILOGY"

Jedi Search, Bantam, 1994.
Dark Apprentice, Bantam, 1994.
Champions of the Force, Bantam, 1994.
Jedi Academy Trilogy, (includes *Jedi Search, Dark
   Apprentice,* and *Champions of the Force,* published
   as one volume), Doubleday, 1994.

STAR WARS: "YOUNG JEDI KNIGHTS" SERIES

(With Rebecca Moesta) *Heirs of the Force,* Boule-
   vard, 1995.
(With Moesta) *Shadow Academy,* Boulevard, 1995.
(With Moesta) *The Lost Ones,* Boulevard, 1995.
(With Moesta) *Lightsabers,* Boulevard, 1996.
(With Moesta) *Darkest Knight,* Boulevard, 1996.
(With Moesta) *Jedi under Siege,* Boulevard, 1996.
(With Moesta) *Shards of Alderaan,* Boulevard, 1997.
(With Moesta) *Crisis at Crystal Reef,* Boulevard,
   1998.
Young Jedi the Lost, Boulevard, 1998.
Jedi Trilogy, Bantam, 1998.
(With Moesta) *Trouble on Cloud City,* Boulevard,
   1998.
(With Moesta) *Return to Ord Mantell,* Boulevard,
   1998.
(With Moesta) *The Emperor's Plague,* Boulevard, 1998.

"STAR WARS" ANTHOLOGIES SERIES

(Editor) *Star Wars: Tales from the Mos Eisley
   Cantina,* Bantam, 1995.
(Editor) *Star Wars: Tales from Jabba's Palace,* Bantam,
   1995.

STAR WARS: "TALES OF THE JEDI" SERIES

Dark Lords of the Sith, Dark Horse Comics, 1996.
The Sith War, Dark Horse Comics, 1996.
Golden Age of Sith, Dark Horse Comics, 1997.
Fall of the Sith Empire, Dark Horse Comics, 1998.

"DUNE" SERIES

(With Brian Herbert) *Dune: House Atreides,* Bantam, 1999.

NONFICTION

The Illustrated Star Wars Universe, illustrated by
   Ralph McQuarrie, with additional art by Michael
   Butkus and others, Bantam, 1995.
(With Rebecca Moesta) *Star Wars: The Mos Eisley
   Cantina Pop-Up Book,* illustrated by Ralph
   McQuarrie, Little, Brown, 1995.
(With Moesta) *Jabba's Palace Pop-Up Book,* illustrated
   by McQuarrie, Little, Brown, 1996.

OTHER

(With L. Ron Hubbard) *Ai! Pedrito,* Bridge Publications, 1998.

Work represented in anthologies, including *Full Spectrum*, volumes I, III, and IV, *The Ultimate Dracula*, and The *Ultimate Werewolf*. Contributor of short stories, articles, and reviews to periodicals, including *Analog*, *Amazing*, and *Fantasy and Science Fiction*. Over two dozen of Anderson's books have been translated for foreign publication; also author of several comic-book series.

■ Adaptations

Audiotape, *The X-Files: Ground Zero*, read by Gillian Anderson, Harper Audio, 1995.

■ Sidelights

Kevin J. Anderson is the author of a daunting array of science-fiction books for young adults, and has emerged as one of the most successful writers in the genre's history. Over ten million books of Anderson's were in print by the late 1990s, and in 1998 he set the world record for largest single-author book signing while promoting his spoof-filled spy thriller, *Ai! Pedrito!*, in Los Angeles. In addition to creating original novels with themes of space exploration and new frontiers, Anderson has written many books in the "Star Wars" series for teen readers under the auspices of Lucasfilm. For a 1999 prequel to the classic sci-fitome *Dune*, Anderson set another record when he was signed to the most lucrative book publishing contract ever drawn up for a science-fiction author.

Anderson was born in 1962 and grew up in a small town in Wisconsin. He recalled in a biography published on his Web site, located at http://www.wordfire.com, that a television film broadcast of the H. G. Wells classic *War of the Worlds* made a tremendous impression upon his five-year-old mind. Originally a radio play, *War of the Worlds* caused a stir when first broadcast in the late 1930s, sending many Americans into a panic, believing that the Earth really was being attacked by Martians. The television movie, based on the radio play, made such an impression upon Anderson that, still too young to read or write well, he drew pictures of the movie scenes the next day.

Anderson wrote his first short story at the age of eight, and two years later bought a typewriter with savings from his allowance. The year he

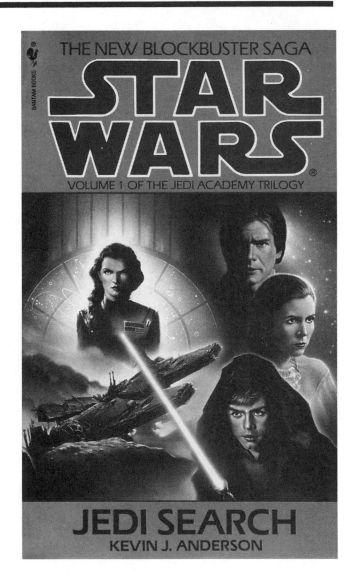

The first volume of the "Jedi Academy" trilogy includes characters from the 1977 film *Star Wars*, including Han Solo and Princess Leia, who are married.

entered high school, he began submitting short stories to science-fiction magazines, but received nothing but peremptory rejection letters. By the time he entered the University of Wisconsin at Madison, he had begun to enjoy minor success with his fiction. After he graduated from college with an honors degree in 1982, he began working for the Lawrence Livermore National Laboratories in Livermore, California. As a technical writer at this important defense-industry complex, Anderson was exposed to ideas and technologies that fired his imagination. He also met his future wife and co-author, Rebecca Moesta, and another future collaborator, a physicist named Doug Beason.

Early Works

Anderson's first published book was *Resurrection, Inc.* which appeared in 1988. Its protagonist is Francois Nathans, founder of a company that recycles human corpses. Nathans owns the technology that can animate the cadavers with a microchip, and, since their human memory has been erased, these "Servants" are used to free the living from difficult, drudge-like, or dangerous labor. When some of the Servants begin to recover their memories, they rebel. One of them possesses inside knowledge about the company because his father, once the greedy Nathans's partner, had been ousted from the partnership. "Although familiar in outline, this first effort is well plotted and lively in the telling," wrote Barbara Bannon in *Publishers Weekly*. As testament to its appeal, *Resurrection, Inc.*, was published in a tenth-anniversary edition.

Anderson's next project was a series of novels based upon the fantasy role-playing games popular with teenagers and young adults in the late 1980s. His 1989 work *Gamearth* introduced Melanie, David, Tyrone, and Scott, a quartet of students deeply involved in a Dungeons-and-Dragons style fantasy game. David begins to think that others are taking the plotted movements and created characters too seriously and wants to quit. To extricate himself, he creates a monstrous character that will destroy the other players' characters. His strategy backfires, however, and the book's ending is a cliffhanger.

In the sequel, *Gameplay*, also published in 1989, the four teens and their two-year-long role-playing game continues. Baffled by some occurrences, they come to realize through their dreams that some of the created characters have begun to make their own moves. The forces of good and evil battle, helped along by a new character who speaks only in advertising and pop-culture platitudes. "Anderson adds a delightfully fresh sense of humor in his character of Journeyman, the clay golem Melanie sends to save the day," noted a reviewer in *Kliatt*.

Collaborates with Beason

Beginning in the early 1990s, Anderson found success with several titles co-authored with his Livermore colleague Doug Beason. The first of these books, *Lifeline*, was published in 1991. It posits a futuristic scenario of an American base

As Han and Leia's young twins study at Luke Skywalker's Jedi Academy, a Dark Jedi plans to kidnap them.

on the Moon, a corporate satellite called Orbitech, and a Soviet counterpart viewed with some suspicion. At the beginning of the story, the American government has agreed to a deal with the Philippines: to retain the leases for their military bases on the Pacific archipelago, the Philippines have been given a space station called Aguinaldo. There, scientist Luis Sandovaal and his team of 1,500 researchers are creating groundbreaking new scientific products. One of these is wall-kelp, a quick-growing edible that provides all necessary nutrients for humans. Aguinaldo is also home to experimental prototypes of fantastic flying creatures that can be transformed into sails for the satellites.

Lifeline's action starts with the space settlers observing nuclear mushroom clouds on Earth. The United States and the Soviet Union have attacked one another, and all space stations are stranded. The Russians on Kibalchick put themselves into suspended animation, while the Americans attempt to find a more immediate solution. When the director of Orbitech, Brahms, turns tyrannical and ejects 150 "under-performing" personnel, Duncan McLaris flees and escapes to the moon base, Clavius. Sandovaal manages to successfully send

Han and Luke must stop the Hutts from building a super-weapon with the power to destroy entire planets.

wall-kelp to the base, and to Orbitech, but then the Soviets unexpectedly awaken, and tensions mount. "The posing and solving of apparently insuperable problems keeps the reader involved in that classic way," stated Tom Easton in *Analog Science Fiction and Fact*, who found fault only with the pacing of the book, and its rapid introduction of technological innovations that come to the rescue. "At the same time, the characters are real enough to engage the reader's sympathy . . . and at the end there is a very real sense of resolution and satisfaction."

Anderson and Beason's second collaboration, *The Trinity Paradox*, appeared in 1991. The novel "demonstrates their collaborative storytelling powers much more effectively," wrote Dan Chow in *Locus*. Its protagonist is Elizabeth Devane, a radical anti-nuclear activist. She and her boyfriend plan to disable a nuclear weapon sitting unguarded in the desert of the American Southwest, but a mishap occurs. He dies, and she is catapulted back into time to Los Alamos, New Mexico during World War II, when Los Alamos was the primary research site for American nuclear-weapons technology. Finding herself in the midst of the feverish race to master nuclear technology at the top-secret national laboratory, Devane realizes that she might be able to sabotage the invention of the atomic bomb.

The Trinity Paradox includes several real scientists in its plot, such as Robert Oppenheimer and Edward Teller, and the "Trinity" of the title takes its name from the site of the first successful test explosion. Devane meets English physicist Geoffrey Fox and tells him something that he in turn reveals to an old college friend now working for Nazi Germany; she also makes math errors on purpose, and attempts to assassinate Oppenheimer. Instead of stopping the Cold War, however, Devane's actions set in motion a new version of Cold War history: the outcome of World War II is affected, and nuclear technology heads in an entirely new direction. Realizing that she possesses the power to change the world, she becomes as dangerous as the scientists she considers traitors to humankind. "Hers is the most chilling of revolutionary beliefs, that with a constituency of one," noted Chow in *Locus*. Rayna Patton reviewed *The Trinity Paradox* for *Voice of Youth Advocates*, and found some fault with the book's credibility at times, such as how Elizabeth manages to work at Los Alamos without security-clearance papers. Nevertheless,

Patton called the book "an interesting read, onewhich will appeal to older high school students interested in physics and science fiction."

Anderson and Beason continued their successful collaboration with the 1993 novel *Assemblers of Infinity*. Set in the early decades of the twenty-first century, the plot centers around a group of scientists who believe an alien invasion may be imminent. A team of investigators is sent to a suspicious site—the Earth's base on the moon—but the mission goes awry when they die under questionable circumstances shortly after landing. Back on Earth, other researchers are positing that the relatively new field of nano-technology (machines run by microprocessors) may have something to do with

that incident and a threat of invasion. Erika Trace, one of the Earth's leading names in nano-technology, is enlisted to help. There are many dynamic characters in this complex plot, and the book won praise from reviewers. *Kliatt* reviewer Bette D. Ammon noted "the premise is riveting and the technology is fascinating," and said that Anderson and Beason created a situation "utterly plausible and frightening—the stuff of which good SF is made." Rosie Peasley reviewed *Assemblers of Infinity* for *Voice of Youth Advocates* and praised its "sophisticated science-fiction concepts," declaring that "the plot hums along at high speed." In a *Booklist* critique, Roland Green compared it to "the techno-thriller, sort of a Tom-Clancy-meets-space-advocacy effort."

Ill Wind was Anderson's fourth collaboration with Beason, a 1995 sci-fi eco-thriller involving a massive oil spill in the San Francisco Bay. The large corporation responsible for this disaster—eager to clean up both the spill and their corporate image as quickly as possible—unleashes an untried new microbe to do the job. Soon the uncontrollable organism begins eating everything made from petroleum products, such as gasoline and plastic. When martial law is declared and the electricity fails, a scientist and two pilots become the heroes who try to save the world.

With their 1996 book, *Virtual Destruction*, Anderson and Beason moved the action closer to home: the story is set at the Livermore Labs, from which Anderson had retired the previous year, and was a timely glimpse into how such national defense labs were forced to re-focus their missions after the end of Cold War tensions. After decades of relying heavily upon federal funding to develop new weapons technology, Livermore and other facilities were challenged to find consumer and private-sector applications for their patents. The conflicts presented by this new era—specifically between profit-minded management and the more altruistic scientists—is the focus of *Virtual Destruction*.

The plots revolves around a virtual reality chamber that produces devastating effects in the real world; Livermore executive Hal Michaelson is discussing with the government possible uses for this chamber in the dangerous realm of nuclear-weapons surveillance. One of Michaelson's researchers, Gary Lesserec, who has been involved with the Virtual RealityLab from its conception, knows that this is not feasible, that even sound recordings can

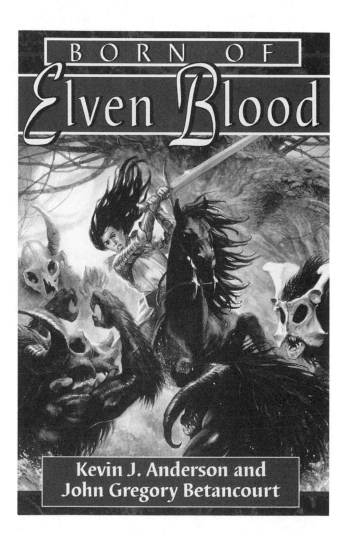

Finding herself in a magical land of elves, a girl embarks on a quest to save her friends from the threat of the trog warriors.

Set in the time of the original Jedi Knights, *Tales of the Jedi: The Sith War,* the story of Qel-Droma's struggle between light and darkness, is told in a comic book format.

trick entrants. Lesserec is about to be fired when Michaelson, his boss, is found dead inside the chamber in the presence of a lethal acid. A Federal Bureau of Investigation agent, Craig Kreident, investigates and uncovers nefarious industrial espionage links to the computer gaming industry. Introducing Kreident changes the feel of the book from sci-fi thriller to detective fiction, but as Tom Easton noted in *Analog,* "[T]here's not much detecting going on here. The tale exists to give us a tour of Livermore, explicate some interesting technology, and discuss the problems the end of the Cold War has given the national labs."

For help with the details in his next book with Beason, Anderson was able to obtain an insider's visit to Kennedy Space Center in Florida. Published in 1997, *Ignition* chronicles the planning and sabotage of a joint U.S.-Soviet mission on the space shuttle *Atlantis.* The first commodore, Colonel Adam "Iceberg" Friese, suffers an accident that cancels his participation. He becomes vitally involved nevertheless when a band of terrorists, organized by a famous Wall Street criminal, take the crew hostage. The pilot's former paramour, Nicole Hunter, an astronaut-turned-launch-controller, is also held hostage, but manages to help Friese battle the gang, some of whom have unusual personal quirks. The realistic details pertaining to the launch pad and prelaunch tensions—somewhat altered for security reasons—make *Ignition* "a nail biter " of a book, according to *Library Journal* reviewer Grant A. Frederickson.

Intrepid FBI agent Craig Kreident reappears in Anderson and Beason's 1998 sci-fi thriller, *Lethal Exposure*. This work is set at another government-funded research facility, the Fermi National Accelerator Laboratory in Illinois. Kreident arrives to investigate the mysterious radiation death of a renowned physicist, Georg Dumenco. A reviewer for *Publishers Weekly* observed that the authors' familiarity with the subject matter and lab environment "gives their latest [book] plenty of scientific authenticity."

Expanding the "Star Wars" Universe

Anderson is also the author of several books in the "Star Wars" series. The plots, aimed at young-adult readers, but popular with Star Wars fans of all ages, help provide panoramic details of the factions, clans, and worlds in this classic saga of good and evil. The first series is set at the Jedi Academy and begins with the 1994 novel *Jedi Search*. Heroic Han Solo is married to Princess Leia, and they have three small children. Other characters from the original 1977 film also appear, such as Luke Skywalker and Chewbacca, and a new one is introduced, the teenager Kyp Durron. Spice mines and a space battle lead to a "rollicking SF adventure," according to Ingrid von Hausen in a review for *Kliatt*. This book and two sequels written by Anderson, *Dark Apprentice* and *Champions of the Force*, were published in 1994 under the collective title *Jedi Academy Trilogy*.

Anderson has written several other "Star Wars" books that are not part of a definitive series. One such work is the 1995 hardcover *Darksaber*, in which the Empire is again attempting to resurrect its former glory. *Darksaber* introduces a new leader of the Hutt group, named Durga, and finds Luke Skywalker in love with a Jedi, Callista, whose special powers have vanished. Many other successful science-fiction writers have authored titles for various "Star Wars" series, but "Anderson leads the pack in both overall popularity and sheer storytelling power," wrote Carl Hays in *Booklist*. Hays further remarked that Anderson's well-developed characters added greatly to their appeal, giving readers a far more in-depth treatment than is possible in the film plots.

With his wife, Rebecca Moesta, Anderson has authored books for the "Young Jedi Knights" series. In this series, the heroes are the offspring of Han Solo and Princess Leia, the teen twins Jacen and Jaina. The first book in the series appeared in 1995, *Heirs of the Force*, and places the two at the fabled Jedi Academy, founded by their uncle, Luke Skywalker. When the teens are captured by a fighter pilot from the evil Empire, they are threatened with stranding on a jungle moon. In *The Lost Ones*, another in the series, also published in 1995, Anderson and Moesta again place Jacen and Jaina in danger. As expected, the fourteen-year-olds ably extricate both themselves and a friend who has been lured astray by the malevolent Dark Jedi Master, Brakiss. The Dark Jedi Force is attempting to revive the empire, creating a Second Imperium that will rule the galaxy. Hugh M. Flick, reviewing *The Lost Ones* in *Kliatt*, declared it, along with its two series predecessors, "well written and will be interesting for Star Wars fans of all ages."

The 1996 book *Lightsabers*, another in the series, features the maimed Tenel Ka, a friend of Jacen and Jaina. Tenel Ka's arm was destroyed when her lightsaber misfired, and out of shame she has exiled herself to the planet Hapes, where she is the crown princess. Jacen and Jaina attempt to help her maintain political stability on her home planet, and convince her to return to the Jedi Academy despite her accident. The fifth book in the Young Jedi Knights series, *Darkest Knight*, came in 1996. In it, Jacen and Jaina travel to Kashyyk, home of Lowbacca and the Wookies. When the Dark Jedis of the Shadow Academy attack Kashyyk, they steal vital computer technology to help build the Second Imperium, but Jacen and Jaina preserve the galaxy once again.

Anderson and Moesta concluded this series with *Jedi under Siege*, published in 1996. The following year they began a new series with *Shards of Alderaan*. Jacen and Jaina, only slightly older now,

---

If you enjoy the works of Kevin J. Anderson, you may also want to check out the following books:

Michael Crichton, *The Andromeda Strain*, 1969.
Dean R. Koontz, *Midnight*, 1993.
Vonda N. McIntyre, *The Crystal Star*, 1994.

are entrusted with the task of rebuilding the Jedi Academy. They expect to take a brief sojourn to the Alderaan system to bring back a chunk of a destroyed planet for their mother, but along the way they are abducted by bounty hunter Boba Fett. As a launch into a new series, "this one keeps the fine tradition going," wrote Flick in a *Kliatt* review.

Anderson has also authored several solo titles outside of the young-adult market that have garnered him definitive praise. His 1994 novel, *Climbing Olympus*, is set on the planet Mars, inhabited by three types of humans.Rachel Dycek, the United Nations commissioner there, is in charge of Lowell Base, but is about to be relieved of her duties. She was once the infamous surgeon who created "adins" (*adin* is Russian for "first"), surgically modified prisoners from Soviet labor camps. Their physiology has been altered so that they can survive on Mars, where they were sent originally to construct a colony.

After the adins rebelled and fled to another part of the planet, Dycek created the "dva" (Russian for "two"), another type of creature, but much less monstrously engineered and in possession of a higher degree of intelligence. The dvas were sent to Mars to create an infrastructure allowing average, non-modified humans to survive there. As the work nears completion, both the dvas and Dycek are being phased out. When a landslide kills a large number of the dva, Dycek visits the site and soon learns that, although adins and dvas were sterilized, the partner of an escaped adin, Boris, is now expecting a child. On the mountain Pavonis Mons, Dycek finds the unbalanced Boris ruling over the remaining adins, and she attempts to right her past wrongs and set the planet toward a harmonious future. Reviewers praised Anderson's vividly drawn portrayals, and Russell Letson in *Locus* called Dycek and Boris "characters as compelling as the technological widgetry of survival augmentation or the extremities of the Martian landscape and climate."

An Amazing Honor

Anderson's rank as a leading American science-fiction writer was reinforced when he was selected to create a companion work to the classic sci-fi novel *Dune* by Frank Herbert. This honor came after he sent a letter to the literary executors of the late author "telling them of my love for *Dune* and wondering if there was ever a possibility of new books," Anderson explained in an interview published on the Web site http://www. anotheruniverse.com. He was teamed with Herbert's son, Brian Herbert, to write the 1999 novel *Dune: House Atreides*, and received for it the most lucrative contract ever signed by science-fiction authors in publishing history.

Their task was to explain some of the relationships and feuds behind the extremely intricate plot of the original book. As *House Atreides* opens, Duke Atreides and his son Leto are attacked by arch-foe House Harkonnen. In the battle, a young boy named Duncan Idaho escapes to the Atreides side. An action of the machine planet Ix infuriates Emperor Elrood and sets in motion a long standing grudge, but Elrood's power is usurped by his own son. Meanwhile, the Bene Gesserits are about to see the fruition of their millennium-long plan to create a perfect being, Kwisatz Haderach. Central to all characters and subplots is the vast wasteland of Dune, where nothing except "Spice" lives. Authors Anderson and Herbert won praise from *Publishers Weekly* for their creation of a complex groundwork for lovers of the original *Dune*. "The attendant excitement and myriad revelations not only make this novel a terrific read in its own right but will inspire readers to turn, or return, to its great predecessor," its critic declared.

Such triumphs were not easily achieved, however. Anderson once won a tongue-in-cheek "Writer with No Future" award at a conference when he produced the most rejection slips among fellow participants. "I have now topped 750 rejections," the writer once stated, "and some people look at me as an 'overnight success.' Hah! My work is very popular now, but it took me a lot of work to get here."

■ Works Cited

Ammon, Bette D., review of *Assemblers of Infinity*, *Kliatt*, May, 1993, p. 12.

Anderson, Kevin J., on-line interview, located at http://www.anotheruniverse.com.

Anderson, Kevin J., comments published on his Website, located at http://www.wordfire.com.

Bannon, Barbara, review of *Resurrection, Inc.*, *Publishers Weekly*, June 3, 1988, p. 83.

Chow, Dan, review of *The Trinity Paradox, Locus,* December, 1991, p. 31.

Review of *Dune: House Atreides, Publishers Weekly,* August 30, 1999, p. 57.

Easton, Tom, review of *Lifeline, Analog Science Fiction and Fact,* May, 1991, pp. 178-180.

Easton, review of *Virtual Destruction, Analog Science Fiction and Fact,*August, 1996, p. 146.

Flick, Hugh M., review of *The Lost Ones, Kliatt,* May, 1996, p. 12.

Flick, Hugh M., review of *Shards of Alderaan, Kliatt,* March, 1997, p. 14.

Frederickson, Grant A., review of *Ignition, Library Journal,* January, 1997, p. 141.

Review of *Gameplay, Kliatt,* January, 1990, p. 16.

Green, Roland, review of *Assemblers of Infinity, Booklist,* February 15, 1993, p. 1041.

Hays, Carl, review of *Darksaber, Booklist,* September 15, 1995, p. 144.

Review of *Lethal Exposure, Publishers Weekly,* June 15, 1998, p. 57.

Letson, Russell, review of *Climbing Olympus, Locus,* August, 1994, p. 27.

Patton, Rayna, review of *The Trinity Paradox, Voice of Youth Advocates,* June, 1992, p. 105.

Peasley, Rosie, review of *Assemblers of Infinity, Voice of Youth Advocates,* August, 1993, p. 159

Von Hausen, Ingrid, review of *Jedi Search, Kliatt,* May, 1994, p. 13.

■ For More Information See

PERIODICALS

Analog Science Fiction and Fact, November, 1992, p. 161; January, 1995, p. 301; December, 1995, p. 162; October, 1996, p. 145.

Booklist, August, 1992, p. 2028; June 1, 1995, p. 1736; March 15, 1996, p. 1244; May 15, 1996, p. 1573; December 15, 1996.

Booktalker, November, 1990, p. 7.

Book Watch, December, 1995, p. 11; January, 1996, p. 10.

Kirkus Reviews, May 1, 1995, p. 570.

Kliatt, July, 1994, p. 54; January, 1996, p. 12; March, 1996, p. 13; p. 51; Spring, 1996, p. 55; July, 1996, p. 16; November, 1996, p. 11.

Library Journal, December, 1990, p. 167; May 1, 1992, p. 133; June, 1995, p. 128; October 15, 1995, p. 91; May 15, 1996, p. 86.

Locus, February, 1989, p. 21; November, 1989, p. 53; October, 1990, p. 50; November, 1990, p. 21; December, 1990, p. 19; January, 1991, p. 54; February, 1991, p. 36; December, 1991, pp. 31, 50; January, 1993, p. 27; July, 1993, p. 39; April, 1994, p. 47.

Magazine of Fantasy and Science Fiction, November, 1988, p. 28; March, 1991, p. 18.

Monthly Review, October, 1996, p. 43.

Necro, fall, 1995, p. 25; spring, 1996, p. 26.

Publishers Weekly, February 7, 1994, p. 85; March 14, 1994, p. 69; May 15, 1995, p. 60; September 4, 1995, p. 54; February 12, 1996, p. 75; April 22, 1996; p. 63; May 13, 1996, p. 30; February 3, 1997, p. 25; February 10, 1997, p. 67; January 11, 1999, p. 20.

School Library Journal, December, 1994, p. 38.

Science Fiction Chronicle, September, 1988, p. 64; March, 1989, p. 38; September, 1990, p. 38; March, 1991, pp. 28, 30; May, 1991, p. 32; April, 1993, p. 30; February, 1994, p. 5; October, 1995, p. 45; December, 1995, p. 59; February, 1996, p. 46.

Voice of Youth Advocates, February, 1990, p. 369; December, 1995, p. 283; October, 1996, p. 214, p. 222.

Wilson Library Bulletin, November, 1990, p. 7.

Poul Anderson

■ Personal

Given name pronounced "pole"; born November 25, 1926, in Bristol, PA; son of Anton William (an engineer) and Astrid (a secretary; maiden name, Hertz) Anderson; married Karen J. M. Kruse (an editorial and research assistant and writer), December 12, 1953; children: Astrid May. *Education:* University of Minnesota, B.S. (with distinction), 1948.

■ Addresses

Home—3 Las Palomas, Orinda, CA 94563. *Agent*—c/o Ted Chichak, Chichak, Inc., 1040 1st Ave., New York, NY 10022.

■ Career

Freelance writer, except for occasional temporary jobs, 1948—. *Member:* Science Fiction Writers of America (president, 1972-73), American Associa-

tion for the Advancement of Science, Mystery Writers of America (northern California regional vice-chairman, 1959). Society for Creative Anachronism, Scowrers (secretary, 1957-62), Elves, Gnomes, and Little Men's Science Fiction Chowder and Marching Society.

■ Awards, Honors

Morley-Montgomery Prize for Scholarship in Sherlock Holmes, 1955; first annual Cock Robin Mystery Award, 1959, for *Perish by the Sword;* Guest of Honor, World Science Fiction Convention, 1959; Hugo Awards, World Science Fiction Convention, 1961, for short fiction "The Longest Voyage," 1964, for short fiction "No Truce with Kings," 1969, for novelette "The Sharing of Flesh," 1972, for novella "The Queen of Air and Darkness," 1973, for novelette "Goat Song," 1979, for novelette "Hunter's Moon," and 1982, for novella "The Saturn Game"; Forry Award for achievement, Los Angeles Science Fantasy Society, 1968.

Nebula Awards, Science Fiction Writers of America, 1971, for "The Queen of Air and Darkness," and 1972, for "Goat Song"; Hugo Award runner-up, World Science Fiction Convention, 1973, for *There Will Be Time;* August Derleth Award, British Fantasy Society, 1974, for *Hrolf*

Kraki's Saga; Gandalf Award, Grand Master of Fantasy, World Science Fiction Convention, 1978.

■ **Writings**

SCIENCE FICTION NOVELS

Vault of the Ages (for children), Winston Press, 1952.

Brain Wave, Ballantine, 1954.

The Broken Sword, Abelard, 1954, revised edition, Ballantine, 1971.

No World of Their Own (bound with *The 1,000 Year Plan* by Isaac Asimov), Ace, 1955, published separately as *The Long Way Home,* Gregg (Rohnert Park, CA), 1978.

Star Ways, Avalon, 1956, published as *The Peregrine,* Ace, 1978.

Planet of No Return (bound with *Star Guard* by Andre Norton), Ace, 1957, published as *Question and Answer,* 1978.

War of the Wing-Men, Ace, 1958, published as *The Man Who Counts,* 1978.

The Snows of Ganymede, Ace, 1958.

Virgin Planet, Avalon, 1959.

The Enemy Stars, Lippincott, 1959.

The War of Two Worlds (bound with *Threshold of Eternity* by John Brunner), Ace, 1959.

We Claim These Stars! (bound with *The Planet Killers* by Robert Silverberg), Ace, 1959.

The High Crusade, Doubleday, 1960.

Earthman, Go Home! (bound with *To the Tombaugh Station* by Wilson Tucker), Ace, 1961.

Twilight World, Torquil, 1961.

Mayday Orbit (bound with *No Man's World* by Kenneth Bulmer), Ace, 1961.

Three Hearts and Three Lions, Doubleday, 1961.

The Makeshift Rocket (bound with the *Un-Man and Other Novellas*), Ace, 1962.

After Doomsday, Ballantine, 1962.

Shield, Berkley, 1963.

Let the Spacemen Beware! (bound with *The Wizard of Starship Poseidon* by K. Bulmer), Ace, 1963, published separately as *The Night Face,* 1978.

Three Worlds to Conquer, Pyramid, 1964.

The Star Fox, Doubleday, 1965.

The Corridors of Time, Doubleday, 1965.

Ensign Flandry, Chilton (Radnor, PA), 1966.

World without Stars, Ace, 1966.

Satan's World, Doubleday, 1969.

The Rebel Worlds, Signet, 1969, published as *Commander Flandry,* Severn House (London), 1978.

A Circus of Hells, Signet, 1970.

Tau Zero, Doubleday, 1970.

The Byworlder, Signet, 1971.

Operation Chaos, Doubleday, 1971.

The Dancer from Atlantis, Doubleday, 1971.

There Will Be Time, Doubleday, 1971.

Hrolf Kraki's Saga, Ballantine, 1973.

The People of the Wind, Signet, 1973.

The Day of Their Return, Doubleday, 1974.

Fire Time, Doubleday, 1974.

A Midsummer Tempest, Doubleday, 1974.

(With Gordon Ecklund) *Inheritors of Earth,* Chilton, 1974.

The Worlds of Poul Anderson (contains *Planet of No Return, The War of Two Worlds,* and *World without Stars*), Ace, 1974.

A Knight of Ghosts and Shadows, Doubleday, 1974, published as *Knight Flandry,* Severn House, 1980.

(With Gordon R. Dickson) *Star Prince Charlie* (for children), Putnam, 1975.

The Winter of the World, Doubleday, 1976.

Mirkheim, Berkley, 1977.

The Avatar, Putnam, 1978.

Two Worlds (contains *Question and Answer* and *World without Stars*), Gregg, 1978.

The Merman's Children, Putnam, 1979.

A Stone in Heaven, Ace, 1979.

Conan the Rebel, Bantam, 1980.

(With Mildred D. Broxon) *The Demon of Scattery,* Ace, 1980.

The Long Night, Pinnacle, 1983.

Orion Shall Rise, Pocket Books, 1983.

Agent of Vega, Ace, 1983.

The Game of Empire, Baen, 1985.

Time Wars, Tor, 1986.

The Year of the Ransom (for children), illustrated by Paul Rivoche, Walker & Co., 1988.

Conan the Rebel #17, Ace, 1989.

No Truce with Kings (bound with *Ship of Shadows* by Fritz Leiber), Tor, 1989.

The Boat of a Million Years, Tor, 1989.

The Shield of Time, Tor, 1990.

The Time Patrol, Tor, 1991.

Inconstant Star, Baen, 1991.

(With others) *Murasaki,* Bantam, 1992.

Harvest of Stars, Tor, 1993.

The Stars Are Also Fire, Tor, 1994.

Harvest the Fire, Tor, 1995.

"THE KING OF YS" FANTASY SERIES; WITH WIFE, KAREN ANDERSON

Roma Mater, Baen, 1986.

Gallicinae, Baen, 1988.
Dahut, Baen, 1988.
The Dog and the Wolf, Baen, 1988.

SHORT STORY COLLECTIONS

(With Gordon R. Dickson) *Earthman's Burden*, Gnome Press, 1957.
Guardians of Time, Ballantine, 1960, revised edition, Pinnacle, 1981.
Strangers from the Earth: Eight Tales of Vaulting Imagination, Ballantine, 1961.
Orbit Unlimited, Pyramid, 1961.
Trader to the Stars, Doubleday, 1964.
Time and Stars, Doubleday, 1964.
Agent of the Terran Empire, Chilton, 1965.
Flandry of Terra, Chilton, 1965.
The Trouble Twisters, Doubleday, 1966.
The Horn of Time, Signet, 1968.
Beyond the Beyond, New American Library, 1969.
Seven Conquests: An Adventure in Science Fiction, Macmillan, 1969.
Tales of the Flying Mountains, Macmillan, 1970.
The Queen of Air and Darkness and Other Stories, Signet, 1973.
The Many Worlds of Poul Anderson, edited by Roger Elwood, Chilton, 1974, published as *The Book of Poul Anderson*, DAW Books, 1975.
Homeward and Beyond, Doubleday, 1975.
Homebrew, National Educational Field Service Association Press (Cambridge, MA), 1976.
The Best of Poul Anderson, Pocket Books, 1976.
The Earth Book of Stormgate, Putnam, 1978.
The Night Face and Other Stories, Gregg, 1978.
The Dark between the Stars, Berkley, 1980.
Explorations, Pinnacle, 1981.
Fantasy, Pinnacle, 1981.
Winners, Pinnacle, 1981.
Cold Victory, Pinnacle, 1981.
The Psychotechnic League, Tor, 1981.
The Gods Laughed, Pinnacle, 1982.
Maurai and Kith, Tor, 1982.
Starship, Pinnacle, 1982.
New America, Pinnacle, 1982.
Conflict, Pinnacle, 1983.
(With Gordon R. Dickson) *Hoka!* (for children), Simon & Schuster, 1983.
Time Patrolman, Pinnacle, 1983.
Annals of the Time Patrol (contains *Time Patrolman* and *Guardians of Time*), Doubleday, 1984.
(With K. Anderson) *The Unicorn Trade*, Tor, 1984.
Past Times, Tor, 1984.
Dialogue with Darkness, Tor, 1985.
(With others) *Berserker Base*, Tor, 1985.

Space Folk, Baen, 1989.
All One Universe, Tor, 1996.

OTHER NOVELS

Perish by the Sword, Macmillan, 1959.
Murder in Black Letter, Macmillan, 1960.
The Golden Slave, Avon, 1960.
Rogue Sword, Avon, 1960.
Murder Bound, Macmillan, 1962.
The Last Viking: The Golden Horn, Zebra, 1980.
The Devil's Game, Pocket Books, 1980.
The Road of the Sea Horse, Zebra, 1980.
The Sign of the Raven, Zebra, 1980.

NONFICTION

Is There Life on Other Worlds?, Crowell, 1963.
Thermonuclear Warfare, Monarch (Derby, CT), 1963.
The Infinite Voyage: Man's Future in Space (for young adults), Macmillan, 1969.

OTHER

(Adaptor) Christian Molbech, *The Fox, the Dog, and the Griffin*, Doubleday, 1966.
(Author of introduction) *The Best of L. Sprague de Camp*, Ballantine, 1978.

Contributor to books including *All about the Future*, edited by Martin Greenberg, Gnome Press, 1955; *The Day the Sun Stood Still: Three Original Novellas of Science Fiction*, Thomas Nelson (Nashville), 1972; *Science Fiction: Today and Tomorrow*, edited by Reginald Bretnor, Harper, 1974; *The Craft of Science Fiction*, edited by Reginald Bretnor, Harper, 1976; *Turning Points: Essays on the Art of Science Fiction*, edited by Damon Knight, Harper, 1977; *Swords against Darkness*, edited by Andrew J. Offutt, Zebra, Volume 1, 1977, Volume 3, 1978, Volume 4, 1979; *The Blade of Conan*, edited by L. Sprague de Camp, Ace, 1979; *Space Wars* (short stories), edited by Charles Waugh and Martin H. Greenberg, Tor, 1988; *Modern Classic Short Novels of Science Fiction*, edited by Gardner Dozois, St. Martin's, 1994.

Also contributor to anthologies, including *Possible Worlds of Science Fiction*, edited by Groff Conklin, Vanguard, 1951; *A Treasury of Great Science Fiction*, edited by Anthony Boucher, Doubleday, 1959; *The Hugo Winners*, edited by Isaac Asimov, Doubleday, 1962; *Space, Time, and Crime*, edited by Miriam Allen de Ford, Paperback Library, 1964; *Monsters of Science Fiction,* Belmont Books, 1964; *The Hugo Winners,* edited by Isaac Asimov, Doubleday, 1971-72; *The Science Fiction Hall of Fame,* edited by Ben Bova, Doubleday, 1973; *The Future at War,* edited by Reginald Bretnor, Ace, 1979. Contributor of short stories and articles, some under pseudonyms A. A. Craig and Winston P. Sanders, to periodicals, including *Astounding Science Fiction, Analog Science Fiction/Science Fact, Boy's Life, Foundation: The Review of Science Fiction, Galaxy, Isaac Asimov's Science Fiction Magazine, Magazine of Fantasy and Science Fiction,* and *National Review.* Writer of a television documentary on the space program for the United States Information Agency, 1963-64. Anderson's books have been translated into eighteen foreign languages.

■ Adaptations

The High Crusade was adapted for a computer game by IRS Hobbies, 1983; "The Longest Voyage," "The Queen of Air and Darkness," "No Truce with Kings," and "The Man Who Came Early" were all adapted for an audio cassette, *Award-Winning Science Fiction by Poul Anderson,* by Listening Library; other stories by Anderson were recorded by Caedmon in 1986 under the title *Yonder—Seven Tales of the Space Age.*

■ Sidelights

The winner of several Nebula and Hugo awards, Poul Anderson is a prolific writer of science fiction and fantasy with well over one hundred novels and short story collections to his credit. Known for writing science fiction that is well-grounded in scientific knowledge, and for fantasy stories involving a heavy dose of Nordic mythology and libertarian values, Anderson is also a poet, translator, and writer of detective and historical novels. Science fiction is, perhaps, the one true cross-over genre; although only a handful of Anderson's works have been specifically written for a juvenile audience, his books and short stories are as popular with young readers as they are with adults. Anderson, who cut his teeth on magazine writing, is "one of the five or six most important writers to appear during the science-fiction publishing boom of the decade following the end of World War II," according to Michael

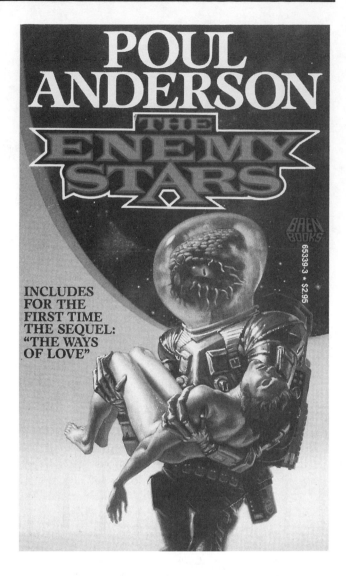

Anderson's 1959 work deals with gravity and the meaning of exploration.

W. McClintock in the *Dictionary of Literary Biography.*

Literary traditions with Anderson go back to Denmark on his mother's side, but his upbringing was not really a literary one. His early years were spent in Port Arthur, Texas, where he navigated a homemade kayak in the family's bayou-like backyard, and where "a neighbor boy made a pet of a small alligator he had found in his," as Anderson recalled in an essay for *Contemporary Authors Autobiography Series (CAAS).* The one negative in his youth was, according to Anderson, school: an "utter emptiness, a purgatory of boredom." Something of an introvert as a child, Anderson relied more on his wits than his athletic prowess to navigate the rough waters of the school yard. At the same time, he was raised with the "strict code of manners of the old South." The Danish influence on both sides of his family was strongly felt: Anderson's mother was born in Denmark, and though his father had been born in the United States, he was educated in Denmark.

When his father was killed in a car accident in 1937, Anderson's secure family life was turned on its head. At first his mother took him and his brother to Denmark in hopes of starting a

This early fantasy novel is concerned with law and chaos.

new life. The war clouds of the late 1930s, however, drove them back to the safety of the United States, first to Maryland and then to Minnesota, where Anderson's mother joined her brother in investing what money the family had left in a farm, though the investment proved unwise. In the countryside around Northfield, Minnesota, Anderson completed junior high and then high school. "Those years are pretty bad in my memory," Anderson recalled in *CAAS*. "I was a total social misfit. . . . Anyway, I had my private world to retreat to, the world of books and, specifically of science fiction." A friend Anderson had earlier made in Maryland, Neil Waldrop, kept in touch with him and sent along copies of pulp magazines that introduced Anderson to the world of science fiction, magazines such as *Thrilling Wonder Stories, Amazing Stories,* and, of course, *Astounding Science Fiction.* He had read Jules Verne and H. G. Wells as a kid; now he was introduced to contemporary practitioners such as Robert Heinlein and Isaac Asimov.

Turned down by the army because of a scarred eardrum resulting from a childhood illness, Anderson enrolled in the University of Minnesota in 1944. "Suddenly I was free," he wrote in *CAAS*. "The old maids and soft young facesof high school were behind me. I was among men, and men whose trade was knowledge. They regarded me as an adult." Initially, Anderson majored in physics, but when he realized how poor his math skills were, he moved into astronomy. He was reading science fiction as avidly as before and was writing his own stories to share with his friend, Waldrop. When Waldrop showed up as a student at the University of Minnesota, the two spent hours together in conversation. One of these midnight talks resulted in Anderson's first published story, "Tomorrow's Children," which dealt with the consequences of the atomic bomb. Anderson's favorite magazine, *Astounding Science Fiction,* took the story, and this sale proved to be a deciding factor in a choice Anderson was then making. Graduating in 1948, he had to decide on a career. "I would never be more than a second-rate scientist," Anderson wrote in *CAAS.* And suddenly writing science fiction for a living seemed a possibility. Several more of his stories had been purchased by magazines; Anderson had also become a member of the Minneapolis Fantasy Society where he came into contact with other people in the writing trade, including Clifford D. Simak and Gordon

R. Dickson. "This was when I settled into a writing career in earnest," he recalled.

Innovative Science Fiction Tales

Anderson sold stories to *Astounding Science Fiction* (which was later renamed *Analog*) and to *Planet Stories.* These early pieces were "blood-and-thunder adventure yarns," according to Anderson, and by 1952 he had published his first novel, *Vault of Ages,* an "apprentice" piece, as McClintock described it in *Dictionary of Literary Biography.* But by his second published science fiction novel, *Brain Wave,* Anderson had "fol-

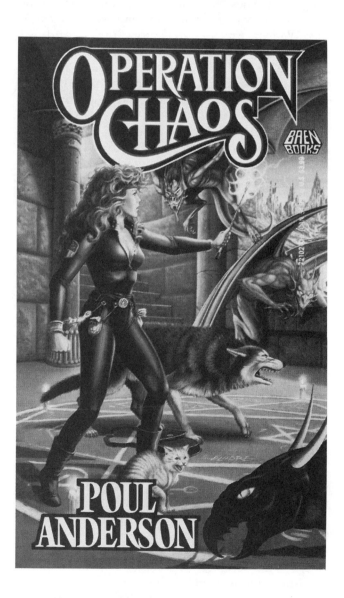

Magical beings populate Anderson's alternative Earth in this 1971 story.

lowed the instruction of H. G. Wells to employ but a single 'marvel' in a story and work out the logical consequences of the innovation," McClintock noted. This logical processing of an innovation is a strong characteristic of Anderson's science fiction. Also, in early stories such as "Sam Hall," in which a bureaucratized government is battled by a computer-generated rebel,and in "Call Me Joe," in which a human escapes the constraints of his body by transferring his personality to a robot, Anderson established some of his most enduring themes. Here is the lone intellect, the individual battling society or other outside forces for freedom; here is the power of reason at work, as well as the use of technology for positive gain.

During the 1950s and 1960s, Anderson wrote a score of novels based on a future history series documenting the Technic Civilization, beginning with *Star Ways.* Many of these short novels are constructed like mysteries or puzzles and also include Anderson's reliance on sound scientific extrapolation. But Anderson was also interested in mythology and Norse legend, and he soon adapted that interest to his writing in the form of fantasy novels. An early fantasy novel of Anderson's is *Three Hearts and Three Lions,* an examination "of the conflict between law and chaos," according to McClintock, which is set in a Carolingian-like world. In succeeding years these twin threads of science fiction and fantasy have occupied most of Anderson's writing output.

Meanwhile, Anderson married, had a child, and settled with his family in the San Francisco Bay area, where he still lives. He became involved in all aspects of the science fiction community, from attending conventions to sharing dinners with fellow writers. In 1958 Anderson published "the two most important novels of the first half" of his career, according to McClintock. *War of the Wing-Men* and *The Enemy Stars* "both feature vividly realized settings. . . . Both utilize to good effect elements of the most current scientific thought," McClintock commented. The political *War of the Wing-Men* introduced the self-indulgent and overweight Nicholas van Rijn, whom Anderson would return to often in his fiction as an unlikely entrepreneurial hero. With *The Enemy Stars,* Anderson worked out the one "marvel"—involving constant and instantaneous gravity—in a story that takes on mythic and mystical pro-

POUL ANDERSON

A conspiracy
to regain the stars...

ORION SHALL RISE

72090-2 ☆ (CAN. $6.50) ☆ U.S. $4.99

BAEN BOOKS

Following a nuclear war, two factions are at odds about the new world they're trying to build.

portions on the meaning of exploration. Notall reviewers found *The Enemy Stars* first rate, however. Roger Baker, writing in *Books and Bookmen*, commented that "the scientific mumbojumbo is just not good enough to blind us to the fact that [Anderson's] characters are more than usually weak stereotypes." *The High Crusade* also continues this literary exploration into the meaning of quest, a celebration of "human courage" and "intelligence," according to McClintock.

Fellow science fiction writer James Blish, writing in the *Magazine of Fantasy and Science Fiction*, labeled Anderson's 1970 work, *Tau Zero*, a water-

shed achievement. Blish called it "the ultimate 'hard science fiction' novel," and went on to note that "everybody else who has been trying to write this kind of thing can now fold up his tent and creep silently away." Here Anderson took the working out of an innovation to the maximum. He posited the question of what would happen to an interstellar vessel travelling at a steady acceleration of one gravity if it were damaged in such a way that its acceleration could not be stopped. Blish noted that Anderson worked out his problem thoroughly like a "born storyteller." This book was followed by *Operation Chaos*, a fantasy set on an alternate Earth where magic is part of everyday life and in which a witch and werewolf are the main protagonists. "The book is well populated and contains a great deal of humor," noted Blish in another *Magazine of Fantasy and Science Fiction* review. While noting that *Operation Chaos* is fundamentally about the contest between law and chaos, Sandra Miesel commented in her monograph *Against Time's Arrow: The High Crusade of Poul Anderson* that the book "celebrates ordinariness. . . . Homely values are soundest: domestic happiness is sweetest. . . . Law is not constraint but protection for these humble realities. Without Law, the very concept of normalcy would vanish. Chaos is ever its foe."

A Writer's Purpose

Such values are not simply empty speeches Anderson puts in the mouths of his characters, but are part of the author's belief system. "If I preach at all," Anderson once told Jeffrey M. Elliot in *Science Fiction Voices #2*, "it's probably in the direction of individual liberty, which is a theme that looms large in my work." Because of this insistence on individual freedom and libertarian values, Anderson is known in science fiction circles as "being fairly far to the right and has been called a reactionary," according to Charles Platt in *Dream Makers, Volume 2: The Uncommon Men and Women Who Write Science Fiction*. Anderson noted in his interview with Platt that if he had to call himself something, "it would be either a conservative libertarian or a libertarian conservative. . . . Basically, I feel that the concepts of liberty that were expressed . . . by people like the Founding Fathers were actually the radically bold concepts from which people have been retreating ever since. And I don't believe that it's necessarily reactionary to say so."

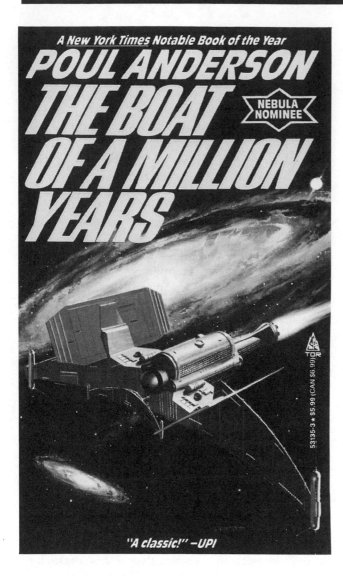

A *New York Times* Notable Book of the Year

POUL ANDERSON

THE BOAT OF A MILLION YEARS

NEBULA NOMINEE

TOR

53135-3 ★ $5.99 (CAN $6.99)

"A classic!" –UPI

Poul tracks the journeys of eight immortals from 310 B.C. to the present in this epic work.

But Anderson has also said that his first job as a writer is to entertain, and that is what he did with the award-winning novelette "The Queen of Air and Darkness" set in a "scientifically plausible Elfland," according to Miesel. Another important fantasy title is *The Merman's Children,* which is based on a Danish ballad depicting the ending of the world of the Faeries. Set in Denmark during the Middle Ages, it relates the battle between the mythic web-footed mermen and the Christian church. Gerald Jonas, writing in the *New York Times Book Review,* noted that the novel was a "hybrid" of fantasy, historical fiction, and science fiction. With 1974's *A Knight of Ghosts and Shadows,* Anderson returned to aspects of the

Technic Empire (specifically its later phases, known as the Terran Empire), and put Dominic Flandry, who has inhabited the pages of much of Anderson's fiction, on center stage. The central conflict in the tale is characteristic of Anderson: the testing of rational judgement in a moral wilderness. A further book in that series includes *The Game of Empire.* Other popular series books by Anderson include his "Time Patrol" books, where time travel and science fiction are mixed neatly together. In the stories and novels of this series, the members of the Time Patrol are charged with the duty of keeping history unchanged by time travellers. *Annals of the Time*

POUL ANDERSON

NATIONALLY BESTSELLING AUTHOR OF THE BOAT OF A MILLION YEARS

HARVEST OF STARS

TOR

51946-9 ★ $5.99 (CAN $6.99)

"Vivid!" –Larry Bond
"An important work!–Omni
"A masterpiece!" –Larry Niven
"The finest!"–John Jakes

"Vivid, fast-paced...A great read!"
–Larry Bond, author of VORTEX

In a future America, a religious cult battles an interplanetary corporation.

Patrol, The Year of the Ransom, and *The Shield of Time* are representative titles in the series. Reviewing *The Shield of Time,* Roland Green noted in *Booklist* that Anderson's "abiding love for history" carried the story's weight. And something of a turning point in Anderson's fiction was 1978's *The Avatar,* a book in which Anderson featured several women as leading characters and in which he attempted to "make sexual passion and an interstellar adventure somehow metaphoric," according to McClintock.

Anderson has never shied away from using his fiction as a way to proclaim his own views. Among the many issues that he has dealt with are those of the safe use of nuclear power and the benefits of space exploration, both of which find a place in *Orion Shall Rise.* This story is an investigation of a world rebuilding itself many generations after a nuclear war. Two main powers—the non-industrial Maurai and the more technology-prone Northwest Union—are at odds about how their new world should progress. "This would be useful in classes discussing our current nuclear debate," concluded Nancy Choice in a *Voice of Youth Advocates* review of the novel. Anderson has also teamed up with his wife, Karen Anderson, on several projects, including the story collection, *The Unicorn Trade,* and the four-volume series, "The King of Ys."

Epic Sagas

More recently, Anderson has turned his hand to epic-length ventures, including *The Boat of a Million Years, The Stars Are Also Free,* and *Harvest of Stars. The Boat of a Million Years* tells the stories of eight immortals who trek through time. Blessed with eternal life, these special few range in time of birth from 310 B.C. to the present day. They slowly find each other on their journeys and band together to try to put meaning into their lives."The novel is fascinating and masterfully done," noted a reviewer in *Kliatt,* adding that the book came "highly recommended." Jonas commented in another *New York Times Books Review* article that Anderson had been writing "solid, serviceable science fiction" for over four decades, but with *The Boat of a Million Years* "he aims higher and succeeds admirably."

Harvest of Stars was another long novel, detailing the future struggle between a North America

that has been taken over by the Avantists, a techno-religious cult dictatorship, and Fireball, an interplanetary corporation and "the last bastion of free-enterprise," according to *Kirkus Reviews.* However, while noting that Anderson had written "wonderful short to medium-length stories," the *Kirkus Reviews* critic concluded that for Anderson to persist "in grinding out ponderous, somnolent, bloated offerings like this is one of science fiction's enduring mysteries." Jonas, in the *New York Times Book Review,* also criticized the book as "overwritten, underimagined and fatally flawed." Others disagreed. Howard G. Zaharoff, writing in *Kliatt,* found *Harvest of Stars* to be a "good, but rather lengthy, read," and *Booklist* contributor John Mort called it "a complex novel" and "a grand meditation."

The Stars Are Also Fire, a sequel to *Harvest of Stars,* covers five centuries and spans several worlds; it is another "epic novel," according to Vicky Burkholder in *Voice of Youth Advocates.* The future world of Earth is controlled by a giant mechanical mind called cybercosm, which rules peacefully over the population. But lost in this placid new world are individuality and the freedom of choice. The mechanical mind now pursues some rebels on distant outposts to bring them into line, especially the Lunar rebels. A *Kirkus Reviews* critic concluded that the book was proof of Anderson's "powerful storytelling talents," but that it also "betrays once again his tendency to hang far too much political, sociological, and technological baggage on the shining thread of the tale." Mort noted in another *Booklist* review that "Anderson's new epic owes clear allegiances to both Heinlein and Asimov and will appeal to their many fans." And a *Publishers Weekly* reviewer commented that Anderson got "back on track" with *The Stars Are Also Fire:* "Where its predecessor was disjointed, unbalanced and clogged with capitalist-libertarian preaching, this novel offers suspense, vivid writing and appealing characters." Third in the series, *Harvest the Fire* follows the adventures of the battle against cybercosm and the Lunarians, but John O. Christensen, writing in *Voice of Youth Advocates,* noted that the novel did not hold up on its own. "Background and plot are not well developed," Christensen commented, "and the characters are less than memorable."

"[There] is a basic attitude, I suppose, which underlies my writing," Anderson said in his interview with Elliot in *Science Fiction Voices #2.* "Namely, that this is a wonderful universe in which to live, that it's great to be alive, and that all it takes is the willingness to give ourselves a chance to experience what life has to offer." Through his science fiction and fantasy, Anderson has attempted to make that attitude toward life manifest. Part of the post-war wave of writers who have helped to make science fiction "legitimate," Anderson employs such elements as humor, politics, puzzles, history, and science in his writing. "I have written quite a lot," Anderson once remarked, "and am proud to have done so, because science fiction is and always has been part of literature. Its long isolation . . . is ending. . . . This is good, because the particular concerns of science fiction have never been parochial. . . . Not that I wish to make exaggerated claims. I merely set forth that science fiction is one human accomplishment, among countless others, which has something to offer the world. Lest even this sound too pompous let me say that at the very least it is often a lot of fun."

■ Works Cited

Anderson, Poul, essay in *Contemporary Authors Autobiography Series,* Volume 2, Gale, 1985, pp. 33-46.

Baker, Roger, "Into the Future," *Books and Bookmen,* August 1972, pp. xii-xiii.

Blish, James, "Books: 'Tau Zero,'" *Magazine of Fantasy and Science Fiction,* March, 1971, pp. 14-15.

Blish, James, "Books: 'Operation Chaos,'" *Magazine of Fantasy and Science Fiction,* December, 1971, p. 25.

Review of *The Boat of a Million Years, Kliatt,* April 1991, pp. 16-17.

Burkholder, Vicky, review of *The Stars Are Also Fire, Voice of Youth Advocates,* February, 1995, p. 343.

Choice, Nancy, review of *Orion Shall Rise, Voice of Youth Advocates,* December, 1983, p. 281.

Christensen, John O., review of *Harvest the Fire, Voice of Youth Advocates,* April, 1996, p. 34.

Elliot, Jeffrey M., "Poul Anderson: Seer of Far-Distant Futures," *Science Fiction Voices #2,* Borgo, 1979, pp. 41-50.

Green, Roland, review of *The Shield of Time, Booklist,* July, 1990, p. 2041.

Review of *Harvest of Stars, Kirkus Reviews,* June 15, 1993, p. 756.

Jonas, Gerald, review of *The Merman's Children, New York Times Book Review,* October 28, 1979, pp. 15-16.

Jonas, Gerald, review of *The Boat of a Million Years, New York Times Book Review,* November 19, 1989, p. 32.

Jonas, Gerald, review of *Harvest of Stars, New York Times Book Review,* September 12, 1993, p. 36.

McClintock, Michael W., "Poul Anderson," in *Dictionary of Literary Biography,* Volume 8: *Twentieth-Century Science-Fiction Writers,* Gale, 1981, pp. 3-12.

Miesel, Sandra, *Against Time's Arrow: The High Crusade of Poul Anderson,* Borgo, 1978.

Mort, John, review of *Harvest of Stars, Booklist,* June 15, 1993, pp. 1733-34.

Mort, John, review of *The Stars Are Also Fire, Booklist,* July 1994, pp. 1892-93.

Platt, Charles, *Dream Makers, Volume 2: The Uncommon Men and Women Who Write Science Fiction,* Berkley, 1983.

Review of *The Stars Are Also Fire, Kirkus Reviews,* June 15, 1994, p. 84.

Review of *The Stars Are Also Fire, Publishers Weekly,* July 18, 1994, p. 239.

Zaharoff, Howard G., review of *Harvest of Stars, Kliatt,* January 1995, p. 12.

■ For More Information See

BOOKS

Benson, Gordon, Jr., and Phil Stephenson-Payne, *Poul Anderson, Myth-Maker and Wonder-Weaver: A Working Bibliography,* 5th revised edition, Borgo, 1990.

Bretnor, Reginald, editor, *The Craft of Science Fiction,* Harper, 1974.

Children's Literature Review, Volume 58, Gale, 2000.

Contemporary Literary Criticism, Volume 15, Gale, 1980, pp. 10-15.

Tuck, Donald H., compiler, *The Encyclopedia of Science Fiction and Fantasy,* Volume 1, Advent, 1974.

Walker, Paul, *Speaking of Science Fiction: The Paul Walker Interviews,* Luna, 1978.

PERIODICALS

Analog, July, 1978, p. 175; January, 1979, p. 172; March, 1981, p. 164; September, 1983, p. 160; October, 1985, p. 179; December, 1993, p. 167.

Kliatt, fall, 1977, p. 10; spring, 1978, p. 11; winter, 1981, p. 11; winter, 1985, p. 16; September, 1991, p. 19; May, 1993, p. 12.

School Library Journal, March, 1977, p. 158; March, 1982, p. 162; August, 1988, p. 105; September, 1988, p. 122.

Times Literary Supplement, April 7, 1966, p. 281; June 29, 1967, p. 573; December 20, 1969, p. 1345; February 2, 1973, p. 129.

Wilson Library Bulletin, January, 1980, p. 323; January, 1995, p. 90.

—Sketch by J. Sydney Jones

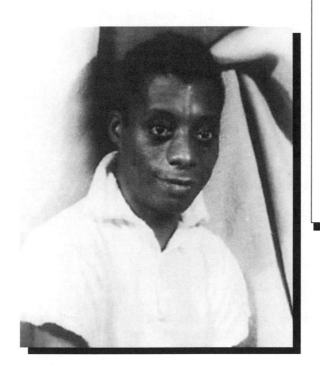

James Baldwin

■ Personal

Born August 2, 1924, in New York, New York, United States; died of stomach cancer December 1 (some sources say November 30), 1987, in St. Paul de Vence, France; son of David (a clergyman and factory worker) and Emma Berdis (maiden name, Jones) Baldwin. *Education:* Graduate of De Witt Clinton High School, New York, NY, 1942.

■ Career

Writer, 1944-87. Youth minister at Fireside Pentecostal Assembly, New York, NY, 1938-42; variously employed as handyman, dishwasher, waiter, and office boy in New York City, and in defense work in Belle Meade, NJ, 1942-46. Lecturer on racial issues at universities in the United States and Europe, 1957-87. Director of play, *Fortune and Men's Eyes,* in Istanbul, Turkey, 1970, and film, *The Inheritance,* 1973. *Member:* Congress on Racial Equality (member of national advisory board), American Academy and Institute of Arts and Letters, Authors League, International PEN, Dramatists Guild, Actors' Studio, National Committee for a Sane Nuclear Policy.

■ Awards, Honors

Eugene F. Saxton fellowship, 1945; Rosenwald fellowship, 1948; Guggenheim fellowship, 1954; *Partisan Review* Fellowship, National Institute of Arts and Letters grant for literature, and National Institute of Arts and Letters Award, all 1956; Ford Foundation grant, 1959; National Conference of Christians and Jews Brotherhood Award, 1962, for *Nobody Knows My Name: More Notes of a Native Son;* George Polk Memorial Award, 1963, for magazine articles; Foreign Drama Critics Award, 1964, for *Blues for Mister Charlie;* D.Litt. from the University of British Columbia, Vancouver, 1964; National Association of Independent Schools Award, 1964, for *The Fire Next Time;* American Book Award nomination, 1980, for *Just Above My Head;* named Commander of the Legion of Honor (France), 1986.

■ Writings

FICTION

Go Tell It on the Mountain (novel), Knopf, 1953.
Giovanni's Room (novel; also see below), Dial, 1956, reprinted, Transworld, 1977.
Another Country (novel), Dial, 1962.
Going to Meet the Man (short stories), Dial, 1965.

(Contributor) *American Negro Short Stories*, Hill & Wang, 1966.

Tell Me How Long the Train's Been Gone (novel), Dial, 1968.

If Beale Street Could Talk (novel), Dial, 1974.

Little Man, Little Man: A Story of Childhood (juvenile), M. Joseph, 1976, Dial, 1977.

Just above My Head (novel), Dial, 1979, published in France as *Harlem Quartet*, Stock, 1987.

NONFICTION

Autobiographical Notes, Knopf, 1953.

Notes of a Native Son (essays), Beacon Press, 1955.

Nobody Knows My Name: More Notes of a Native Son (essays), Dial, 1961.

The Fire Next Time, Dial, 1963.

(Author of text) Richard Avedon, *Nothing Personal* (photographic portraits), Atheneum, 1964.

(With others) *Black Anti-Semitism and Jewish Racism*, R. W. Baron, 1969.

(With Kenneth Kaunda) Carl Ordung, editor, *Menschenwuerde und Gerechtigkeit* (essays delivered at the fourth assembly of the World Council of Churches), Union-Verlag, 1969.

(With Margaret Mead) *A Rap on Race* (transcribed conversation), Lippincott, 1971.

No Name in the Street (essays), Dial, 1972.

(With Francoise Giroud) *Cesar: Compressions d'or*, Hachette, 1973.

(With Nikki Giovanni) *A Dialogue* (transcripted conversation), Lippincott, 1973.

The Devil Finds Work (essays), Dial, 1976.

(With others) John Henrik Clarke, editor, *Harlem, U.S.A.: The Story of a City Within a City*, Seven Seas [Berlin], 1976.

The Evidence of Things Not Seen, Holt, 1985.

The Price of the Ticket: Collected Nonfiction 1948-1985, St. Martin's, 1985.

(With others) Michael J. Weber, editor, *Perspectives: Angles on African Art*, Center for African Art, 1987.

PLAYS

The Amen Corner (first produced in Washington, D.C., at Howard University, 1955, produced on Broadway at Ethel Barrymore Theatre, April 15, 1965), Dial, 1968.

Giovanni's Room (based on novel of same title), first produced in New York City at Actors' Studio, 1957.

Blues for Mister Charlie (first produced on Broadway at ANTA Theatre, April 23, 1964), Dial, 1964.

One Day, When I Was Lost: A Scenario (screenplay; based on *The Autobiography of Malcolm X*, by Alex Haley), M. Joseph, 1972, Dial, 1973.

A Deed for the King of Spain, first produced in New York City at American Center for Stanislavski Theatre Art, January 24, 1974.

Also author of *The Welcome Table*, 1987.

OTHER

Jimmy's Blues: Selected Poems, M. Joseph, 1983, St. Martin's, 1985.

Early Novels and Stories, Library of America (New York City), 1998.

Collected Essays, Library of America, 1998.

Contributor of book reviews and essays to numerous periodicals in the United States and abroad, including *Harper's, Nation, Esquire, Playboy, Partisan Review, Mademoiselle*, and *New Yorker*.

■ **Adaptations**

The Amen Corner was adapted as a musical stage play, *Amen Corner*, by Garry Sherman, Peter Udell and Philip Rose, and produced on Broadway at the Nederlander Theater, November 10, 1983. *Go Tell It on the Mountain* was dramatized under the same title for the Public Broadcasting System's *American Playhouse* series, January 14, 1985.

■ **Sidelights**

A self-proclaimed disturber of the peace and subversive outsider whose modest goal was to change the world, James Baldwin is considered one of the most important American writers since World War II. As Horace A. Porter noted in his critical study, *Stealing the Fire: The Art and Protest of James Baldwin*, the African American writer "established a remarkable record. He wrote about race and sexuality for almost four decades. He published twenty-two books, among them six novels, a collection of short stories, . . . plays, several assortments of essays, a children's book, a movie scenario, and . . . a chapbook of poems." Baldwin was a self-made man and self-created persona, unique in American letters of the time. Born illegitimate, Baldwin was also both black and gay in a time of racial and sexual intolerance. He was the grandson of a slave and the stepson of a Harlem preacher and was for a time a preacher himself.

But Baldwin's personal message came best not from the pulpit, but from the pen, a fact he discovered early on in his career. With a high school education, Baldwin filled out an intellectual arsenal with independent study, becoming in time one of the foremost spokesmen on racism in America. He also wrote daringly and openly about his own homosexuality, and was able to do so with a sense of security by transplanting himself to France in 1948. As Baldwin wrote in his book of essays, *Nobody Knows My Name,* "I left America because I doubted my ability to survive the fury of the color problem here. . . . I wanted to prevent myself from becoming merely a Negro; or, even, merely a Negro writer."

But Baldwin never became a true expatriate; he held on to American citizenship, living in the States off and on for the next forty years, but also making homes for himself in France, Turkey, and Switzerland. An international, Baldwin could maintain a skeptical, critical eye about his native country, one that he employed in the writing of such well known novels as *Go Tell It on the Mountain, Giovanni's Room, Another Country, Going to Meet the Man,* and *Tell Me How Long the Train's Been Gone,* as well as in his hard-hitting essays and social criticism collected in *Notes of a Native Son, Nobody Knows My Name, The Fire Next Time,* and *No Name in the Street.*

Baldwin "addressed complex social issues in his novels and in his essays," according to Porter. He took as his themes racism, homosexuality, hypocrisy, the moral bankruptcy of the United States, the role of the artist in society, and a myriad other social woes. As Porter noted, "[Baldwin] is considered by many critics and readers to be an essayist who poses as a novelist. Other critics complain about the highly autobiographical content of his novels; they see Baldwin as a thinly disguised surrogate for his protagonists." Still others say that Baldwin's primary goal in his writings was a search for identity: he never knew who his father was, nor over the course of his life, did he ever seem to be at home in any one country. Yet Baldwin the artist was little concerned with such criticism. He had a job, and that was to write and to make a difference with his writing. His greatest wish was

to be, as he often said, an honest man and a good writer. He wanted to last.

Up to the end of his life, ill with stomach cancer, he continued to write, hoping to put the finishing touches on his biography of Martin Luther King, Jr., a man Baldwin much admired. When he died on December 1, 1987, his work was not finished. His funeral, held at the Cathedral Church of St. John the Divine in Manhattan, was the first held there since Duke Ellington's in 1974, and was attended by 5,000 friends and relatives mourning the passing of a considerable talent. Tributes from the writers Maya Angelou and Toni Morrison stirred the gathered mourners. Another black writer, Amiri Baraka, giving the main eulogy, reminded the congregation that Baldwin "lived his life as witness," and that he was "God's black revolutionary mouth." And Baldwin himself was there at the funeral, on tape, singing "Precious Lord, take my hand, lead me on," as Baldwin's biographer, David Leeming reported in his *James Baldwin.* The preacher boy from Harlem and the internationally acclaimed writer were united at last. Leeming summed up Baldwin the man: "He was a man, like most people, with evident neuroses. He was not a saint, he was not always psychologically or emotionally stable. But he *was* a prophet."

Growing Up in Harlem

Born on August 2, 1924, in New York City's Harlem Hospital, James Arthur Jones was the illegitimate child of Emma Berdis Jones. Three years after the birth, his mother married David Baldwin, a preacher originally from New Orleans, and James Jones became James Baldwin. "Illegitimacy and an almost obsessive preoccupation with his stepfather were constant themes in the life and works of James Baldwin," noted Leeming. "The circumstance of his birth . . . was to symbolize for him the illegitimacy attached to an entire race within the American nation."

His stepfather, a disillusioned and bitter man, had recently migrated from New Orleans to Harlem. There were eight children produced in the union between Emma Berdis Jones and David Baldwin; the father was hard pressed to support such a large family. Strict, repressive, racist, and tyrannical, David Baldwin was one of the strongest influences in James Baldwin's development.

His father criticized young James at every possibility, calling him ugly because of his large, bulging eyes, calling him ignorant and hopeless. "He was righteous in the pulpit and a monster in the house," Baldwin told the poet and novelist Robert Penn Warren in *Who Speaks for the Negro?* "Maybe he saved all kinds of souls, but he lost his children, every single one of them. And it wasn't so much a matter of punishment with him: he was trying to kill us. I've hated a few people, but actually I've hated only one person, and that was my father."

"I guess the one thing my father *did* for me was that he taught me how to *fight*," Baldwin once told Fern Marja Eckman in the *New York Post.* "I had to know how to fight because I *fought* him so hard. He taught me—what my real *weapons* were. Which were patience. And a kind of ruthless determination. Because I had to *endure* it; to go under and come back *up;* to *wait.*" Another positive side effect of such a repressive childhood was that Baldwin was saved from the dangers of the Harlem streets where drug abuse, crime, and white racism were tearing the community apart. Baldwin was kept so busy at home trying to help his mother care for his eight brothers and sisters, that he had no time for the violent life on the streets. And added to the hard economic times endemic to Harlem was the Great Depression gripping all of America during Baldwin's youth.

Baldwin took refuge in books, reading voraciously and indiscriminately. He would later brag that he went through all the volumes in Harlem's two libraries, and then had to go downtown to the New York Public Library on Forty Second Street for more sustenance. Dickens was a favorite author for him, his rags to riches stories being the perfect palliative for Baldwin, whose own life could have filled the pages of the Englishman's novels. Another refuge was his mother who nurtured him where his father abused him, and outside the home, Baldwin was fortunate in finding other supportive adults. At his first public school, P.S. 24, he had one of the few black principals in New York. For Baldwin, this woman was living proof that a black person could make it to the top, that a black person was not doomed to menial positions.

Also at P.S. 24 he formed a strong bond with one of his teachers, a young white woman from the Midwest whom he called "Bill" Miller. Miller took an interest in her young student, encouraging his

Baldwin's classic novel reveals elements of the black experience by following several generations of one family.

bookish-ness, helping him in his first efforts at writing. She and her sister took young Baldwin to the theater, and it was on one such outing that he witnessed the Orson Welles, all-black production of *Macbeth* at the Lafayette Theater. Baldwin sat through the performance entranced; his love for the theater was confirmed that day. Baldwin was also a fan of the movies, loving in particular the screen adaptation of Dickens's *A Tale of Two Cities.* Miller, an ardent leftist politically, helped to form the young Baldwin's social conscience.

Baldwin moved on to junior high school at P.S. 139, where he continued his writing and came under the influence of the black poet, Countee Cullen, director of the school's literary club. This club became another refuge for Baldwin, whose slight frame and love for books made him a target for schoolyard jest. While in junior high, Baldwin was made editor of the school newspaper, the *Douglass Pilot.* It was also during these years that Baldwin underwent a religious conversion, becoming a member of Mount Cavalry of the Pentecostal Faith Church, eventually reaching the level of junior minister. Baldwin's life was receiving a challenge from another quarter as well, for he was accepted to the De Witt Clinton High School in the Bronx, a predominantly white school, many of whose students were Jewish. This was a new world for Baldwin, and here he met several people who would become life-long friends. Richard Avedon, the future photographer, was one of these; Baldwin worked with him on the school's literary magazine, the *Magpie,* and would much later collaborate with Avedon on a picture book of America, *Nothing Personal.*

His experiences at De Witt Clinton were beginning to make him question his new-found religiosity, as was his budding sexuality. At sixteen he fell in love with an older man, a Harlem racketeer, and began to come to grips with his sexual identity. Another formative influence was a friendship with the older black artist, Beauford Delaney, a man who showed Baldwin that a black could make it in the world of art. By seventeen, Baldwin had become disillusioned with the church. "Being in the pulpit was like being in the theater," Baldwin later wrote in *The Fire Next Time.* "I was behind the scenes and knew how the illusion worked. I knew the other ministers and knew the quality of their lives. And I don't mean to suggest by this the 'Elmer Gantry' sort of hypocrisy concerning sensuality; it was a deeper, deadlier, and more subtle hypocrisy than that, and a little honest sensuality, or a lot, would have been like water in an extremely bitter desert. I knew how to work a congregation until the last dime was surrendered. . . ." With all this turmoil in his private life, Baldwin did not graduate from high school with his class; he did so, however six months later, in 1942. At this point, his youth in Harlem was coming rapidly to an end.

Writer in the Making, Writer in Exile

Baldwin's stepfather had been in declining health for some time; a deteriorating mental condition forced him to give up work and Baldwin needed to earn money to held support his family. Another De Witt Clinton school chum found him a job in Belle Mead, New Jersey, working on the construction of the Army Quartermaster Depot. Here Baldwin experienced firsthand the sort of discrimination and racism that Harlem had insulated him from. Working with Southerners, he had a miserable time of it, but lived frugally and sent part of his paycheck to his family in Harlem. By 1943 his stepfather died and his mother gave birth to a baby daughter, the last child of her union with David Baldwin.

Baldwin decided that it was time for him to make an all-out commitment to writing. Moving to Greenwich Village, he supported himself as a waiter while devoting the rest of his time to the writing of his first novel, at onepoint called "Crying Holy" and then later changed to "In My Father's House." A chance meeting with the black novelist Richard Wright led to a Eugene F. Saxton Memorial Trust Award for Baldwin, but Baldwin was unable to finish this first manuscript during the tenure of his award. Disappointed at what he saw as a failure in his craft, Baldwin searched for new forms of expression, turning to the essay. He sold a book review to *Nation,* and then did reviews for *The New Leader,* writing on what was then called the Negro problem. One such article, "The Harlem Ghetto," about anti-Semitism in the black community, was published by the influential journal of the American Jewish Committee, *Commentary,* and made a name for Baldwin as a new voice in social commentary. His articles were in demand now, and in 1948 he published his first short story, "Previous Condition," in the pages of *Commentary.* The story of a black artist exiled between two worlds—that of the whites as well as of the blacks—announced a powerful theme that would recur in most of Baldwin's writing: the story of dispossession and a search for identity.

A Rosenwald Fellowship helped to finance Baldwin's next great experiment—life outside of the United States. Though he had earned a name for himself as an essayist, he had yet to produce the major work he knew he was capable of. "I was past caring," he told W. J. Weatherby in *James Baldwin: Artist on Fire.* "My whole life had become a gamble. I wasn't really choosing France, I was getting out of America. I had no idea what might happen to me in France, but I was very clear what would happen if I remained in New York." In

Paris, Richard Wright and Beauford Delaney had both taken up residence before Baldwin, and when he arrived there he was nearly broke and spoke no French. Things did not go well for Baldwin at first, as he was arrested over a silly incident involving a stolen bed sheet from a hotel, but still the new climate was hospitable to him. He began to find his own identity as a human rather than as a black man or as a bisexual. "Everybody's Protest Novel," an essay which attacked the traditional protest novel from *Uncle Tom's Cabin* to Wright's *Native Son,* was an early product of his Paris sojourn, and freedhim to find his own course in fiction, as well.

Baldwin continued working on his first novel, influenced not only by the other American writers in Paris, such as James Jones, Philip Roth, William Styron, and Norman Mailer, but also his readings of other authors, including the great prose stylist, Henry James. Just when he was about to give up on this first novel, a close friend took him away to a chalet in Switzerland where Baldwin finally finished what now was titled *Go Tell It on the Mountain.* The book, so many years in the making, was finally published in 1953, and laid to rest some of the ghosts surrounding his relationship with his stepfather. The story of John Grimes who must come to grips with the cruel treatment of his father as well as with the power of religion, *Go Tell It on the Mountain* is highly autobiographical. As John W. Roberts noted in *Dictionary of Literary Biography,* "John Grimes is Baldwin seeking in the movies, the streets of Harlem, religion, and a silent mother the answers to questions hidden in the recesses of familial memory. And he is young Baldwin polishing his intellectual armor in hopes of using it as a weapon against the forces that would destroy him in his present environment." Set in Harlem's Temple of the Fire Baptised and on the day of John's fourteenth birthday, the novel uses a complex mix of flashbacks along with its internal point of view to focus on the boy's religious conversion. Divided into three parts, the novel takes the reader through an introduction of the Grimes clan—much resembling Baldwin's own family—and John's guilt over his budding sexuality and hatred of whites in part one. Part two is a flashback recounting of the Grimes's family background centering upon three prayers, and focusing on three characters, Florence, Elizabeth, and Gabriel, born between 1875 and 1900, who migrate to the North. In the third part John is converted before the altar. Though not actually a religious novel, the book is full of biblical language and references; irony is one of the main weapons of Baldwin in this debut novel. Though having experienced a religious revelation, John really has not changed by the end of the novel.Religion does not set him free.

Critical reception of this first book was generally positive. Harvey Curtis Webster, writing in *Saturday Review,* felt that "Mr. Baldwin's first novel is written as skillfully as many a man's fifth essay in fiction," and concluded that while the novel "fulfills a great deal, [it] promises more." Anthony West noted in *The New Yorker* that *Go Tell It on the Mountain* "is a first novel of quite exceptional promise, centering on a church in Harlem," while Donald Barr dubbed the novel "beautiful" and "furious" in the *New York Times.* Granville Hicks, originally writing in the *New Leader,* commented, "There is a new name to be added to the list of serious and talented young writers—that of James Baldwin," and went on to call this debut novel "a very fine book." This novel of a teenager getting religion on his fourteenth birthday was accomplished with "intense reality," Hicks felt. Colin MacInnes, in a critical evaluation of Baldwin's Works in *Encounter,* described his first novel as "a densely-packed, ominous, sensual, doom-ridden story, lit by rare beauty, love and human penetration. The theme is life and religion and how both, wonderful and terrible, can create and destroy. . . ." And in his critical study of Baldwin, the Baldwin scholar Louis H. Pratt wrote in his *James Baldwin,* "*Go Tell* stands as an honest, intensive, self-analysis, functioning simultaneously to illuminate self, society, and mankind as a whole."

A Man of Letters

Baldwin returned to the U.S. for a time at the publication of his first novel; returning to France he began work on his first play, *The Amen Corner,* which mines much of the same ground as did *Go Tell It on the Mountain.* Within the next few years he finished his play, which was produced first at Howard University, published his first collection of essays, *Notes of a Native Son,* and also completed the manuscript of his second novel, *Giovanni's Room,* which he had trouble at first placing because of its themeof homosexuality. In *Notes of a Native Son,* Baldwin collected ten essays published in journals such as *Commentary* and *Partisan Review,* writings largely autobiographical or impressionistic on topics from race to the protest novel to movies.

Writing in the *New York Times Book Review*, Langston Hughes felt that the essays were "thought-provoking, tantalizing, irritating, abusing and amusing," and that "[f]ew American writers handle words more effectively in the essay form than James Baldwin."

Baldwin ultimately published his second novel, *Giovanni's Room*, in England, and once the book proved successful there, it was brought out in America. A departure for Baldwin, the novel had no black characters. Instead, it focussed on the tall, blond American, David, who ping-pongs back and forth between his fiancée, Hella, and his Italian lover, Giovanni. "Nevertheless," pointed out Fred L. Standley in *Dictionary of Literary Biography*,

JAMES BALDWIN

"A STRAIGHT-FROM-THE-SHOULDER WRITER, WRITING ABOUT THE TROUBLED PROBLEMS OF THIS TROUBLED EARTH WITH AN ILLUMINATING INTENSITY."
—LANGSTON HUGHES, THE NEW YORK TIMES BOOK REVIEW

NOTES OF A NATIVE SON

The author examines various subjects from an African American perspective in this 1955 collection of essays.

"the principal concerns of the novel are similar to those of previous books—the search for sexual awareness and psychological identity; the complexity of the father-son relationship; the paradox of the relation between freedom and attachment; the painful and baffling complexity of relations among male and female, male and male."

Critical response to the book was mixed. Roberts, for example, in *Dictionary of Literary Biography*, called it "one of Baldwin's finest creations," while noting that it was a "failure" as a novel. A negative conceptualization of David results from his failure to resolve his sexual conflict, according to Roberts. Other reviewers felt that Baldwin handled his theme sensitively. David Karp, writing in *Saturday Review*, commented that Baldwin "has taken a very special theme and treated it with great artistry and restraint. . . . Mr. Baldwin has managed to instill in one reader, at least, a greater tolerance, a fresher sense of pity." William Esty, writing in *The New Republic*, noted that Baldwin "successfully avoids the cliché literary attitudes" and "insists on the painful, baffling complexity of things."

After publication of *Giovanni's Room*, Baldwin began work on a third novel, *Another Country*, feeling that he had not fully explored America's racial and sexual attitudes and biases. Still not finished with the novel by the summer of 1956, he returned to the United States for inspiration and found a country embroiled with the civil rights battle and desegregation. Temporarily abandoning his novel, he traveled to the South to be part of the struggle. Back in New York he became involved with the theater, 'apprenticing' with the director Elia Kazan for a time and writing essays for various periodicals. Returning to work on his novel, he lived in the guest cottage at William Styron's place in Connecticut, then moved on to Istanbul, where he finished the manuscript.

Meanwhile came publication of *Nobody Knows My Name*, "a brilliant . . . collection of essays," according to Irving Howe in the *New York Times Book Review*. Reviewing the selection in *Commonweal*, James Finn wrote that *Nobody Knows My Name* "is confirmation that James Baldwin is one of America's finest writers. . . . What sets Baldwin apart from even the best of his contemporaries is that he is an unproclaimed moralist. . . ." In a critical evaluation of much of Baldwin's writings, David Littlejohn noted in *Black on White* that Baldwin "is the most powerful and important American essayist of the post-war period, perhaps of the century," and that *Notes of a Native Son* and *Nobody Knows My Name* will maintain their place among the small collection of genuine American classics."

Another Country

Baldwin's third novel, *Another Country*, was published on June 25, 1962 and represents, according to Standley in *Dictionary of Literary Biography*, "the author's *magnum opus* in fiction." Once again, Baldwin deals with his twin themes of race and sex in a very ambitious novel both in scope as well as in terms of technique. Like all rich novels, *Another Country* can be read on various levels. "In one sense, the novel contains several stories, interrelated and interwoven, of people trying to come to terms with their identities," according to John W. Roberts in *Dictionary of Literary Biography*. Race and sex are both defining attributes of the characters. And on another level, "the novel deals with pain and the role of pain in allowing one to become a complete person," according to Roberts.

Told in four sections whose stories sometimes intersect, intertwine, and converge, *Another Country* follows the lives and fortunes of four couples: a black jazz drummer, Rufus Scott and his Southern white girl friend, Leona; the black woman, Ida Scott, Rufus's sister, and her lover, an Italian-American named Vivaldo Moore; a white couple, Richard and Cass Silenski, who do not deal well with the changes brought on by the success of Richard's book; and Eric Jones and his male lover Yves, both white. Eric intertwines with the others in his affairs with Cass and Vivaldo. All of these characters somehow connect with the others in "a kind of phantasmagoria of interracial and intersexual relations among friends and strangers in New York City," as Standley explained. "In *Another Country* Baldwin explores the possibilities of the Afro-American blues tradition to deal with the chaos of twentieth-century life," noted Roberts. All of them artists, either singers or writers or actors, the characters represent for Baldwin a cross-section of that other country in which he dwelt, be it in Europe or the United States.

Much of Baldwin's work has drawn both praise and indignation, and critical response to *Another Country* was typically mixed. Though it was

Baldwin's big work, some critics have found it deeply flawed. "*Another Country* is a novel whose parts are more successful than the whole," remarked Finn in *Commonweal*. "There are passages where Baldwin is equal to his intentions. . . . And those are enough, not entirely to save the book but to make it more interesting and more rewarding that the 'great' works held up for universal admiration with such implacable regularity." Paul Bone, writing in *The Negro Novel in America*, called the novel "a failure on the grand scale," noting that the book "drowns in a torrent of rhetoric." And Paul Goodman dubbed *Another Country* "mediocre" in the *New York Times Book Review*.

Other critics had more positive words for the book. Edgar Z. Friedenberg remarked in *The New Republic* that "Baldwin is the least sentimental of novelists," and that *Another Country* was "a magnificent moral cliffhanger," while Littlejohn commented that "*Another Country* reminds the reader that James Baldwin is still one of the genuine stylists of the English language." Standley summed up the contribution of *Another Country* to American letters and society: "Baldwin has been audacious enough, prior to most other artists, to grapple candidly with the usually taboo subjects of American society and culture: interracial sexual intercourse, homosexuality as a normative mode of experience, and bisexuality as a real phenomenon."

At Home and Abroad

While living in the United States off and on throughout the Sixties, Baldwin became involved with civil rights leaders from Martin Luther King, Jr. to Malcolm X to James Meredith and Medgar Evers. Following publication of *Another Country*, Baldwin came out with a book of two essays in *The Fire Next Time*, a drama, *Blues for Mister Charlie*, and *Going to Meet the Man*, a book of short stories. In *The Fire Next Time*, Baldwin once again tackles the subject of race, in the form of letters to his nephew in the first essay of the collection, who is about to enter the world of racial conflict. The second essay, "Down at the Cross," is part autobiography about Baldwin's life in Harlem, and part a look at the Black Muslims. Stephen Spender, reviewing the book in *Partisan Review*, noted, "The great contribution of Mr. Baldwin is that he finds words to express what one knows to be true: how it feels to be an American Negro. . . . Within his own works he has solved the problem of integration: not by

This novel addressed race relations in the wake of the Civil Rights Movement.

love, but by the imagination using words which know no class nor color bars."

In 1964 Baldwin completed *Blues for Mr. Charlie,* his third play, which was produced in New York in April of that year. Based on his work in the South with Medgar Evers and partly on the case of a young black man in Mississippi who was killed and whose murderer was let off, *Blues for Mr. Charlie* focuses on the life of Richard Henry and is told in flashbacks. Returning from the North, Richard refuses to bow to the norms of Southern society and is killed for such impudence. His killer in turn is let off when he lies about a supposed assault on his wife by the black man. The message: blacks must go it on their own and not rely on the so-called integrity of the white community. In the *New York Times,* Howard Taubman

concluded that Bald-win's speeches "lay bare the heart of the Negro's suffering and explain the iron of his determination." Philip Roth however, writing in the *New York Review of Books,* felt that the play was "soap opera designed to illustrate the superiority of blacks over whites. . . . There is no glory or hope, not a shred of it, to be found in the life of either the black man or the white. What these characters give evidence to, what the play seems to be about really, is the small-mindedness of the male sex."

That same year saw Baldwin's collaboration with his old schoolmate Avedon on the photo-essay, *Nothing Personal,* a look at contemporary America. More indicative of Baldwin's prose strengths of the time are the stories gathered in the 1965 collection, *Going to Meet the Man,* tales which "sing with truth dug out from pain," according to Daniel Stern writing in *Saturday Review.* "The stories in *Going to Meet the Man* demonstrate with stunning effect that James Baldwin has no need of racial or sexual special pleading," Stern concluded. Stories such as "The Outing," "Come out of the Wilderness," "Sonny's Blues," and "The Previous Condition" span Baldwin's writing career to the time, and introduce his major themes in compressed fashion. "James Baldwin's most valuable quality as a writer is authenticity," declared John Rees Moore in *The Hollins Critic,* concluding that Baldwin's "endeavor is to show us—even to the point of hallucination—that the public life and the private life are an indivisible whole, that sanity cannot exist half slave and half free."

Baldwin's last novel of the productive 1960s was *Tell Me How Long the Train's Been Gone,* the story of a black actor, Leo Proudhammer, whose life story unfolds in flashbacks as he is recuperating from a heart attack. The son of migrants to Harlem, Proudhammer knows personally of poverty and racism. He is now cut off both from the black community because of his success, and from the white community because of his color. He must decide if he will play a part in the black struggle for equality and join the civil rights movement. In flashbacks the reader learns of his youth, of his early love for a white actress, a doomed love not only because of her color but also because of his bisexuality. A young militant black, with whom Leo has an affair, helps to show Leo the optimism inherent in the civil rights movement and in the end it appears Leo will become part of the movement.

Critical reception for this novel was again mixed. John Thompson, for example, writing in *Commentary*, found the book to be "a masterpiece by one of the best living writers in America . . . the book will move you to tears." Others were not so complimentary. The author Mario Puzo called the book "a simple-minded, one-dimensional novel with mostly cardboard characters" in the *New York Times Book Review*. Puzo went on to complain of "a polemical rather than narrative tone, weak invention, and poor selection of incident." Puzo concluded, "It becomes clearer with each book he publishes that Baldwin's reputation is justified by his essays rather than his fiction. . . . It is possible that Baldwin believes this is not tactically the time for art, that polemical fiction can help the Negro cause more. . . . But perhaps it is now time for Baldwin to forget the black revolution and start worrying about himself as an artist, who is the ultimate revolutionary."

By 1970 Baldwin had had enough of living in America again. The assassinations of so many black leaders—Malcolm X, Martin Luther King, Jr., Medgar Evers—had taken their toll on Baldwin and the country as a whole. Following a long illness, he returned to Europe and bought a farmhouse in the French countryside at St. Paul de Vence. Though he would still "commute" between continents, this would become his permanent home until his death in 1987.

The Final Years

A further book of essays appeared in 1972, *No Name in the Street*, the subject matter of which is, according to Charles Deemer in *The Progressive*, "the struggle of the artist trapped in history." A screenplay adaptation of *The Autobiography of Malcolm X* was also published in 1972, an effort with "[p]lenty of heart . . . but not enough soul," as Anthony Bailey described it in the *New Statesman*. Baldwin describes his frustrations with Hollywood as well as the world of American movies in the essays in the 1976 collection, *The Devil Finds Work*, a "visionary" and "unusual" work according to Eric Rhode in *Sight and Sound*.

Baldwin also pursued fiction in his later works. *If Beale Street Could Talk*, a novel again set in Harlem and told from the point of view of a nineteen-year-old narrator, Tish Rivers, pregnant and unmarried. The father of her unborn child, Fonny,

is in jail on rape charges—a crime he is innocent of—and it is unlikely he will be released in time for the birth. Tish's attempts to get Fonny out of jail form the heart of this novel, Baldwin's first in six years. Again employing flashback, Baldwin explores Tish and Fonny's romance, and their struggle to find some happiness in the world. Baldwin takes on the U.S. judicial system in this novel as well as a religion that keeps its people down.

Again, critical reception of Baldwin's novel was highly mixed. Walter Clemons in *Newsweek* found the book to be "an almost total disaster," and

Baldwin presents a realistic view of African-Americans and the criminal justice system in a story emphasizing the people behind the issues.

Peter Ackroyd writing in *The Spectator* noted that the book "is composed of largely cardboard, since stereotypes are the only possible vehicles for the single-minded passions, wordless joys and lengthy silences which Baldwin insists upon discovering in every basement." However, Joyce Carol Oates, writing in the *New York Times Book Review* called the novel "a moving, painful story." Oates concluded, "It is so vividly human and so obviously based upon reality, that it strikes us as timeless— an art that has not the slightest need of esthetic tricks, and even less need of fashionable apocalyptic excesses." David Thomas commented in *The Listener*, "*If Beale Street Could Talk* celebrates this new-found capacity for self-creation. It is a sort of fable about the Negro's quest for cultural freedom in the alien environment of New York."

A departure for Baldwin was the 1977 juvenile book, *Little Man, Little Man,* a coming of age story set in Harlem. Two years later he published perhaps his most ambitious novel, *Just Above My Head,* at nearly 600 pages surely his longest book. Focusing on the gospel singer Arthur Hall and his family, the novel becomes something of a journey into another country—that of the soul and the senses. By metaphor, the book is also a contemporary history of blacks in America, tracing a network of family and friends through the South and Harlem over the course of a generation. The book looks at the civil rights movement, the Korean War, Harlem's storefront churches, white racism and homosexuality.

"*Just Above My Head* reveals a calmer, less bitter, more mature Baldwin," noted Roberts in *Dictionary of Literary Biography.* "[It] is a long, complex novel," Roberts continued. "It is instructive to note that in the novel Baldwin has finally brought together and completely resolved many of the issues raised in earlier works." Baldwin himself felt that this last novel presented his work in full, that he had come full circle from *Go Tell It on the Mountain.* The critics, as usual, were of varied opinions. Reviewing thetitle in *Washington Post Book World,* the writer Edmund White called Baldwin "the warmest, the most companionable, the least ironic" of all well-known novelists of the day, and commented that while *Just Above My Head* is not a perfect novel," it did give readers a "comprehensive and comprehending examination of race and sexuality. . . ." John Romano applauded Baldwin's effort to create a "saga in the contemporary mode," in the *New York Times Book Review,* but concluded "there is

If you enjoy the works of James Baldwin, you may also want to check out the following books:

Charles Dickens, *Oliver Twist,* 1837-39.
William Styron, *The Confessions of Nat Turner,* 1967.
Countee Cullen, *Copper Sun,* 1927.

too much that is inchoate, unrealized." And Stanley Crouch, reviewing this sixth novel in *The Village Voice,* felt that while large sections of the book stood up with the best Baldwin had written, it was still the fact that "Baldwin's sentimental and poorly argued attempt to present homosexuality as some form of superior erotic enlightenment . . . continually slackens the power" of the novel. Richard Gilman remarked in *The New Republic* that *Just Above My Head* was "a melancholy piece of creation, swollen . . . meandering, awkwardly colloquial, and pretentiously elevated by turns," while on the other hand Whitney Balliet called Baldwin a "A prophet, a master of exhortation," in *The New Yorker.*

Baldwin did not publish for several years thereafter, and then came out with a book of poems in 1983, *Jimmy's Blues,* as well as a further foray into nonfiction with his 1985 *The Evidence of Things Not Seen.* The latter was a meditation on the series of child murders in Atlanta, Georgia from 1979 to 1980. Baldwin used the murders and the arrest of the perpetrator as a springboard to look at race and society in late twentieth century America. The following year he was inducted into France's Legion of Honor for his body of work. Increasingly, however, Baldwin suffered from poor health. Two heart attacks set him back, and then in 1987 he was diagnosed with stomach cancer. He continued working on projects from dramas to biography while passing his last days at his home in St. Paul de Vence. He died there on December 1, 1987, with many friends in attendance, at the age of 63.

As Fred Standley noted in *Dictionary of Literary Biography Yearbook, 1987,* "As novelist, essayist, dramatist, and social critic, [Baldwin's] corpus demonstrates unequivocally both a sustained productivity and a consistent and sensitive human perspective. At times alternately praised and damned by blacks and whites alike, he never lacked an audience." Nor has his appeal waned since his death. If anything there has been something of a Baldwin revival," according to Dwight A. McBride in the introduction to the 1999 *James Baldwin Now.* Since 1990 there have been a plethora of new dissertations on the author, and his inclusion in the Library of America insures Baldwin a place in the American canon. As McBride noted, Baldwin was "one of the most prolific and influential African American writes ever to live. . . . [His] life was committed to struggle."

■ Works Cited

Ackroyd, Peter, review of *If Beale Street Could Talk, The Spectator,* July 6, 1974, p. 22.

Bailey, Arthur, "Black and White," *New Statesman,* November 3, 1972, pp. 643-44.

Baldwin, James, *Nobody Knows My Name,* Dial, 1961.

Baldwin, James, *The Fire Next Time,* Dial, 1963.

Balliet, Whitney, "Father and Son," *The New Yorker,* November 26, 1979, pp. 218-19.

Baraka, Amiri, "We Carry Him as Us," *New York Times Book Review,* December 20, 1987, pp. 27, 29.

Barr, Donald, "Guilt Was Everywhere," *New York Times,* May 17, 1953, p. 5.

Bone, Robert A., "James Baldwin," *The Negro Novel in America,* Yale University Press, 1965, pp. 215-29.

Clemons, Walter, "Black and Blue," *Newsweek,* May 27, 1974, p. 82.

Crouch, Stanley, "Cliches of Degradation," *The Village Voice,* October 29, 1979, pp. 39, 42.

Deemer, Charles, "James Baldwin's Baptism," *The Progressive,* August, 1972, pp. 37-38.

Eckman, Fern Marja, "James Baldwin," *New York Post,* January 15, 1964.

Esty, William, "The Cities of the Plain," *The New Republic,* December 17, 1956, p. 26.

Finn, James, "Critics' Choices for Christmas: 'Nobody Knows My Name'," *Commonweal,* December 8, 1961, pp. 288, 290.

Finn, James, "The Identity of James Baldwin," *Commonweal,* October 26, 1962, pp. 113-16.

Friedenberg, Edgar Z., "Another Country for an Arkansas Traveler," *The New Republic,* August 27, 1962, pp. 23-26.

Gilman, Richard, review of *Just Above My Head, The New Republic,* November 25, 1979, pp. 30-31.

Goodman, Paul, "Not Enough of a World to Grow In," *New York Times Book Review,* June 24, 1962, p. 5.

Hicks, Granville, "Go Tell It on the Mountain," *Literary Horizons: A Quarter Century of American Fiction,* New York University Press, 1970, pp. 87-90.

Howe, Irving, "A Protest of His Own," *New York Times Book Review,* July 2, 1961, p. 4.

Hughes, Langston, "From Harlem to Paris," *New York Times Book Review,* February 26, 1956, p. 26.

Karp, David, "A Squalid World," *The Saturday Review,* December 1, 1956, p. 34.

Leeming, David, *James Baldwin: A Biography,* Knopf, 1994.

Littlejohn, David, *Black or White: A Critical Survey of Writing by American Negroes,* Viking, 1966.

MacInnes, Colin, "Dark Angel: The Writing of James Baldwin," *Encounter,* August, 1963, pp. 22-33.

McBride, Dwight A., "Introduction," *James Baldwin Now,* New York University Press, 1999, pp. 1, 8.

Moore, John Rees, "An Embarrassment of Riches: Baldwin's 'Going to Meet the Man'," *The Hollins Critic,* December, 1965, pp. 1-2.

Oates, Joyce Carol, review of *If Beale Street Could Talk, New York Times Book Review,* May 19, 1974, p. 2.

Porter, Horace A., *Stealing the Fire: The Art and Protest of James Baldwin,* Wesleyan University Press, 1989, pp. 11, 12, 14.

Pratt, Louis H., *James Baldwin,* Twayne, 1978, p. 51.

Puzo, Mario, "His Cardboard Lover," *New York Times Book Review,* June 23, 1968, pp. 5, 34.

Rhode, Eric, review of *The Devil Finds Work, Sight and Sound,* Autumn, 1976, p. 260.

Roberts, John W., "James Baldwin," *Dictionary of Literary Biography,* Volume 33: *African-American Fiction Writers after 1955,* Gale, 1984, pp. 3-16.

Romano, John, "James Baldwin Writing and Talking," *New York Times Book Review,* September 23, 1979, pp. 3, 33.

Roth, Philip, "Channel X: Two Plays on the Race Conflict," *New York Review of Books,* May 28, 1964, pp. 10-13.

Spender, Stephen, "James Baldwin: Voice of a Revolution," *Partisan Review,* Summer, 1963, pp. 256-60.

Standley, Fred L., "James Baldwin," *Dictionary of Literary Biography,* Volume 2: *American Novelists Since World War II, First Series,* Gale, 1978, pp. 15-22.

Standley, Fred L., "James Baldwin," *Dictionary of Literary Biography Yearbook, 1987,* Gale, 1988, pp. 219-25.

Stern, David, "A Special Corner on Truth," *Saturday Review,* November 6, 1965, p. 32.

Taubman, Howard, "Common Burden: Baldwin Points Duty of Negro and White," *New York Times,* May 3, 1964.

Thomas, David, "Too Black, Too White," *The Listener,* July 25, 1974, p. 125.

Thompson, John, "Baldwin: The Prophet as Artist," *Commentary,* June, 1968, pp. 67-69.

Warren, Robert Penn, *Who Speaks for the Negro?,* Random House, 1965.

Weatherby, W. J., *James Baldwin: Artist on Fire,* Donald I. Fine, 1989.

Webster, Harvey Curtis, "Community of Pride," *Saturday Review,* May 16, 1953, p. 14.

West, Anthony, "Sorry Lives," *The New Yorker,* June 20, 1953, p. 93.

White, Edmund, review of *Just Above My Head, Washington Post Book World,* September 23, 1979, pp. 5, 9.

■ **For More Information See**

BOOKS

Balakian, Nona, and Charles Simmons, editors, *The Creative Present: Notes on Contemporary Fiction,* Doubleday, 1963.

Bigsby, C. W. E., *Confrontation and Commitment: A Study of Contemporary American Drama,* University of Missouri Press, 1967.

Bigsby, C. W. E., editor, *The Black American Writer,* Volume I: *Fiction,* Volume II: *Poetry and Drama,* Everett/Edwards, 1969.

Bobia, Rosa, *The Critical Reception of James Baldwin in France,* Peter Lang, 1997.

Brustein, Robert, *Seasons of Discontent: Dramatic Opinions 1959-1965,* Simon & Schuster, 1965.

Burgess, Anthony, *The Novel Now: A Guide to Contemporary Fiction,* Norton, 1967.

Campbell, James, *Talking at the Gates,* Viking, 1991.

Champion, Ernest A., *Mr. Baldwin, I Presume: James Baldwin—Chinua Achebe, A Meeting of the Minds,* University Press of America, 1995.

Chapman, Abraham, editor, *Black Voices: An Anthology of Afro-American Literature,* New American Library, 1968.

Cleaver, Eldridge, *Soul on Ice,* McGraw-Hill, 1968.

Cohn, Ruby, *Dialogue in American Drama,* Indiana University Press, 1971.

Concise Dictionary of American Literary Biography: The New Consciousness, 1941-1968, Gale, 1987.

Contemporary Authors Bibliographical Series, Volume I: *American Novelists,* Gale, 1986.

Contemporary Literary Criticism, Gale, Volume 1, 1973, Volume 2, 1974, Volume 3, 1975, Volume 4, 1975, Volume 5, 1976, Volume 8, 1978, Volume 13, 1980, Volume 15, 1980, Volume 17, 1981, Volume 42, 1987, Volume 50, 1988, Volume 67, 1992, Volume 90, 1996.

Cook, M. G., editor, *Modern Black Novelists: A Collection of Critical Essays,* Prentice-Hall, 1971.

Culture for the Millions, Van Nostrand, 1959.

Dance, Daryl, *Black American Writers: Bibliographical Essays,* St. Martin's, 1978.

Dictionary of Literary Biography, Volume 8: *Twentieth-Century American Dramatists,* Gale, 1981.

Eckman, Fern Marja, *The Furious Passage of James Baldwin,* M. Evans, 1966.

French, Warren, editor, *The Fifties: Fiction, Poetry, Drama,* Everett/Edwards, 1970.

Frost, David, *The Americans,* Stein & Day, 1970.

Gayle, Addison, Jr., *The Way of the World: The Black Novel in America,* Anchor Press, 1975.

Gibson, Donald B., editor, *Five Black Writers: Essays on Wright, Ellison, Baldwin, Hughes, and LeRoi Jones,* New York University Press, 1970.

Gottfried, Ted, *James Baldwin: Voice from Harlem,* F. Watts (New York City), 1997.

Harris, Trudier, *New Essays on Go Tell It on the Mountain,* Cambridge University Press (New York City), 1995.

Hesse, H. Ober, editor, *The Nature of a Humane Society,* Fortress, 1976.

Hill, Herbert, editor, *Anger and Beyond,* Harper, 1966.

Howe, Irving, *A World More Attractive: A View of Modern Literature and Politics,* Horizon Press, 1963.

Hyman, Stanley Edgar, *Standards: A Chronicle of Books for Our Time,* Horizon Press, 1966.

Jothiprakash, R., *Commitment as a Theme in African American Literature: A Study of James Baldwin and Ralph Ellison,* Wyndham Hall Press (Bristol, IN), 1994.

Kazin, Alfred, *Contemporaries,* Little, Brown, 1962.

Kazin, Alfred, *Bright Book of Life: American Novelists & Storytellers from Hemingway to Mailer,* Little, Brown, 1973.

Kenan, Randall, *James Baldwin,* Chelsea House (New York City), 1994.

King, Malcolm, *Baldwin: Three Interviews,* Wesleyan University Press, 1985.

Kinnamon, Kenneth, editor, *James Baldwin: A Collection of Critical Essays,* Prentice-Hall, 1974.

Klein, Marcus, *After Alienation: American Novels in Mid-Century,* World Publishing, 1964.

Lumley, Frederick, *New Trends in 20th Century Drama: A Survey Since Ibsen and Shaw,* Oxford University Press, 1967.

Macebuh, Stanley, *James Baldwin: A Critical Study,* Joseph Okpaku, 1973.

Major, Clarence, *The Dark and Feeling: Black American Writers and Their Work,* Joseph Okpaku, 1974.

Moeller, Karin, *The Theme of Identity in the Essays of James Baldwin,* Acta Universitatis Gotoburgensis, 1975.

Moore, Harry T., editor, *Contemporary American Novelists,* Southern Illinois University Press, 1964.

O'Daniel, Therman B., *James Baldwin: A Critical Evaluation,* Howard University Press, 1977.

Panichas, George A., *The Politics of Twentieth-Century Novelists,* Hawthorn, 1971.

Podhoretz, Norman, *Doings and Undoings,* Farrar, Straus, 1964.

Rosenblatt, Roger, *Black Fiction,* Harvard University Press, 1974.

Sheed, Wilfrid, *The Morning After,* Farrar, Straus, 1971.

Simon, John, *Uneasy Stages: Chronicle of the New York Theatre,* Random House, 1975.

Sontag, Susan, *Against Interpretation and Other Essays,* Farrar, Straus, 1966.

Standley, Fred and Nancy Standley, *James Baldwin: A Reference Guide,* G. K. Hall, 1980.

Standley, Fred and Nancy Standley, editors, *Critical Essays on James Baldwin,* G. K. Hall, 1981.

Sylvander, Carolyn Wedin, *James Baldwin,* Frederick Ungar, 1980.

Tachach, James, *James Baldwin,* Lucent Books (San Diego), 1996.

Turner, Darwin T., *Afro-American Writers,* Appleton, 1970.

Washington, Bryan R., *The Politics of Exile: Ideology in Henry James, F. Scott Fitzgerald, and James Baldwin,* Northeastern University Press, 1995.

Weatherby, William J., *Squaring Off: Mailer vs. Baldwin,* Mason/Charter, 1977.

Williams, John A. and Charles F. Harris, editors, *Amistad I: Writings on Black History and Culture,* Random House, 1970.

Williams, Sherley Anne, *Give Birth to Brightness: A Thematic Study in Neo-Black Literature,* Dial, 1972.

PERIODICALS

America, March 16, 1963.
American Scholar, winter, 1994, p. 102.
Atlanta Constitution, May 19, 1976.
Atlantic, July, 1961; July, 1962; March, 1963; July, 1968; June, 1972.
Atlas, March, 1967.
Black Scholar, December, 1973-January, 1974.
Black World, June, 1972; December, 1974.
Books and Bookmen, August, 1968; September, 1972; December, 1979.
Book Week, May 31, 1964; September 26, 1965.
British Journal of Sociology, June, 1966.
Bulletin of Bibliography, January-April, 1965; May-August, 1968.
Chicago Tribune, September 16, 1979; October 10, 1979; November 15, 1985; December 16, 1987; November 15, 1989.
Christian Science Monitor, July 19, 1962.
College Language Association Journal, Number 7, 1964; Number 10, 1966; March, 1967.
Commentary, November, 1953; January, 1957; December, 1961; December, 1979; December, 1985.
Commonweal, May 22, 1953; December 7, 1962; October 12, 1973; June 24, 1977.
Critical Quarterly, Summer, 1964.
Critique, Winter, 1964-65.
Cross Currents, Summer, 1961.
Detroit Free Press, December 2, 1987; December 8, 1987.
Ebony, October, 1961.
Ecumenical Review, October, 1968.
Encounter, July, 1965.
English Journal, May, 1973.
Esquire, July, 1968.
Freedomways, Summer, 1963.
Globe & Mail (Toronto), January 11, 1986.
Harper's, March, 1963; September, 1968.
Hudson Review, Autumn, 1964; Autumn, 1968.
Intellectual Digest, July, 1972.
Life, May 24, 1963; June 7, 1968; June 4, 1971; July 30, 1971.
London Magazine, December, 1979-January, 1980.
Lone Star Book Review, January-February, 1980.
Look, July 23, 1968.
Los Angeles Times Book Review, December 1, 1985.
Mademoiselle, May, 1963.
Massachusetts Review, Winter, 1964.
Midcontinent American Studies Journal, Fall, 1963.
Muhammad Speaks, September 8, 1973; September 15, 1973; September 29, 1973; October 6, 1973.
Nation, July 14, 1962; November 17, 1962; March 2, 1963; December 13, 1965; April 10, 1972; June 10, 1968; July 3, 1976; November 3, 1979.
National Observer, March 6, 1967; June 3, 1968.
National Review, May 21, 1963; July 7, 1972.
Negro American Literature Forum, Spring, 1969; Winter, 1972.
Negro Digest, June, 1963; October, 1966; April, 1967.

New Leader, June 3, 1968; May 27, 1974; May 24, 1976.

New Republic, August 7, 1961; November 27, 1965; August 17, 1968; June 15, 1974; December 30, 1985.

New Statesman, July 13, 1962; July 19, 1963; December 4, 1964; June 28, 1974; February 25, 1977; November 29, 1985.

Newsweek, February 4, 1963; June 3, 1969.

New Yorker, November 25, 1961; August 4, 1962; July 8, 1974.

New York Herald Tribune Book Review, June 17, 1962.

New York Review of Books, December 17, 1964; December 9, 1965; June 29, 1972; June 13, 1974; December 6, 1979; January 21, 1988.

New York Times, May 3, 1964; April 16, 1965; May 31, 1968; February 2, 1969; May 21, 1971; May 17, 1974; June 4, 1976; September 4, 1977; September 21, 1979; September 23, 1979; November 11, 1983; January 10, 1985; January 14, 1985; June 22, 1989.

New York Times Book Review, December 12, 1965; June 2, 1968; May 28, 1972; May 2, 1976; May 24, 1984; December 9, 1987.

New York Times Magazine, March 7, 1965.

Nickel Review, February 27, 1970.

Observer, November 24, 1985; April 6, 1986.

Partisan Review, Winter, 1966.

People, January 7, 1980.

Philadelphia Inquirer, December 2, 1987; December 9, 1987; December 14, 1987.

Queen's Quarterly, Summer, 1965.

San Francisco Chronicle, June 28, 1962.

Saturday Review, July 1, 1961; July 7, 1962; February 2, 1963; February 8, 1964; May 2, 1964; June 1, 1968; May 27, 1972; June 15, 1974; January 5, 1980.

South Atlantic Quarterly, Summer, 1966.

Southern Humanities Review, Winter, 1970.

Southern Review, Summer, 1985.

Spectator, July 12, 1968; January 11, 1986; April 26, 1986.

Studies in Short Fiction, Summer, 1975; Fall, 1977.

Time, June 30, 1961; June 29, 1962; November 6, 1964; June 7, 1968; June 10, 1974.

Times (London), May 15, 1986; January 19, 1987; January 22, 1987; December 2, 1987; January 31, 1989.

Times Educational Supplement, December 27, 1985.

Times Literary Supplement, July 26, 1963; December 10, 1964; October 28, 1965; July 4, 1968; April 28, 1972; November 17, 1972; June 21, 1974; December 21, 1979; August 2, 1984; January 24, 1986; September 19, 1986.

Tri-Quarterly, Winter, 1965.

Twentieth-Century Literature, April, 1967.

Village Voice, January 12, 1988.

Vogue, July, 1964.

Washington Post, October 15, 1979; September 9, 1983; September 25, 1983; August 14, 1989.

Washington Post Book World, September 11, 1977; October 27, 1985; December 9, 1987.

Western Humanities Review, Spring, 1968.

World Literature Today, Spring, 1980.

Yale Review, October, 1966.

■ Obituaries

PERIODICALS

Chicago Tribune, December 2, 1987.

Los Angeles Times, December 2, 1987.

New York Times, December 2, 1987; December 9, 1987.

Times (London), December 2, 1987.

USA Today, December 2, 1987.

Washington Post, December 2, 1987.*

—Sketch by J. Sydney Jones

Joan Bauer

■ Personal

Born in River Forest, IL; married; children: Jean.

■ Addresses

Home—Darien, CT. *Agent*—c/o Putnam Publishing Group, 200 Madison Ave., New York, NY 10016.

■ Career

Author. Has also worked as an advertising and marketing salesperson, a writer for magazines and newspapers. and a screenwriter.

■ Writings

Squashed, Delacorte, 1992.
Thwonk, Delacorte, 1995.
Sticks, Delacorte, 1996.
Rules of the Road, Putnam, 1998.
Backwater, Putnam, 1999.

■ Awards, Honors

Delacorte Prize for First Young Adult Novel, for *Squashed;* Top Ten Best Books for Young Adults selection, American Library Association, 1999, for *Rules of the Road.*

■ Sidelights

"There are two things you can count on in a book by Joan Bauer. One, it will make you laugh. And two, the girl who is telling the story will be really good at something, but not something you'd expect," Amazon.com reviewer Patty Campbell commented in a review of Bauer's 1999 novel *Backwater.* Bauer, an advertising salesperson-turned-writer, has written five books, which have earned her a reputation as a deft spinner of engaging, off-beat tales about young adult themes. "While the general perception of young adult literature is that it's all dark and depressing, many worthy writers of the genre produce work of wit and hilarity," noted "Rising Star," a website feature of the *Bulletin of the Center for Children's Books.* "Joan Bauer is Exhibit A in this category; her characters' narration is smart, funny, and original."

In a 1996 *Alan Review* article entitled "Humor, Seriously," Bauer explained that she uses levity to "teach young people to use laughter against the storms of life." After quoting Mark Twain, who once said that "Humor must speak the truth," Bauer explained, "Finding that truth in characters for me evolves through a process of layering—determining where the characters have been, what they've experienced, what they've overcome and failed abysmally at—that's when the truth of who they are emerges and the voice becomes concrete." For Bauer, humor also reveals that "the person or character has moved from seeing life as a series

DELL ·U.S. $3.99
CAN. $4.99

JOAN BAUER

The problems of a sixteen-year-old girl all revolve around her desperate wish to produce a prize-winning pumpkin in this 1992 work.

of problems or things done to them, and has moved into greater clarity and control of the situation." Being someone who knows from first-hand experience about the trials and tribulations of a difficult youth, Bauer works to help teens through their problems and boost their self-esteem through her fiction—both as entertainment and as mild therapy for those who are coping with the problems and pressure of growing up nowadays.

Joan Bauer was born in River Forest, Illinois, the eldest of four sisters. The girls were raised by their mother, a teacher with a lively sense of humor; Bauer's father played little role in her up-

bringing. Responding to a question in a 1999 interview that is posted on the Web site of her publisher, Penguin-Putnam, the writer described her father, as "a very messed up man—an alcoholic [who was] married four times, a chronic gambler." Bauer was close to her grandmother, who lived with the family; the woman, a gifted storyteller, engaged the imaginations of her granddaughters with wonderful tales, which she told in a colorful, animated style, using a range of voices. Bauer recalled in the Penguin-Putnam interview, "[My grandmother] taught me the significance of humor and how it intersects our daily lives."

Humor Brings Hope

Bauer's teen years were difficult. Her grandmother suffered from Alzheimer's disease, and when Bauer was twenty, her father committed suicide. She revealed in the Penguin-Putnam interview that day was "the saddest day of my life." Shortly before her father's death, Bauer had gone to Iowa, where he was living, to seek him out. "I confronted him on several things," Bauer told the interviewer. "I learned from that experience that there are times in life when we have choices—we can continue to be victims or we can move forward to be healthy people." Applying the same direct, pro-active approach in her fiction, Bauer's characters confront problems in their relationships head-on as they attempt to deal with them.

In the Penguin-Putnam interview, Bauer explained the connection of her real life teen experiences to her storylines this way: "Because so much was not positive for me, I want to write positive stories. Because so much was painful for me, I want to show ways to overcome pain with emotional health, relationships, and humor. Because I desperately needed ties to my father, I write a great deal about complex fathers. . . . Because I never had a huge group of friends when I was growing up, I write about kids who tend to be loners." Bauer's protagonists are consistent in that they are role models for teens as they move past their problems by working through them. Bauer told her interviewer, "My first drafts are usually quite serious because I'm getting the real serious underpinnings of the stories and characters in place." As she edits her first draft, she adds the humor, which she feels is vital to telling her stories: "I see laughter as being a bridge between pain and redemption," she says. "When we can laugh about something difficult, what we're really saying is that we've moved from the pain of it to thehope." Before she types out the story, Bauer spends a great deal of time researching occupations of her characters, activities the characters engage in, and the scenes where the action takes place. She then writes detailed biographies about her characters before she begins fleshing out the story, treating her own acquaintance with her characters as real and integral to bringing them to life in the imaginations of her readers.

Bauer's teenage daughter, Jean, and her friends help Bauer to stay current on American youth culture. Being a fan of her mother's work, Jean Bauer offers suggestions and comments regarding her mother's characters, helping the author to fo-

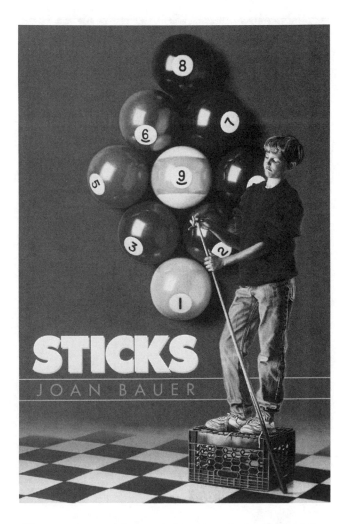

When a potential new coach comes along, Mickey just might have a shot at winning the nine-ball championship in this 1996 novel.

cus on what interests teens; in her Penguin-Putnam interview, Bauer described her daughter as "one of the world's great teenagers." Placing great value on the input and response of her readers, Bauer doesn't take for granted the letters she receives from her readership.

Bauer started working at various jobs when she was still a pre-teen; she was an assistant typing teacher, waitress, and a freelance writer. Bauer began a decade-long career in advertising sales in her early twenties. Although she was successful, she eventually grew frustrated with the lack of creativity in her job and, as she recalled in her Penguin-Putnam interview, she "ended up with a few ulcers and was singularly miserable. It was then that I finally began to listen to my heart, quit my job, and started writing." Bauer began in journalism, then tried her hand at screenwriting, before finding achieving success in young adult fiction. Like many writers, Bauer confesses to a love/hate relationship with writing. "I write because I have to," she told the Penguin-Putnam interviewer. "I love writing, and yet there are times when it is painfully difficult. I see the world through metaphor, and stories have always been a way for me to explain the world." Bauer recognizes that writing is her forte and therefore a path she pursues naturally. During difficult periods, she said in her Penguin-Putnam interview, "My faith in God, my family, and my close friends keeps me going as a writer."

Stories of Teens Coming of Age

Bauer's writing debut was an auspicious one. A reviewer for the *Bulletin for the Centre for Children's Books* praised *Squashed* for its "humor and tenderness," and the book won the 1992 Delacorte Press Prize for a first novel. Like all of her subsequent tales, *Squashed* is narrated by the chief protagonist in the first-person. Ellie Morgan is a slightly overweight teenager who is determined to raise a champion pumpkin she calls Max. Ellie is resolute in mustering up the inner strength and agricultural savvy required to successfully care for Max, who requires an exceeding amount of tender loving care. In one of Ellie's asides to the reader regarding the art and strain of rasing a champion pumpkin, she explains, "Not all vegetables are this draining. Lettuce doesn't bring heartache. Turnips don't ask for your soul. Potatoes don't care where you are or even where they are. Tomatoes cuddle up to anyone who'll give them mulch and sunshine. But giants like Max need you every second. You can forget about a whiz-ban social life." Ellie has loved pumpkins since the first time she saw Cinderella at the age of five. Her hometown of Rock River, Iowa, boasts of its prize-winning pumpkin-growing in its motto: "Our pumpkins we prize; Our rights we will maintain." As Max already weighs three hundred pounds in August, Ellie has a good chance of winning this year's Rock River Pumpkin Weigh-In, where she could earn a dollar per pound, as well as respect in the town. Ellie's motivational specialist father, who wants more than farming for his daughter, is concerned that she is neglecting herself by devoting so much time to her pumpkin. Ellie's grandmother, in contrast, views her granddaughter's attention to Max as instrumental in helping her to build her self-esteem.

The story takes the reader through Ellie's vigorous "battle of the patch," as she dubs it. Ellie stands on watch against vandals and pumpkin bandits;she sprays and composts; she cleans Max with Windex; she warms him against the fall chill; she plays music for him and talks to him; she injects a concoction of buttermilk and Orange Crush into his stem. The reader may reflect on the nurturing of a child by a mother when Ellie declares, "There is something about a grower's presence that calls a vegetable to greatness." In the end, the ordinary girl from Iowa achieves an extraordinary accomplishment through her care of her beloved Max; she emerges as a heroine.

Bauer's second novel, *Thwonk* (1995), teaches readers something about the ingredients for true romance—in other words, what we initially think we want in a mate may not be what can truly bring lasting happiness. A.J. (Allison Jean) McCreary is a Connecticut high-school senior with a passion for photography. When she stumbles upon a stuffed Cupid doll that magically comes to life, A.J. is offered the doll's help in one of the following areas: academics, career, or romance. She chooses the latter, specifically a love-tipped arrow for the heart of Peter Terris, a boy who is handsome, popular, and totally unaware of A.J.'s existence. She is set on Peter taking her to the school's King of Hearts Dance—hence the title "thwonk," which is the sound of an arrow shot from Cupid's bow. With the doll's help, Peter becomes pathetically infatuated with A.J., but it's not long before she finds his attentions her an-

noying. What's more, A.J. discovers that Peter is wanting in wit and smarts, areas in which she excels. A.J.'s drollery in relating her story to readers sharply contrasts with Peter's dullness and goofiness. As the plot progresses and A.J.'s skill in photography develops, she learns more about herself and what's really important to her. Her talents are even acknowledged and rewarded by her previously distant filmmaker father.

Several reviewers praised *Thwonk* and lauded Bauer for her writing. Alice Casey Smith of *School Library Journal* praised the book as a "silly, offbeatnovel . . . [that] revels in the vagaries, insecurities, and uncomfortable realities of teen love." Suzanne Curley of the *Los Angeles Times*

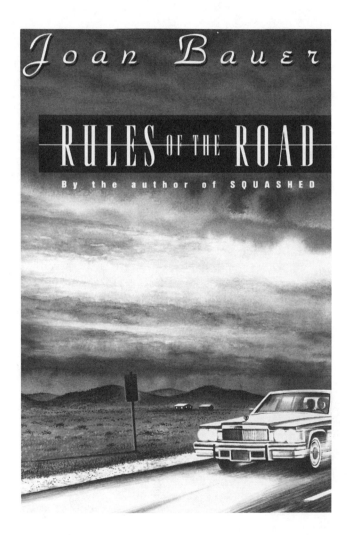

When Jenna is hired to drive a shoe model and a shoe salesman across the country, she learns some important lessons about life.

Book Review described it as "a first-class comic romance," while Deborah Stevenson of *The Bulletin of the Centre for Children's Books* noted that "Bauer's forcefully funny writing remains stylish from start to finish."

Novels Get Noticed

By now, it was apparent that Bauer was beginning to hit her stride as a writer; *Sticks* (1996), her third novel, was nominated for the 1998-1999 Mark Twain Award; it is another light-hearted teen novel with a message. The protagonist is ten-year-old Mickey Vernon, who dreams of winning the nine-ball tournament hosted by his family's pool hall. His rival is town bully Buck Pender. At age thirteen, Buck is bigger than Mickey and stronger than him. However, Mickey learns during the story that physical size and strength aren't everything. Superior technique and using his brain will help him beat Buck in the big tournament. As Mickey prepares for the match, his brilliant friend Arlen shows him the mathematics of pool and assists him in becoming skilful in the geometric strategy of the game. Meanwhile, Joseph Alvarez, an old friend of Mickey's late father comes to town. An old poolshark himself, he takes Mickey under his wing, in the process becoming a sort of father figure to the boy. Mickey's mother objects to her son's relationship with Joseph, forbidding it. Since Mickey narrates the story, the reader is drawn into his struggle to win the tournament from Buck while soothing the tensions between his mother and Joseph.

Reviewer Todd Morning of *School Library Journal* liked *Sticks*, writing that "the winning characterizations may make this a book to be enjoyed by kids who like pool and even some who don't." Janice Del Negro of *Booklist* echoed that assessment. "Bauer's characterizations are well drawn, their personalities three-dimensional even when they only appear briefly, and Mickey is not only a credible ten-year-old but also a likable narrator," DelNegro noted. "Good characters, humor, and an engaging plot make this a solid piece of middle-grade fiction." An anonymous *Publishers Weekly* reviewer took a markedly different view, however, complaining that the novel was likely to disappoint fans of Bauer's previous work since "Mickey lacks the emotional spark needed to engage an audience and his contrived world leaves readers feeling unfulfilled."

J O A N   B A U E R

Ivy Breedlove journeys through the Adirondack Mountains in search of the eccentric relative who might help her find a place in her family.

Rules of the Road (1998), Bauer's next book, is the story of sixteen-year-old Chicago-resident Jenna Boller, a young woman with a talent for selling shoes. Not only does Jenna have the knack for servicing the needs and footwear tastes of customers, she is dedicated to the business. Shortly after obtaining her driver's license, Elden Gladstone, president of Gladstone shoes, offers Jenna the job of chauffeuring her to Texas for a stockholders' meeting. The novel chronicles the twosome's adventure south, during which Jenna learns about her own strengths and capabilities, while picking up important values in loyalty and service to others. Jenna is also confronted with betrayal and greed through the dirty deeds of Mrs. Gladstone's slimy son Elden, who is trying to swindle his mother out of her shoe empire through corporate

If you enjoy the works of Joan Bauer, you may also want to check out the following books:

Alden R. Carter, *Growing Season*, 1984.
Sheila Solomon Klass, *To See My Mother Dance*, 1981.
Candice Ransom, *The Love Charm*, 1991.

takeover maneuvering. Together, Jenna and Mrs. Gladstone embark on a mission to save the business.

Along the way, Jenna befriends a salesman, a longtime member of Alcoholics Anonymous. She wishes her own father, a current alcoholic, were more like him. After the salesman is killed by a drunk driver, Jenna alerts police to her own father's drunk driving. Reflecting on her experiences, she concludes, "It seemed to me that the people who made the rules of the road had figured out everything that would help a person drive safely right down to having a sign that tells you you're passing through a place where deer cross. Somebody should stick up some signs on the highway of life. 'CAUTION: JERKS CROSSING.' Blinking yellow lights when you are about to do something stupid. Stop signs in front of people who could hurt you. Green lights shining when you're doing the right thing. It would make the whole experience much easier."

Reviewer Cindy Darling Codell of *School Library Journal* hailed *Rules of the Road* as "Bauer's best [novel] yet;" Candace Deisley of the *Voice of Youth Advocates* praised it as "a remarkable book, presenting lessons of respect for others, courtesy, and honesty gently, but persistently." A reviewer for *Publishers Weekly* voiced a contrary opinion, lamenting that "the story quickly runs out of gas" and that "a supporting cast of stock characters and forced dialogue may disappoint readers of [Bauer's] previous novels."

Backwater (1999), Bauer's most recent effort, is a tale of a sixteen-year-old girl's journey to find her roots and to discover her emotional, intellectual, and physical limits. Ivy Breedlove comes from a family of lawyers, and being an intelligent girl, she is naturally expected to pursue a legal career. However, her real passion in life is studying his-

tory. While tracing her family tree, a project started as a birthday gift for her Great Aunt Tib, Ivy discovers female relatives who were mavericks in that they followed their own interests, and left behind family expectations for them. Ivy becomes obsessed with wanting to learn more about her father's sister Josephine, "Aunt Jo"; aided by a colorful guide known as Mountain Mama, Ivy sets out to meet her. Aunt Jo is a hermit sculptor who lives in the wilderness of the Adirondack Mountains. During Ivy's quest for knowledge and historical revelation, she learns important lessons about herself and the essence of family.

A *Publishers Weekly* reviewer described *Backwater* was "a compelling, though ultimately uneven outing" that readers might in the end find "to be too far-fetched." However, reviewer Jean Franklin of *Booklist* liked the novel considerably more. "This warm, funny patchwork quilt of a book . . . will keep readers turning the pages to the last." Franklin added that taken with *Rules of the Road*, *Backwater* provides "a dynamite mother-daughter book discussion."

On the strength of such comments, Bauer's five novels have won her many fans among teen readers, parents, librarians, and teachers. The author revealed in her Penguin-Putnam interview that a new book she is writing centers on a theme of honor and politics. "And yes, it's fiction," she added jokingly.

■ Works Cited

Review of *Backwater*, *Publishers Weekly*, June 7, 1999, p. 84.

Bauer, Joan, "Humor, Seriously," *ALAN Review*, winter, 1996.

Bauer, Joan, interview on *Penguin-Putnam* Web site, located at http://www2.penguinputnam.com.

Campbell, Patty, review of *Backwater*, *Amazon.com* Web site, located at http://www.amazon.com.

Coddell, Cindy Darling, review of *Rules of the Road*, *School Library Journal*, March, 1998, p. 208.

Curley, Suzanne, "A Few Well-Placed Arrows," *Los Angeles Times Book Review*, February 26, 1995, p. 9.

Deisley, Candace, review of *Rules of the Road*, *Voice of Youth Advocates*, June, 1998, p. 120.

Del Negro, Janice, review of *Sticks*, *Booklist*, May 1, 1996, p. 1505.

Franklin, Jean, review of *Backwater*, *Booklist*, May 15, 1999, p. 1687.

Morning, Todd, review of *Sticks, School Library Journal,* June, 1996, p. 120.

Review of *Rules of the Road, Publishers Weekly,* February 23, 1998, p. 77.

Smith, Alice Casey, review of *Thwonk, School Library Journal,* January, 1995, p. 134.

Review of *Squashed, Bulletin of the Center for Children's Books,* October, 1992, p. 36.

Stevenson, Deborah, review of *Thwonk, Bulletin of the Center for Children's Books,* January, 1995, p. 158.

Review of *Sticks, Publishers Weekly,* June 10, 1996, p. 100.

■ For More Information See

PERIODICALS

Booklist, January 1, 1995, p. 814; July, 1997, p. 1830; February 1, 1998, p. 77.
Horn Book, May-June, 1998, p. 339.
New York Times Book Review, June 20, 1999, p. 21.
Publishers Weekly, February 27, 1995, p. 104.
School Library Journal, June, 1999, p. 126.

—Sketch by Melissa Walsh Doig

Francesca Lia Block

the 1980s list from *Booklist*, YASD Best Book Award, and Recommended Books for Reluctant Young Adult Readers citation, all 1989, all for *Weetzie Bat*; Recommended Books for Reluctant Young Adult Readers citation, 1990, for *Witch Baby*; Best Books of the Year citation from the ALA, Recommended Books for Reluctant Young Adult Readers citation, Best Books citation from the *New York Times*, and Best Fifty Books citation from *Publishers Weekly*, all 1991, all for *Cherokee Bat and the Goat Guys*; Best Books of the Year citations from *School Library Journal* and the ALA, and Recommended Books for Reluctant Young Adult Readers, all 1993, all for *Missing Angel Juan*.

■ Writings

YOUNG ADULT NOVELS

Weetzie Bat, HarperCollins, 1989.
Witch Baby, HarperCollins, 1990.
Cherokee Bat and the Goat Guys, HarperCollins, 1991.
Missing Angel Juan, HarperCollins, 1993.
The Hanged Man, HarperCollins, 1994.
Baby Be-Bop, HarperCollins, 1995.
Girl Goddess #9: Nine Stories, HarperCollins, 1996.
Dangerous Angels: The Weetzie Bat Books, HarperCollins, 1998.
I Was A Teenage Fairy, HarperCollins, 1998.
Violet and Claire, HarperCollins, 1999.

FOR ADULTS

Ecstasia, New American Library, 1993.

■ Personal

Born December 3, 1962, in Hollywood, CA; daughter of Irving Alexander (a painter) and Gilda (a poet; maiden name, Klein) Block. *Education:* University of California, Berkeley, B.A., 1986. *Politics:* Democrat. *Hobbies and other interests:* Dance, film, vegetarian cooking.

■ Addresses

Home—Studio City, CA. *Agent*—Julie Fallowfield, McIntosh & Otis, 310 Madison Ave., New York, NY 10017.

■ Career

Writer. *Member:* Authors Guild, Authors League of America, Phi Beta Kappa.

■ Awards, Honors

Shrout Fiction Award, University of California, Berkeley, 1986; Emily Chamberlain Cook Poetry Award, 1986; Best Books of the Year citation from the American Library Association (ALA), Best of

Primavera, New American Library, 1994.

POETRY

Moon Harvest, illustrated by Irving Block, Santa Susanna Press, 1978.
Season of Green, illustrated by Irving Block, Santa Susanna Press, 1979.

OTHER

Author of screenplays of *Cherokee Bat and the Goat Guys* and (with James Edward Quinn) *Luna and Rosa* and *Zeroes Journey.* Contributor of short stories to anthologies, including *Am I Blue?,* edited by Marion Dane Bauer, 1994; *When I Was Your Age,* edited by Amy Ehrlich, 1994; and *Soft Tar,* a benefit for a global children's organization, 1994.

■ **Sidelights**

Only a few years after her first publication, Francesca Lia Block has already carved out a unique piece of young adult turf for herself and the characters she has created. With the publication in 1989 of *Weetzie Bat,* she set the agenda for a new direction in young adult novels: stories of Los Angeles subculture replete with sex, drugs, and rock 'n roll—for the nineties. With a cast of characters ranging from Weetzie Bat, a punk princess in pink, to her lover, My Secret Agent Lover Man, and her best friend Dirk and *his* boyfriend, to their common offspring, Witch Baby and Cherokee, Block's novels create postmodernist fairy tales where love and art are the only cures in a world void of adult direction. Praised and criticized for her edgy tales of urban adventure, Block is still somewhat in awe of her instant success and of the stir her books are creating. "I wrote *Weetzie Bat* as a sort of valentine to Los Angeles at time when I was in school in Berkeley and homesick for where I grew up," the author once stated in an interview. "It was a very personal story. A very personal love letter. I never expected people to respond to it the way they have. I never imagined I could reach other people from such a very personal place in me."

But reach people the stories have. Block's "technicolor lovesong to Los Angeles," as *Publishers Weekly* writer Diane Roback described *Weetzie*

Bat, sold steadily through several printings. There have been three sequels to that original novel and a fourth is in the works, each one focusing on a different character and exploring new variations on the theme of the curative power of love and art. "The whole experience is magical," Block said of the success of her series. And there is something a little magical about Block's life as well.

Born in Hollywood, the center of the modern fairy tale industry, she was exposed to the power of art and creativity from an early age. Her parents were both artists: her father, who died in 1986, was a well-known painter and teacher and one-time special effects technician and writer for Hollywood studios; her mother is a poet who once wrote a children's poetry book. "My parents taught me that you could be creative in this world. That it was possible," Block remarked. Books were always part of her life. "I can't remember not having books. There were trips to the library for books and there were books all around our home. It feels like I was always able to read." In addition to traditional childhood favorites such as Charlotte Zolotow's *Mr. Rabbit and the Lovely Present,* Randall Jarrell's *Animal Family,* and Maurice Sendak's *Where the Wild Things Are,* Block was also greatly influenced by Greek mythology and legend. "My father used to tell me bits of the *Odyssey* for my nighttime story," she recalled. "It was an incredibly rich upbringing."

Creating stories is something that has been with Block from an early age. "I remember walking around the house," she once said, "telling stories to myself. Or sometimes like-minded friends would get together with me and we would make up stories together." This knack for telling stories soon grew into a passion. "I always wanted to be a writer," Block recalled. "Even when I was really small. My mom would write down things I said before I could write them, and that somehow validated my thoughts and expression. Made them worth recording. Soon I was writing short poems." Growing up in the Hollywood area was also an enriching experience for Block, who came into daily contact with the world of art and creative talent. Her family lived in the San Fernando Valley and she attended North Hollywood High, but her fondest memories of the time are after-school activities. "I really pushed myself hard in school, so I didn't enjoy it," she said. "My parents didn't expect or demand it of me; it was just something I felt I had to do. I liked the creative side of school, but largely the experience was unsatisfying."

Cruising the Streets of Hollywood

A teenager in the late 1970s, Block and her friends were fond of going into Hollywood after school. "When I was 17 years old, my friends and I used to drive through Laurel Canyon after school in a shiny blue vintage Mustang convertible," Block wrote in an article for the *Los Angeles Times Book Review*. "The short distance of the canyon separating us from Hollywood made that city a little enchanted." Once in Hollywood they would hang out at Schwab's soda fountain, check out the street scene with all the punk costumes, cruise Sunset Strip, or frolic at the Farmer's Market. It was on one such trip that Block first saw the prototype of Weetzie: "A punk princess with spiky bleached hair, a very pink '50s prom dress and cowboy boots," as she described her. It was a momentary glimpse of a hitchhiker that stayed with her over the years, and later a name came with the apparition, for she saw a pink Pinto on the freeway with a driver who looked like that hitchhiker and with a license plate spelling "WEETZIE." The character of this punk princess would ferment for another six years before coming to full bloom in Block's first novel. She continually made up stories about Weetzie and drew her innumerable times: Block came to know Weetzie long before she first wrote about her in a novel.

"I lived a little bit of the Weetzie lifestyle in those years," Block once said in an interview. "Being around creative people, a little bit on the edge, listening to bands like X, being a part of the punk scene because it was something different and expressive." But soon the punk scene took on a violent edge with beatings at concerts and punks wearing swastikas, and the specter of AIDS had appeared. Block left Los Angeles to attend college in Berkeley, California, where she fell in love with the modernist poetry of H. D. (Hilda Doolittle) and the magic realism of Colombian novelist Gabriel Garcia Marquez. "College was a very intense time. I took a course with Jayne Walker in modernist poetry my first year and loved its mix of concrete images and classical references." She also took a poetry workshop with Ron Loewinsohn, developing her poetry into short-short stories and then longer short stories, all with a minimalist influence to them. "And then came my father's illness, and I got increasingly homesick for L.A. and stressed out at school," Block remembered. "I started to write *Weetzie* at that time. It's a nostalgic look at that time and place. A sort of therapy for me."

"I wrote Weetzie Bat *as a sort of valentine to Los Angeles at time when I was in school in Berkeley and homesick for where I grew up. It was a very personal story. A very personal love letter. I never expected people to respond to it the way they have. I never imagined I could reach other people from such a very personal place in me."*

—Francesca Lia Block

The therapy worked. Block graduated from the University of California and weathered her father's death. She returned to Los Angeles, took a job in a gallery, lived alone, and wrote. It was a very productive time for Block, during which she completed the manuscript of an adult novel and another young adult title, as well as several pieces of short fiction. Of course, Block did not know at the time that she was writing "young adult." "I just wrote," she once explained. "Never mind the genre. I would write maybe with a friend in mind as the reader, but never gave a thought to whether the books were for adults or not."

In 1989 a friend at the gallery where Block worked, children's illustrator Kathryn Jacobi, read the manuscript of *Weetzie Bat*, was impressed, and sent it off to the writer and editor Charlotte Zolotow at HarperCollins. Zolotow—continuing the magic—liked the book, told Block that she wanted to bring it out as a young adult title, and also encouraged Block to go further with the characters, that there seemed to be more stories there. "I was incredibly lucky that the manuscript went to Charlotte," Block said. "I loved her work as a child and here *she* was liking mine in return."

Weetzie Bat tells the story of Weetzie and her gay friend Dirk—the only person who seems to understand her—who set up house together in a cottage Dirk's grandmother has left him in Los Angeles. Soon they fill it with a loving extended family (Weetzie Bat's divorced, booze-ridden parents have left a vacuum in this regard). Dirk finds the surfer Duck, Weetzie finds My Secret Lover Man, and even their dog finds a mate. Together they make underground movies and much more. Soon a baby they name Cherokee is born, and the extended family take it as natural that it should belong to all of them. Even the abandoned Witch Baby, reminder of a dalliance My Secret Lover Man has had, is taken in as one of the family. Love is the connecting rod here, the one thing that makes life possible. "I hear that rats shrivel up and die if they aren't like, able to hang out with other rats," Duck says at one point. And this band of punk, hip youth learn that lesson well. "I don't know about happily ever after," Weetzie muses at the end of the book, "but I know about happily."

A modern fairy tale, *Weetzie Bat* blends Block's love of modernist poetry with magical realism— there's a genie granting three wishes and an evil witch—to come up with a potent narrative of love and loyalty in an age of pessimism and AIDS. Using a mixture of L.A. slang and inventive personal hip talk, Block created an "off-beat tale that has great charm, poignancy, and touches of fantasy," wrote Anne Osborn in *School Library Journal. New York Times Book Review* contributor Betsy Hearne also praised the author's style: "Block's far-ranging free association has been controlled and shaped into a story with sensual characters. The language is inventive California hip, but the patterns are compactly folkloristic and the theme is transcendent."

Controversy Surrounds Work

In spite of such glowing reviews, the book still caused a minor uproar among other reviewers and some librarians. Patrick Jones, writing in *Horn Book,* summed up and put such criticism into context: "It is not that the sex [in Block's books] is explicit; it is not. It is just that Block's characters *have* sex lives. . . . In the age of AIDS—whose ugly shadow appears—anything less than a 'safe sex or no sex' stance is bound to be controversial." Jones points out that the homosexual relationship between Dirk and Duck was also hard for some reviewers to deal with, as was the communal rearing of the baby, Cherokee. This alternate family lifestyle, so validating for teenager readers whose own lives seldom fit the "Father

Knows Best" model, became a sore spot for some. But Block recounted the story of one such critic in her *Los Angeles Times Book Review* article. Having heard of this purportedly perverse book, Frances V. Sedney of the children's department of the Harford, Maryland, County Library read it, then wrote a letter in the novel's defense: "This short novel epitomizes the 'innocent' books where the *reader's* mind and experience make all the crucial difference." *Weetzie Bat* went on to be shortlisted for the ALA Best Book of the Year as well making the Recommended Books for the Reluctant Young Adult Reader list.

"I don't know about happily ever after, but I know about happily."

—from *Weetzie Bat*

Following the advice of her editor, Charlotte Zolotow, Block went on to enlarge the stories of other characters from *Weetzie Bat.* In 1990 she published *Witch Baby,* a novel "reminiscent of a music video," Maeve Visser Knoth wrote in *Horn Book.* "Scenes and sensory images flash across the page; characters speak in complicated slang and create a safe haven for themselves in the midst of a shifting, confusing world." Witch Baby stumbles and sometimes crashes through the book, searching for her own identity, trying to understand her place in the scheme of things, looking for an answer to her own poetic question: "What time are we upon and where do I belong?" Witch Baby, endowed with tilted purple eyes and a Medusa head of black hair, collects newspaper clippings of tragedies in an attempt to understand the world. Ultimately Witch Baby is able to find her real mother and then can deal with her place in the extended family of Weetzie Bat.

As Ellen Ramsay noted in *School Library Journal,* Block is "a superior writer and has created a superior cast of characters," and in *Witch Baby* she "explores the danger of denying life's pain." This assessment mirrors what the author herself says about her work. "My books talk about tolerance," Block explained, "though I never consciously think of themes like that as I write. I guess my general theme is the value of love and art as healers. That you must face the darkness, acknowledge it and still have hope. I think that is what is important in life."

With the next installment of the Bat family saga, Block further pursued the theme of family loyalty and the importance of love and a balance of spiritual powers in the world. *Cherokee Bat and the Goat Guys* opens with the "adults," Weetzie Bat and others, off on a filming expedition in South America. Teenage Cherokee and Witch Baby are left under their own direction and soon they team up with Raphael Chong Jah-Love and Angel Juan Perez to form a rock band, the Goat Guys. These four receive and depend on powerful gifts from a Native American family friend, Coyote, to perform. They are an instant hit, but quickly the euphoria goes to their heads and "everything begins to fly apart in wild and outrageous ways," according to Gail Richmond in *School Library Journal,* as the band loses itself in sex and drugs. "The group descends into the bacchanalian hell of the nightclub scene with tequila and cocaine, skull lamps and lingerie-clad groupies drenched in cow's blood," noted Patty Campbell in a *New York Times Book Review* article. When Angel Juan slashes himself while performing, Cherokee figures it is time to turn in their magic totem gifts to Coyote and "be cleansed of the pain and guilt," according to Campbell. "An emotionally charged story with a contemporary message," Richmond noted, and Roback and Richard Donahue, writing in *Publishers Weekly,* similarly observed: "This latest effort provides yet another delicious and deeply felt trip to Block's wonderfully idiosyncratic corner of California."

It is this very idiosyncratic nature of much of Block's work that has also prompted some criticism. Ramsay praised the quality of Block's work but wondered if she was not "just a tad too Southern California cool for broad appeal." Campbell, in an overview on Block's work in *Horn Book,* argued however that "many novels are set in New York, and . . . no one thinks those books are strange or labels them as depicting 'an alternate lifestyle' because the characters ride to work on the subway or shop at Bloomingdale's. . . . Why should the second largest city in the United States be perceived so differently? It is doubly puzzling considering that America sees Los Angeles every night on television."

> "My books talk about tolerance, though I never consciously think of themes like that as I write. I guess my general theme is the value of love and art as healers. That you must face the darkness, acknowledge it and still have hope. I think that is what is important in life."
>
> —Francesca Lia Block

Puzzling or not, Block moved the action of her next young adult novel, *Missing Angel Juan,* to New York when Witch Baby's boyfriend, Angel Juan, takes off on his own musical career in the Big Apple. Witch Baby misses him and soon follows Angel Juan to New York, and the book is about her search for him—aided by the ghost of Weetzie's father—through the nightmare world of Manhattan. Her search ultimately takes her into the subways of New York, with "strong echoes of Orpheus' descent into Hades," as Michael Cart noted in *School Library Journal.* But in the end Witch Baby realizes she has to leave Angel Juan to find his own way, as she must find hers. "Love will come," she muses, "because it always does, because why else would it exist, and it will make everything hurt a little less. You just have to believe in yourself." Like its predecessors, *Missing Angel Juan* is "an engagingly eccentric mix of fantasy and reality, enhanced—this time—by mystery and suspense," Cart remarked. And Judy Sasges, writing in *Voice of Youth Advocates,* likewise called the story "imaginative, mystical, and completely engaging."

Examines Mature Themes

With her fifth young adult title, *The Hanged Man,* Block explored even more mature themes, this time looking at the "descent of a woman into madness of a sort," as the author stated. Set in the same L.A. club scenes as the Weetzie books, *The Hanged Man* is about the darker side of life. The story deals with a young woman named Laurel, who is struggling with her emotions in the wake of the death by cancer of her father, with whom she has had an incestuous relationship. "Block's prose moves like a heroin trip through the smog and wet heat, heavy flowers, and velvet grunge of Hollywood," reviewer Vanessa Elder wrote in *School Library Journal.* "There is lots of fairy tale imagery," Block said of the work, "but there is also an ominous side. It's about obsession and being haunted by the past. This time the cure, the healing power, is much more art than love. In that sense I feel I am in a sort of transition in my writing. So much of my earlier stuff was about searching for love, and in fact love was missing in my own life. But now that exists for me. The result is less of a yearning tone in my books."

In 1995, Block returned to the world of Weetzie Bat with the novel *Baby Be-Bop.* This book is actually a prequel to those earlier ones in that it tells the story of Weetzie's friend Dirk, and of how he deals with the realization that he is gay. "What might seem didactic from lesser writers becomes a gleaming gift from Block," a *Publishers Weekly* reviewer wrote. "Her extravagantly imaginative settings and finely honed perspectives remind the reader that there is magic everywhere."

Block's next two books *Girl Goddess #9* and *I Was a Teenage Fairy* deal with similar themes: young people fighting to come to grips with a rapidly changing world and their place in it. *Girl Goddess #9* is a collection of nine short stories about girls, which are arranged chronologically; the first tales in the book are about toddlers, while the last one concerns a young woman entering college. The stories are written in Block's "funky, richly sensual style," Dorie Freebury of *Voice of Youth Advocates* noted, and the characters "are painfully real, facing the challenges of life that can make or break one's spirit."

The novel *I Was a Teenage Fairy* is a modern-day fairy tale about an eleven-year-old girl named Barbie who is being pushed into modeling by her mother. The appearance of an acid-tongued, finger-sized fairy named Mab changes Barbie's life and eventually helps her overcome the emotional trauma of being molested by a well-known photographer, whose crime is ignored by the girl's mother. According to a critic in *Publishers Weekly,* "The prose, less obviously lush than in previous books, sustains steady crescendos of insight. This fairy tale is too pointedly a social critique to be entirely magical, but its spell feels real."

Block's next novel, *Violet and Claire,* is the story of the friendship that develops between Violet and Claire, two teenage girls as different as night and

If you enjoy the works of Francesca Lia Block, you may also want to check out the following books:

Marion Dane Bauer, *Am I Blue? Coming out From the Silence,* 1994.
Hazel Rochman, *Who Do You Think You Are? Stories of Friends and Enemies,* 1993.
Walter Dean Myers, *Crystal,* 1987.

day. Seventeen-year-old Violet is an aspiring screenwriter and filmmaker, and an outsider at her high school. Past depression and a suicide attempt have left her hard-edged and isolated; she devotes her time to studying the films she loves and to writing her own screenplay. Then she meets Claire, a poet with glittering gauze fairy wings sewn on the back of her Tinker Bell T-shirt, and the two become fast friends. As the novel unfolds, the friendship between Violet and Claire is tested as the girls are divided by personal ambition and the intrusion of the outside world. Violet is willingly seduced by a rock star, who gets her a job with a screen agent, while Claire enrolls in a poetry workshop and becomes attached to the instructor. The action reaches its peak at a wild party the girls attend after Violet sells a screenplay. Claire flees into the desert, and Violet follows in search of her. "Block excels in depicting strong and supportive friendships between teen girls," wrote Debbie Carton in *Booklist,* "and *Violet and Claire* is at its best when the two protagonists reach past their own pain to help each other." According to a *Kirkus Reviews* critic, "Fans of the author's previous works will take to this one; newcomers will be captured by the rainbow iridescence of Block's prose."

In addition to her books for teenagers, Block has published two adult titles, *Ecstasia* and *Primavera.* "My adult titles explore much the same ground as my young adult ones," Block once declared. "Greek myth plays in these as well, and they deal with my eternal theme of art and love as healing forces. They are a longer format, though, with more poetry and actual song lyrics in the text. They are poetic fantasies set in mythic landscapes." Block plans to continue writing in both fields, but finds particular satisfaction in her young adult titles, which, after the retirement of

Zolotow; are now edited by Joanna Cotler. "There is a certain openness and receptivity in young readers," Block said. "I've found a real depth of feeling from kids who have written to me. It's so hard for these kids in the time of AIDS. And they are still so full of hope, though I see a lot of despair, as well."

"I hope my work is poetic," Block once said. "I want my books to be contemporary fairy tales with edge. And I love the magical realism in my work. It's not as if you can escape the world. You're in the world. You're part of it. But there is solace and hope through the magic. There is something of another world. Hope, but in a grounded way." It is exactly this sense of hope that Block has given her readers and that has led to her success. She has validated their experience by writing about it. "One of the things about *Weetzie Bat* is that it has given readers freedom to take their own contemporary culture and write about it themselves seriously as fiction or poetry. In letters from my readers I see that I have done something of the same service as my mother did for me writing down my early stories. I have made this other culture real and worthy. My readers discover it's okay to write about whatever is important to them and do it in a poetic way. Writing has saved my life in a way. Being able to express myself creatively was the way I could survive at certain parts of my life. If I can give others that message, that their lives and experiences are worth writing about, I would be very happy."

■ Works Cited

Review of *Baby Be-Bop, Publishers Weekly,* July 31, 1995, p. 82.

Block, Francesca Lia, *Weetzie Bat,* HarperCollins, 1989.

Block, Francesca Lia, *Witch Baby,* HarperCollins, 1990.

Block, Francesca Lia, "Punk Pixies in the Canyon," *Los Angeles Times Book Review,* July 26, 1992, pp. 1, 11.

Block, Francesca Lia, *Missing Angel Juan,* Harper-Collins, 1993.

Block, Francesca Lia, in a telephone interview with J. Sydney Jones for *Something about the Author,* June 9, 1994.

Campbell, Patty, review of *Cherokee Bat and the Goat Guys, New York Times Book Review,* September 20, 1992, p. 18.

Campbell, Patty, "People Are Talking about . . . Francesca Lia Block," *Horn Book,* January/February, 1993, pp. 57-63.

Cart, Michael, review of *Missing Angel Juan, School Library Journal,* October, 1993, p. 148.

Carton, Debbie, review of *Violet and Claire, Booklist,* September 1, 1999, p. 122.

Elder, Vanessa, review of *The Hanged Man, School Library Journal,* September, 1994, p. 238.

Freebury, Dorie, review of *Girl Goddess #9, Voice of Youth Advocates,* February, 1997, p. 326.

Hearne, Betsy, "Pretty in Punk," *New York Times Book Review,* May 21, 1989, p. 47.

Review of *I Was a Teenage Fairy, Publishers Weekly,* September 21, 1998, p. 86.

Jones, Patrick, "People Are Talking about . . . Francesca Lia Block," *Horn Book,* November/December, 1992, pp. 697-701.

Knoth, Maeve Visser, review of *Witch Baby, Horn Book,* January/February, 1992, pp. 78-79.

Osborn, Anne, review of *Weetzie Bat, School Library Journal,* April, 1989, pp. 116-17.

Ramsay, Ellen, review of *Witch Baby, School Library Journal,* September, 1991, p. 277.

Richmond, Gail, review of *Cherokee Bat and the Goat Guys, School Library Journal,* September, 1992, p. 274.

Roback, Diane, "Flying Starts: Francesca Lia Block," *Publishers Weekly,* December 22, 1989, p. 27.

Roback, Diane, and Richard Donahue, review of *Cherokee Bat and the Goat Guys, Publishers Weekly,* July 20, 1992, p. 251.

Sasges, Judy, review of *Missing Angel Juan, Voice of Youth Advocates,* December, 1993, p. 287.

Review of *Violet and Claire, Kirkus Reviews,* September 15, 1999, p. 1497.

■ For More Information See

BOOKS

Children's Literature Review, Volume 33, Gale, 1994.

PERIODICALS

Booklist, August, 1992, p. 2004; October 1, 1996, p. 340.

Bulletin of the Center for Children's Books, December, 1993, p. 115; September, 1994, p. 6; October, 1996, p. 49; September, 1999, p. 5.

English Journal, December, 1990, p. 78; October, 1991, pp. 94-95.

Five Owls, January-February, 1999, p. 66.

Horn Book, September/October, 1992, p. 587.

Los Angeles Times Book Review, November 12, 1995, p. 4.

New Yorker, November 25, 1991, p. 148.

New York Times Book Review, January 19, 1992, p. 24; February 26, 1995, p. 21.

Publishers Weekly, March 10, 1989, p. 91; July 18, 1994, pp. 246-47.

School Library Journal, December, 1993, p. 24; September, 1994, p. 238; December, 1998, p. 118; September, 1999, p. 218.

Voice of Youth Advocates, December, 1995, pp. 297-98; February, 1997, p. 326.

—Sketch by J. Sydney Jones, updated by Ken Cuthbertson

Judith Clarke

■ Personal

Born August 24, 1943, in Sydney, Australia; daughter of Kenneth Edward (a production supervisor) and Sheila Iris (Grey) Clarke; married Rashmi Desai (an anthropologist), December 27, 1968; children: Yask. *Education:* University of New South Wales, B.A. (with honors), 1964; Australian National University, M.A. (with honors), 1966.

■ Addresses

Home—31 Alice St., Mt. Waverley, Melbourne 3149, Australia.

■ Career

Teacher, librarian, lecturer, and writer.

■ Awards, Honors

The Heroic Life of Al Capsella was shortlisted for the New South Wales Premier's Award, 1989, and was named an editors' choice by *Booklist,* 1990, and a best book for young adults by the American Library Association, 1990; *Al Capsella and the Watchdogs* was shortlisted for the New South

Wales Premier's Award, 1990, was named talking book of the year by Variety Club, 1991, and a best book for young adults by the New York Public Library, 1992; Victorian Premier's Award for Young Adult Novel, 1998, for *Night Train.*

■ Writings

The Heroic Life of Al Capsella, University of Queensland Press (St. Lucia, Queensland, Australia), 1988, Henry Holt (New York, NY), 1990.

The Boy on the Lake (stories), University of Queensland Press, 1989, revised edition published as *The Torment of Mr. Gully: Stories of the Supernatural,* Henry Holt (New York, NY), 1990.

Teddy B. Zoot, illustrated by Margaret Hewitt, Henry Holt, 1990.

Al Capsella and the Watchdogs, University of Queensland Press, 1990, Henry Holt (New York, NY), 1991.

Luna Park at Night, Pascoe Publishing (Apollo Bay, Victoria), 1991.

Al Capsella on Holidays, University of Queensland, 1992, published as *Al Capsella Takes a Vacation,* Henry Holt, 1993.

Riff Raff, Henry Holt, 1992.

Friend of My Heart, University of Queensland Press, 1994.

Big Night Out, Shorts (Norwood, South Australia), 1995.

Panic Stations (short stories), University of Queensland Press, 1995.

Night Train, Penguin (Ringwood, Victoria, Australia), 1998.

The Lost Day, Henry Holt, 1999.

Angels Passing By, Puffin (Ringwood, Victoria, Australia), 1999.

■ Sidelights

Judith Clarke writes incisive fictional novels for teens that have earned praise for their humor and deft handling of weighty issues. This former teacher and librarian, who is a parent herself, enjoyed her first taste of success as an author with *The Heroic Life of Al Capsella*, a 1988 novel set in Clarke's native Australia. Two other novels featuring the likable teen followed, and in these and subsequent young-adult titles that deal with more serious topics or crises, the universal appeal of Clarke's protagonists and their dilemmas have prompted reviewers to note that the books should undoubtedly resonate with a global readership as well. After the success of Clarke's debut as a writer—*The Heroic Life* earned a finalist's spot in a government-sponsored literature competition in Australia—nearly all of her books have been published in the United States by Holt.

Clarke was born in Sydney in 1943 and earned an advanced degree from the Australian National University in 1966. Two years later she married an anthropologist, with whom she had a son, Yask. The author once stated: "Although I didn't write much during the period when my own family was young—probably because I was consumed with just the kind of parental anxieties that dog the parents in the 'Capsella' series—I can remember very clearly my first attempt at writing. I was very young, probably about four, had not gone to school yet, and had no idea of how to 'write' in the sense of forming actual letters. My mother had given me an empty notebook to draw in, and I used it to write a 'book' (it even had chapters) about a doll who'd fallen from her pram and had a series of horrendous adventures. The actual 'writing' was a kind of scribble—long wavy lines—but the story itself was a heartrending tale, and when I finished it, I gave it to my uncle to read. I watched him closely, expecting him to dissolve into sympathetic tears, but to my amazement and fury he burst out laughing. Perhaps this un-

This first installment of a series set in Australia finds Al wishing his eccentric parents could be more like other people.

settling experience is what turned me toward comedy so many years after."

Introducing Al Capsella

The hero of the Al Capsella series is actually named Almeric, an odd name with which his parents have saddled him in just one example of their loving eccentricity and the first in a series of burdens fully outlined in the 1988 debut, *The Heroic Life of Al Capsella*. The work was published in the United States two years later. Al is fourteen and wishes his parents were conformist and "normal," rather than intellectual and decidedly different from the other households he observes.

His mother writes romance novels and wears secondhand clothes, while his father is a university professor who finds it difficult to keep up on the yard work that is the hallmark of perfection in their suburban community. Al states that the ideal set of parents would be "perfectly ordinary and unobtrusive, quiet and orderly, well dressed and polite, hardworking and as wealthy as possible."

On a visit to the home of his grandparents—whose household is a veritable model of the ordinary—"Al discovers what 'normal' is with a vengeance," noted Ronald A. Van De Voorde in *School Library Journal.* Stephanie Zvirin, in *Booklist,* commended Clarke for her ability to craft oddly endearing adult characters that provide Al with the appropriate amount of teen angst, yet "beneath the comic veneer she has created," Zvirin opined, "lurks a fondness and respect for people—even parents—despite their strange ways."

In her next book, *Al Capsella and the Watchdogs,* Clarke depicts Al attempting to forge a life for himself as a more independent teenager. He feels that parents worry far too much—they give him permission to attend a party, for instance, but then his mother borrows a dog and takes it for a walk in order to spy on him and his friends. When his grandparents come for a visit, Al realizes that his mother endured—and still endures—the same constant, overprotective hovering he experiences. Zvirin, reviewing it for *Booklist,* again praised Clarke as a writer with a unique ability to relate to teens; the cast of adult characters in the Capsella series, she noted, "ring true in surprising, subtle ways."

A third book in the series appeared with a revised American title *Al Capsella Takes a Vacation* in 1993. Now sixteen, Al is able to convince his parents that he and his friend are mature enough for their own holiday at Christmastime, when it is summer in Australia. Lured by another friend's exaggerations, they cart their surfboards off to what they envision as their beachfront party paradise. Instead they find themselves in a deadly dull rural nightmare two-hundred miles inland; a leech-filled pond awaits, and they are forced to fend for themselves, even to the point of cooking their own food. "Al's wry, almost deadpan narrative is the perfect vehicle for describing a fantasy vacation gone awry," remarked Zvirin in *Booklist.* Clarke's attempt to age her protagonist and show some character development did not escape the notice of *School Library Journal* reviewer Kathy Piehl. "The maturing Al has grown a bit reflective, and a new poignancy surfaces in his consideration of the world," noted Piehl.

Examines Mature Themes

With her 1994 young adult novel *Friend of My Heart,* Clarke began addressing more serious issues in her fiction. The work revolves around a shy, overweight boy whose grandparent suffers from senile dementia, a difficult situation prompted by the author's own experience with her mother. Another trying event that occurred in the author's household spurred Clarke to delve into even more realistic plots for her fiction: the

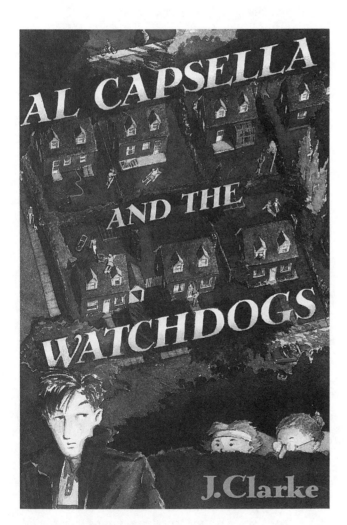

Al struggles for independence from his parents in this sequel to *The Heroic Life of Al Capsella.*

JUDITH CLARKE

THE LOST DAY

When a teen disappears in this 1999 work, his friends' responses showcase their own difficult lives.

at a crossroads in life, and Clarke attempts to give an accurate example of the stress and strain teens face from parents, school, economics, and their peers. Anne Briggs, who reviewed *The Lost Day* for *Magpies,* called it a "clever and memorable book" and praised Clarke for her ability to merge "the most original and lyrical language with perfectly realised teenage slang," as well as for the series of "brilliant vignettes" that reveal Vinny, Jasper, and the cast of other characters. The work was published in the United States in 1999.

If you enjoy the works of Judith Clarke, you may also want to check out the following books:

Ron Koertge, *The Harmony Arms,* 1992.
Gordon Korman, *Losing Al's Place,* 1990.
Joel L. Schwartz, *Upchuck Summer's Revenge,* 1990.

---

suicide of a friend of her teenage son. As Clarke told *Magpies* interviewer Margot Hillel, "I would find it very hard to write books like the Capsella series any more, because I would be thinking in the back of my mind that it wasn't actually true. Nothing bad could ever happen to Al Capsella or within the structure of those stories."

Clarke's 1997 novel *The Lost Day* explores what happens when a friend mysteriously disappears. Australian teens Vinny and his friend Jasper spend a Saturday evening at the Hanging Gardens, but Jasper is still sad over a breakup with his girlfriend and doesn't notice when Vinny disappears. He is still missing the next day, and the effect this has on Jasper and several other friends makes up the bulk of the action in the novel. All seem

Clarke's 1998 novel *Night Train* won unstinting praise for presenting depression and suicide in an empathetic manner. Luke, the young protagonist, feels increasingly isolated from those around him. Clarke begins the novel at the end of Luke's life, retracing his last weeks. Because of a learning disability, he does poorly in school, though he is intelligent. Teachers and school officials fail to recognize the depth of his problem, and the bad grades and expulsions cause his father to treat him harshly. His mother and sister fail to sympathize, mired in their own problems, and it is only his youngest sister, Naomi, who tries to show Luke that someone needs him.

Luke's only comfort comes from the sound of the night train, but he begins to question his own sanity when he learns that no one else hears it. Jane Connolly, writing in *Magpies,* commended Clarke for her deft handling of the difficult subject matter. "By providing the end before the beginning, Clarke changes this story from simply one of despair and ultimate death to an examination of the care we provide or deny young people in obvious need," Connolly declared. "The story becomes a powerful question about responsibility."

Clarke sometimes feels compelled to answer charges that her work is too starkly realistic for young adults. She disagrees and supports her belief with the strongly approving letters she receives from her teen readers. "I want people to read my books and feel a kind of empathy, to feel that they understand how it is," Clarke told Hillel in *Magpies*. "That's what I want really, I want a child to read a book and think that's just like me or that's how it is for me, and there is somebody who understands. I do believe that something you read in a book can change your life for good."

■ Works Cited

Briggs, Anne, review of *The Lost Day, Magpies,* March, 1997, p. 37.

Connolly, Jane, review of *Night Train, Magpies,* May, 1998, pp. 36-37.

Hillel, Margot, interview with Judith Clarke, *Magpies,* March, 1999, pp. 14-16.

Piehl, Kathy, review of *Al Capsella Takes a Vacation, School Library Journal,* May, 1993, p. 124.

Van De Voorde, Ronald A., review of *The Heroic Life of Al Capsella, School Library Journal,* July, 1990, p. 88.

Zvirin, Stephanie, "Guffaws, Giggles, and Good Old-Fashioned Roars," *Booklist,* March 15, 1990, p. 1429.

Zvirin, Stephanie, review of *Al Capsella and the Watchdogs, Booklist,* August, 1991, p. 2140.

Zvirin, Stephanie, review of *Al Capsella Takes a Vacation, Booklist,* July, 1993, p. 1957.

■ For More Information See

PERIODICALS

Bulletin of the Center for Children's Books, July-August, 1990, p. 261; November, 1999, pp. 86-87.

Kirkus Reviews, June 1, 1993, p. 718.

Kliatt, September, 1999, p. 6.

Reading Time, November, 1999, p. 32.

School Library Journal, August, 1991, p. 195.

Voice of Youth Advocates, December, 1999, p. 329.*

Douglas Coupland

■ Personal

Born December 30, 1961, on a Canadian military base in Baden-Sollingen, Germany; son of Douglas Charles Thomas (a doctor) and C. Janet (Campbell) Coupland. *Education:* Attended Emily Carr College of Art and Design, Vancouver, Canada, 1984; completed a two-year course in Japanese business science, Hawaii, 1986.

■ Addresses

Home—Vancouver, British Columbia, Canada. *Office*—c/o Pantheon Books, 201 E. 50th St., New York, NY 10022-7703.

■ Career

Writer, sculptor, and editor. Host of *The Search for Generation X* (documentary), PBS, 1991.

■ Writings

Generation X: Tales for an Accelerated Culture (novel), St. Martin's (New York City), 1991.

Shampoo Planet (novel), Pocket Books (New York City), 1992.
Life after God (short fiction), Pocket Books, 1994.
Microserfs (novel), ReganBooks (New York City), 1995.
Polaroids from the Dead (essays and short fiction), ReganBooks, 1996.
Girlfriend in a Coma (novel), ReganBooks, 1998.
(With Kip Ward) *Lara's Book: Lara Croft and the Tomb Raider Phenomenon*, Prima Publishing (Rocklin, CA), 1998.
Miss Wyoming, Pantheon Books, 2000.

Contributor of articles to periodicals, including *New Republic*, *New York Times*, *Spin*, *Wired*, and *Saturday Night*.

■ Sidelights

What started as a handbook to 1990s hip culture written by would-be sculptor Douglas Coupland ended up being a call to arms to a generation that, until he defined it, had gone unnamed, a generation he called Generation X. These 1990s "twentysomethings" finally had a face when Coupland, after receiving a $22,500 advance to write a *Preppie Handbook*-type guide, observed and detailed the generation to a tee in his 1991 book *Generation X: Tales for an Accelerated Culture*. He invented succinct and witty tag-words that clearly described what it was the members of this generation were feeling and trying to say. Coupland

"A groundbreaking novel."

—*Los Angeles Times*

TALES FOR AN ACCELERATED CULTURE

DOUGLAS COUPLAND

Through the characters in this 1991 novel, Coupland spoke to a new generation as no one had previously.

was then deemed the "voice of a generation"—a title he claimed he did not want and tried to shake off in his subsequent writings. Still, he was known for his witty, detailed observations of culture and society, and in addition to publishing seven books, wrote for magazines like *Wired, Spin, New York Times,* and *New Republic.*

Coupland's *Generation X* characters, Andy, Dag, and Claire, are twentysomethings living in the retirement community of Palm Springs, California. The three share a quick recall of 1970s TV shows, all have "McJobs" ("low pay, low status, low future"), a listless view of the future, and an ironic and jaded sense of the world. What Coupland described through his characters sounded very familiar to many real-life American twentysomethings. But everyone did not understand Generation X's cynicism, struggle and sensibilities. According to Coupland himself in an interview with Jeffrey Favre of the *Chicago Tribune,* "You either get it or you don't, but in general they (older people) don't. There's no point trying to explain

it." The generation born between the early 1960s and early 1970s were then given the name—for marketing, entertainment, and political discussions—Generation X. Until Coupland, no one had been able to successfully study, market to, or analyze this group.

The newly named Generation X seemed to have understood Coupland's point. According to a *People* article, when *The Seattle Post-Intelligencer* asked for reader responses to the book, it received over 100 replies. One 26-year-old woman wrote, "We leave the overachievement to the elder siblings, the prison cells of those office jobs to the thirtysomethings, and we live off Mom and Dad as long as the umbilical cord will stretch." A 29-year-old man responded, "I'm cynical. I'm wary. I'm tired. This book has helped me realize just how many of 'us' there are."

Leftovers from *Generation X*'s beginnings as a handbook appear in the book's margins—definitions of Coupland's made-up terms that serve to further define the mode and manner of its subjects. A "Bleeding Ponytail" is an "elderly, sold-out baby boomer who pines for hippie or presellout days," "Lessness" is "a philosophy whereby one reconciles oneself to diminishing expectations of material wealth," and "101-ism" means "the tendency to pick apart, often in minute detail, all aspects of life, using half-understood pop psychology as a tool."

Critics either praised Coupland's edgy, glossary-type sides as hip and smart, or panned them for being distracting. In a *New Statesman* review of *Generation X*, critic John Williams found a balance and commented, "Underneath the fancy-dan trappings, though, *Generation X* is a surprisingly endearing read . . . self-conscious as hell, but charming, too." *Vanity Fair* critic Bruce Handy wrote of *Generation X:* "By turns clever and irritating, *Generation X* was in essence a conventional story of bored, alienated youth, but one that heralded the arrival of a new genre. . . . More than an uneven first novel, this was a canny pop-culture manifesto." *Generation X* topped best-seller lists, sold over 150,000 copies in North America alone, and was translated into 13 languages. Based on the book's success, Coupland hosted a public-television documentary called *The Search for Generation X.* He also turned down a request from White House policy analysts for advice about Generation X.

Compelled to Write Fiction

Like his characters in *Generation X*, Coupland grew up in the 1960s and 1970s. Raised in Vancouver, British Columbia, Coupland went to art school to become a sculptor, traveled to Hawaii to study Japanese business science, then took an internship in Japan. He ended up writing for a Toronto magazine and collaborating on a comic strip called *Generation X*. It was then that he was approached to turn the comic series into a handbook. "It had awoken something inside me, and once it woke up, I literally had to stop doing magazine articles," he told Robin Abcarian of the *Los Angeles Times*. "I had to do the fiction." Coupland's first book, which he shies away from talking about, was "such a wretched book," he told Favre in the *Chicago Tribune*, that it wasn't even released.

In his next novel, *Shampoo Planet*, Coupland tried to distance himself from Generation X by writing about the generation born ten years later, whom he called "global teens." These hair-product-obsessed teenagers often have parents who were 1960s hippies, and see hope for the future in corporate America. Having learned the hard way with *Generation X* what it's like to be called the voice of a generation, Coupland tried to stress, as with *Generation X*, that he had just written a fictional book based on his observations of society. "With Generation X, what started out as characters in a book became representatives of a broad layer of people, and of changing times," Coupland said in an interview with *Maclean's* writer Victor Dwyer. "Still, they were just characters in a novel. That is all they are in the new book, too."

Tyler Johnson, *Shampoo Planet*'s main character, is a college student who lives in the northeastern United States. Johnson and his two siblings were raised by their mother, a divorced hippie. He reads a magazine called *Young Achiever*, desperately wants a job at a local high-tech firm, and has to inspect the house for his mom's hashish before friends come over. He keeps a collection of shampoo and hair-care products that his mom calls his "shampoo museum" and his girlfriend calls a "landfill starter kit." But Tyler, the aspiring yuppie, has a theory: "What's on top of your head says what's inside your head," the character says in *Shampoo Planet*. "Once hair goes, all else follows." The story shows Tyler going through a change that starts with a breakup with his girlfriend and is evidenced by his reaction to the

SHAMPOO PLANET
DOUGLAS COUPLAND

"Having called Coupland's first book a *Catcher in the Rye* for our time, I repeat myself. Nobody has a better finger on the pulse of the twenty-something generation...."
—Louise Bernikow, *Cosmopolitan*

THE REVELATORY BESTSELLER BY THE AUTHOR OF *LIFE AFTER GOD*

In this 1992 work, the author examines the phenonenon of parents who grew up in the 1960s raising children of the 1990s.

sight of a forest that's been clear-cut—he's brought to tears.

Coupland didn't make as big a hit with *Shampoo Planet* as he did with *Generation X*. Critic Sophfronia Scott Gregory commented in *Time*, "The characters never really do anything. . . . Coupland wants very much to be the voice of this generation, but he must understand that its stories are intriguing enough to stand on their own. He does not have to dance around hair gels and alternative music to tell them." *Entertainment Weekly* critic Margot Mifflin gave the novel a D-plus grade and called it "Neither political enough to be satiric nor substantial enough to be stirring." Dwyer gave the book mixed praise when he wrote in *Maclean's*, "Without the pique of his first book, but with all of its punch, *Shampoo Planet* shows a maturing author artfully evoking the hopes and dreams of a generation that has good reason to have little of either."

By 1994, Coupland had had enough of Generation X. All of his writing about consumerism, listless youth, and pop culture seemed to finally catch up with him after *Shampoo Planet*. He longed to get away from his observations of contemporary culture and decided to research the Irish potato famine of 1845-1847. But try as he might to avoid them, stories "started popping out of me," he told Mike Snider of *USA Today*. So he collected these stories into *Life After God*. The book was the result of a change Coupland said he was

Coupland explores the spiritual issues of the first generation of Americans to be raised largely without a spiritual foundation.

undergoing. "The Other World . . . is more 'real' than our everyday allegedly real world of keyboards, coffee mugs, Toyotas and newspapers, etc.," he told Snider, "and is hence more worthy of exploration." So Coupland explored his gravitation toward the religious, which came about during a period of "loss and mortality." In the book, he states that his generation was the first "raised without religion." Coupland's parents were not religious when he was growing up—religious holidays such as Easter or Christmas were not observed. In *Life After God*, Coupland's characters face coping with life without faith, and the eternal questions of life, death, and human origins are posed.

Brenda Peterson had nothing good to say about *Life After God* in her *New York Times* review. "It drones where it might delve, it skims where it might seduce, it hoards where it might offer sustenance," Peterson wrote. "The range of character and emotion is so slight as to be undetectable. Presented with such and unmoving feast, a reader might starve to death." Peterson concluded, "The author withers all he creates." Although "[t]hereare flashes of genuine wit and surprise," wrote Handy in *Vanity Fair*, "reading the stories in *Life After God* becomes not unlike spending an evening in a bar with an old school friend you quickly realize you've outgrown." Coupland also appeared in a series of 30-second spots on MTV in which he read excerpts from *Life After God* over video-type graphics.

Watching the Workers

After the introspection of *Life After God*, Coupland returned to his position as cultural observer. *Wired* magazine hired him to write a continuing fiction series about a small group of Microsoft employees. It started with a cover story called "Microserfs," that was published in the January 1994 issue. "You see yourself in his writing," *Wired* managing editor John Battelle told Snider in *USA Today*. In preparation for the story, Coupland "actually moved in with some" Microsoft computer coders. "I Gorilla-in-the-Mist-ed with all these people," he said in *USA Today*. "What I saw is that they really think they are designing the code which feeds the machine that will design the machine that will design the machine that will design the machine that will one day give answers," Coupland told Favre in the *Chicago Tri-*

DOUGLAS COUPLAND

microserfs

"Coupland continues to register the buzz
of his generation with a fidelity that should shame
most professional Zeitgeist chasers."

—*New York Times Book Review*

This 1995 bestseller deals with corporate culture and the individual's search for a life outside of it.

bune. "Even if you pretend you're not being religious, you're actually being more religious than you even realize."

Coupland's experience developed into another novel, 1995's *Microserfs*. In the book, Coupland follows the lives of Daniel Underwood and his five roommates—all Microsoft coders who live together in a college dorm-type environment, work sixteen-hour days, and are obsessed with Microsoft chairman Bill Gates. Again, his characters are 1970s TV buffs, and define their personalities by listing their dream *Jeopardy* categories. Underwood's roommate Susan's list: 680XO assembly language, cats, early 1980s haircut bands, "My secret affair with Rob in the Excel Group," license plate slogans of America, plot lines from *The*

Monkees, and the death of IBM. Known as a perceptive observer and gatherer of details, Coupland also was criticized by some critics for his lack of story and plot development. Jay McInerney wrote in the *New York Times,* "Mr. Coupland is an acute observer of the non-natural world, and he indulges his gifts to such an extent that plot junkies may grow impatient."

Coupland then paired twenty-four mini-essays and short fictions with forty-two black-and-white photos in 1996's *Polaroids From the Dead*. Most of the written pieces had already appeared in magazines like *Spin* and *New Republic,* among others. In them, he visits the former East Berlin, nuclear tourist sites in Los Alamos, New Mexico, ponders James Rosenquist's gigantic pop painting *F-111,* and writes a "Letter to Kurt Cobain," the late singer for the rock band Nirvana. *Rolling Stone* critic Jim DeRogatis wasn't impressed. He wrote, "I'd call him [Coupland] a charlatan and a poseur. . . . he's actually something much worse: a self-important bore. If he *is* the voice of my generation, he's speaking in a dreadfully dull monotone."

Examining the Modern World

In his 1998 work, *Girlfriend in a Coma*, Karen Ann McNeil, a pregnant, seventeen-year-old girl, falls into a coma in 1979 and reawakens eighteen years later to "a dramatically different world," wrote Coupland, "one without the Berlin Wall and one with AIDS, computers, and radicchio." She thinks modern society is more soulless than the one she fell asleep in, and doesn't understand her thirty-something friends' unhappiness in life. McNeil then foresees a deadly sleeping virus that wipes out most of the world's population. While Anthony Duignan-Cabrera wrote in *People* that *Girlfriend in a Coma* was Coupland's "strongest novel to date," he went on to write that "*Coma* is hampered by many of its own plot and character devices." *New York Times* critic Laura Miller was less gracious. "While Coupland seems to mean well, to sincerely hunger after such ideals as 'truth' and 'meaning'," she wrote, "he brings to the task of novel writing the aptitudes or a marketing executive. Or . . . as a trend analyst, he's a Porsche," adding "But as a novelist, he's more like a Gremlin, underpowered and oddly truncated."

As with *Life After God*, Coupland attempted with *Girlfriend in a Coma* to lose the sense of irony he'd

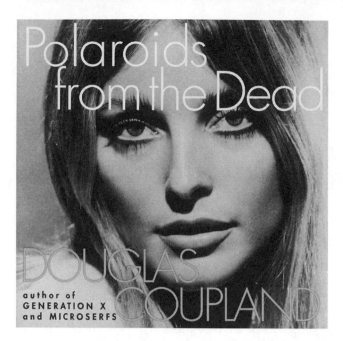

In this 1996 work, Coupland defines American culture by examining its subcultures and stories, both public and private.

become known for with *Generation X* and *Shampoo Planet.* "What I know and what I'm really comfortable around is irony—ironic people, ironic situations, ironic everything," he told Philip Marchand in a *Toronto Star* interview. "But you're not going to get to heaven rehashing Mary Tyler Moor re-runs. You just have to give all that up. It still has its place. . . . But what I'm saying is, you're not going to get better than you are just doing irony or being ironical."

Also in 1998, Coupland became a published cyber world observer, as well, with *Lara's Book: Lara Croft and the Tomb Raider Phenomenon*, a study of Lara Croft, the sexy, powerful star of the successful action-adventure video game Tomb Raider whom millions of video gamers had fallen in love with. In the book, Coupland's thoughts on the Lara Croft sensation are paired with an original adventure called "Air Tibet." "Harold Adams Innes, a media critic from the 1960s said, 'We become what we behold.' Well, at the moment there are certainly millions of people out there beholding Lara," Coupland said in a press release. "I'm darn curious to see what these people will become and I think this book is an exploration of that." In "Air Tibet," Coupland got to flex his flair for fan-

tasy fiction. He had Croft kicking in airplane windows—which she has trouble squeezing through, due to her ample bosom—and generally wreaking havoc on a power-hungry bad guy and his bodyguards, all while trying to control the mysterious powers of an ancient pair of jewels.

If you enjoy the works of Douglas Coupland, you may also want to check out the following books and films:

The works of Francesca Lia Block, including *Dangerous Angels: The Weetzie Bat Books,* 1998, and *Violet and Claire,* 1999.
Rob Thomas, *Rats Saw God,* 1996.
Reality Bites, a film starring Winona Ryder and Ben Stiller, 1994.

Although Coupland was often criticized for his lack of plot, many critics, including Philip Marchand in the *Toronto Star,* believed "He capitalized on his strengths—a keen eye for the details of culture, a gift for anecdote, a hyper-active intelligence." And Coupland was quick to offer a reason. "Remember, the only fiction I've ever written is what's on the bookseller's shelf," he wrote in an e-mail interview with Dennis Romero of the *LosAngeles Times.* "There's no high-school short stories. My education has been entirely public." And to those who gave him the "voice of a generation" title he loathed, he wrote, "I'm never out to prove anything. I just follow my fascinations."

■ Works Cited

Abcarian, Robin, "Boomer Backlash," *Los Angeles Times,* June 12, 1991.
DeRogatis, Jim, review of *Polaroids from the Dead, Rolling Stone,* July 11-25, 1996, p. 90.
Duignan-Cabrera, Anthony, review of *Girlfriend in a Coma, People,* April 13, 1998, p. 31.
Dwyer, Victor, "Puberty Blues: An Author Scans a New Generation," *Maclean's,* August 24, 1992, p. 60.
Favre, Jeffrey, "Douglas Coupland Tries, Largely in Vain, To Ignore 'Generation X,'" *Chicago Tribune,* March 14, 1994.

Gregory, Sophfronia Scott, "The Stories Left Untold," *Time*, October 19,1992, p. 78.

Handy, Bruce, "'X' Marks the Schlock: Slacking Towards Bethlehem with Author Douglas Coupland," *Vanity Fair*, March, 1994, pp. 92, 94.

Marchand, Philip, "Coupland in Trivial Pursuit," *Toronto Star*, March 18, 1998.

Marchand, Philip, "Doug Coupland and the Human World," *Toronto Star*, October 7, 1995.

McInerney, Jay, "Geek Love," *New York Times*, June 11, 1995, p. 54.

Mifflin, Margot, review of *Shampoo Planet*, *Entertainment Weekly*, September 11, 1992, p. 85.

Miller, Laura, "The Gen X Files," *New York Times*, April 12, 1998, p. 9.

Neill, Michael, and Nancy Matsumoto, "X Marks the Angst," *People*, October 14, 1991, pp. 105-6.

Peterson, Brenda, "The Bomb and Burger King," *New York Times*, May 8, 1994, p. 13.

Prima Publishing press release, July 16, 1998.

Romero, Dennis, "On-Line with the Ex Mr. Gen X," *Los Angeles Times*, May 31, 1995.

Snider, Mike, "The X Man," *USA Today*, March 7, 1994, p. D1.

Williams, John, review of *Generation X*, *New Statesman*, May 29, 1992, p. 40.

■ For More Information See

BOOKS

Contemporary Literary Criticism, Volume 85, Gale, 1995.

PERIODICALS

Booklist, November 15, 1992, p. 578.

Books in Canada, September, 1991, pp. 50-51; April, 1992, p. 13; October, 1992; September 1995, p. 30.

Byte, October, 1995, p. 49.

Canadian Forum, January, 1993, p. 41; June, 1994, p. 44; December, 1995, p. 50.

Christian Century, October 5, 1994, p. 905.

Entertainment Weekly, August 25, 1995, p. 106.

Esquire, March, 1994, pp. 170-71.

Fortune, September 18, 1995, p. 235.

Globe and Mail (Toronto), September 5, 1992, p. C8.

Library Journal, February 15, 1994, p. 187.

Maclean's, April 25, 1994, p. 62; June 26, 1995, p. 54.

Nation, June 26, 1995, p. 934.

New Criterion, April, 1994, pp. 79-80.

New Statesman and Society, July 29, 1994, p. 39; November 10, 1995, p. 37.

Newsweek, January 27, 1992, p. 58; June 19, 1995, p. 12.

New York, June 5, 1995, p. 50.

Observer, August 7, 1994, p. 22.

Paragraph, fall, 1994, pp. 32-33.

People, April 25, 1994, pp. 31-32; July 10, 1995, p. 30.

Progressive, January, 1994, p. 42.

Publishers Weekly, February 1, 1991, p. 77; June 15, 1992, p. 82; December 20, 1993, p. 48; May 13, 1996, p. 66; January 26, 1998, p.68.

Quill and Quire, February, 1994, p. 24; June, 1994, p. 38; May, 1995, p. 7; July, 1995, p. 51; May, 1996, p. 1.

Saturday Night, March, 1994, pp. 8-9.

Time, October 19, 1992, p. 78.

Times (London), June 4, 1992, p. 6.

Times Literary Supplement, February 19, 1993, p. 23; August 5, 1994, p. 18; November 10, 1995, p. 22.

Voice Literary Supplement, November, 1992, p. 25.

ON-LINE

Coupland, Douglas, official homepage on the World Wide Web, located at http://www.coupland.com.

Coupland, Douglas, online biography, located at http://www.altculture.com/.index/aentries/c/couplandxx.html (October 18, 1999).

"The Coupland File," located at http://www.geocities.com/SoHo/Gallery/5560 (October 16, 1999).

—Sketch by Brenna Sanchez

Richard Donner

■ Personal

Born Richard D. Schwartzberg on April 24, 1930, in New York, NY; married Lauren Shuler-Donner (a producer).

■ Addresses

Home—Los Angeles, CA. *Agent*—Creative Artists Agency, c/o Michael Ovitz, 9830 Wilshire Blvd., Beverly Hills, CA 90210-1825.

■ Career

Director and producer, best known as the director of *Lethal Weapon* and its sequels, and as co-executive producer of the television series *Tales from the Crypt*.

■ Credits

FILM DIRECTOR

X-15, United Artists, 1961.
Salt and Pepper, United Artists, 1968.
The Omen, Twentieth Century-Fox, 1976.

Superman, Warner Bros., 1978.
The Final Conflict, Twentieth Century-Fox, 1981.
Inside Moves, Associated Film Distributors, 1981.
(Also executive producer) *The Toy*, Columbia, 1982.
(Also producer) *Ladyhawke*, Warner Bros., 1985.
(And producer with others) *The Goonies*, Warner Bros., 1985.
(Also producer) *Lethal Weapon*, Warner Bros., 1987.
(Also producer) *Scrooged*, Paramount, 1988.
(Also producer) *Lethal Weapon 2*, Warner Bros., 1989.
(And producer with others) *Radio Flyer*, Columbia, 1992.
(Also producer) *Lethal Weapon 3*, Warner Bros., 1992.
(Also producer) *Maverick*, Warner Bros., 1994.
Assassins, Warner Bros., 1995.
Conspiracy Theory, Warner Bros., 1997.
Lethal Weapon 4, Warner Bros., 1998.

TELEVISION EXECUTIVE PRODUCER

(With Joel Silver, Robert Zemeckis, Walter Hill, and David Giler) *Tales from the Crypt* (series), HBO, 1989—.

TELEVISION DIRECTOR; MOVIES

Senior Year, CBS, 1974.
Lucas Tanner (pilot for series), NBC, 1974.
A Shadow in the Streets, NBC, 1975.
Sarah T.—Portrait of a Teenage Alcoholic, NBC, 1975.

Also director of *Lola* (also known as *Twinky*), 1969.

■ **Sidelights**

Probably best known for his action–packed commercial movie hits like the *Lethal Weapon* series, director and producer Richard Donner has influenced several generations of viewers beginning with his early television work in the 1960s. Baby boomers were impacted by some of his very successful television credits, including *The Twilight Zone, The Fugitive, The Man from U.N.C.L.E.,* and *Gilligan's Island.* Generation X viewers grew up with his more fantastic feature films, including *Superman, The Goonies, Ladyhawke,* and *The Lost Boys.* Donner's films display a vast array of genres with broad audience appeal. In a *Premiere* article by John

Donner's 1976 horror film *The Omen* established him as a major director.

Clark, Donner states that he "likes action and a strong storyline." Although not hailed as a "true film creator," Donner has shared with audiences the characters and stories that most interested him. He has also not shied away from darker scripts simply to do pictures with less risk and more commercial appeal. Yet, despite his steady career success, Donner has remained gracious,considering himself lucky to be doing what he loves.

Born in New York City on April 24, 1930, Richard Donald Schwartzberg attended Packer Junior College and New York University. His first love was acting, but a director told him that he had difficulty taking direction. This caused Donner to reassess, and in the late fifties, he moved to the Los Angeles area to begin working as a director. According to John Clark in *Premiere,* Donner's big break came when he directed Steve McQueen in *Wanted: Dead or Alive.* From there, he embarked on a highly successful television directing career, working on such series as: *Perry Mason, The Loretta Young Show, Route 66, The Wild Wild West, Ghost Story, Circle of Fear, The Six-Million Dollar Man, Kojak, Tales from the Crypt* (which he also produced), and others. It was not until 1976 that Donner established himself as a major movie director with the horror film, *The Omen.* He followed *The Omen* with a string of hits between 1976 and 1998, including the *Lethal Weapon* series, *Maverick,* and *Conspiracy Theory,* which prompted a frequent collaboration with Mel Gibson. Donner's highly successful track record, spanning four decades, can be greatly attributed to his adaptability—a quality enormously necessary in Hollywood.

Makes Film Directing Debut

Donner's first venture as a director in the feature film marketplace was the popular and controversial *The Omen.* Often compared to *The Exorcist* and *Rosemary's Baby,* this 1976 horror film revolves around Damien, the proverbial Antichrist. The film stars Gregory Peck and Lee Remick as the foster parents of Damien. Suspense builds as strange and violent occurrences can all be traced back to the child. Peck eventually gains the help of a priest in figuring out the abomination behind Damien's covert misdeeds, and is told to go to Italy to enlist the aid of an old exorcist. Peck returns from Italy commissioned to kill the child with a special set of daggers, only to find his wife has been murdered. Ready to strike the deathblow to Damien,

Peck is killed by police, and the President of the United States raises the child.

Reviews of the film ranged from cold to tepid, based mostly on its questionable premise and seeming absurdity. Vincent Canby in the *New York Times* stated that, "*The Omen* is like Gregory Peck's performance—dignified, grave, and so hollow-headed it rattles." He also claimed that the film was, "nuttily put together" and that Donner had, "a superb way of dismissing any small detail that might give some semblance of conviction to the proceedings." Jack Kroll in *Newsweek* bolstered, "*The Omen* is a dumb and largely dull movie." But Richard Schickel in *Time* stated that Donner, "has a smooth way of burying absurdity in atmospherics, and does well with his set pieces." He goes on to say that "*The Omen* speaks well of . . . the virtues of solid commercial craftsmanship." Despite the luke-warm reviews, the film created quite a stir amongst the United States Catholic Conference and raised many sociological questions at the time of its release. According to Jay Robert Nash and Stanley Ralph Ross in *The Motion Picture Guide*, the Catholic Conference proclaimed the film, "One of the most distasteful ever to be released by a major studio." However, the film was a huge commercial success, which was followed by two sequels, *Damien—Omen II*, and *The Final Conflict. The Omen* seemed to suffer by comparison to *The Exorcist* and *Rosemary's Baby*, but the film did show the sociologically unnerving appeal of the Devil, Satan and Antichrist persona, and helped establish Donner's commercial success.

Donner's next big film was the much anticipated feature film, *Superman*, starring Christopher Reeve, Margot Kidder, Marlon Brando, Gene Hackman, and a host of other celebrities. Although advertising for the film began in May 1974 at the Cannes Film Festival, the film finally opened as the big Christmas movie of 1978. The film was expensive and suffered its share of behind-the-scenes production problems, but the critical consensus was summedup in a *Time* magazine review as "pure fun, fancy and adventure." The film opens on Superman's home planet of Krypton, as his father, Jor-El (played by Brando) exercises his leadership prior to the destruction of the planet. The child is sent to Earth to be raised by foster parents as Clark Kent (played by Reeve). When his foster parents die, Clark Kent/Superman is compelled by a magic crystal to go to the Arctic, to learn his true purpose and identity. Shortly after making his debut

as Superman, the "man of steel" meets ace newspaper reporter, Lois Lane (played by Kidder), and gains the support of civilians and law enforcement, while capturing Lois' romantic attention. Unaware that the villain, Lex Luthor (played by Hackman) and his sidekick are planning to destroy the world, Superman grants Lois an interview and takes her flying. Learning that Superman is threatening his plans for world domination, Lex Luther traps him with Kryptonite (Superman's only weakness), depleting all of his super powers. The villains' plan unfolds successfully and Lois Lane is killed. But Luthor's sidekick feels sorry for Superman and frees him. Nothing is too late for the man of steel. He circles the earth, turning time backwards, so the damage can be undone, and Lois doesn't die. Justice prevails and Superman is off to new adventures.

Released on the heel of the groundbreaking special effects of *Star Wars*, *Superman* was both criticized and praised. Vincent Canby, in a *New York Times* review stated, "The movie does nothing lightly or quickly . . . [it] proceeds at the panel-by-panel pace of a comic strip. . . . The special effects are mostly very good." Donner, who had started out directing action sequences for television, had worked with his technicians to devise several ways to fool the audience with regard to Superman's flight, and critics and audiences believed it. Much praise was given to Christopher Reeve who was described as having "unyielding dignity and sobriety," by *Village Voice* reviewer Andrew Sarris. Donner and his producers were praised by critics for their smart casting decisions. The choice to cast Marlon Brando did return to haunt Donner and the production team. According to a *Time* article, Brando's agent approached Donner stating that the actor felt his character, Jor-El, should be played "like a green suitcase." Donner and his producers asked for a meeting with Brando, wherein Brando then said, "Maybe the people on Krypton should look like bagels." Finally, Donner replied that "all the kids . . . would know that Superman's father was not a bagel."

Plagued by several versions of the script, contract negotiations, a slow production start, changes of filming locations and media ballyhoo, the film was also criticized for an unevenness of tone. In *The Motion Picture Guide* Jay Robert Nash and Stanley Ralph Ross stated, "Donner's direction manages to tie up the episodes of the story, working best in the film's more intimate moments." On a personal

Christopher Reeve played the title role in Donner's popular 1978 film *Superman.*

note, John Clark in *Premiere*, shed some light on Donner's tribulations regarding the *Superman* saga. While shooting *Superman*, Donner was also shooting footage for *Superman II*, when Richard Lester was chosen to finish the sequel. Donner, who is an uncredited director on the film, seemed to suffer anguish over Lester's cut. Donner stated, "I assume he cut out an awful lot of my work simply because he wanted his name on the screen as director."

With the sting of *Superman II* behind him, Donner again demonstrated his adaptability with his next project, *Inside Moves*. Jack Kroll from *Newsweek* stated, "the movie's final feeling is one of sweetness and gritty dignity." Robert Hatch in *Nation*, agreed with the film's ad, it "will make you feel good." The story itself is simply about the human condition. Rory, played by John Savage, has thrown himself out of an office window, feeling that no one cares about him anymore. Patched up and hobbling, he is taken in by a group of misfits: a publican, a bartender, a waitress, a junkie and several cripples. Feeling he finally has a sense of belonging, Rory begins to make the dreams of his newfound family come true. He wins the heart of the waitress, helps the bartender play basketball, and helps the pub make money. Jack Kroll of *Newsweek* was quick to point out that the film could easily have become a tearjerker. But he affords Donner his due in seeing that the sentimentality was not overdone, stating "Donner has directed with a strong, quiet sense of human nuance that includes enough irony. . . ."

Revisits the Fantastic

Although one of Donner's next features, *Ladyhawke,* was somewhat panned by critics as too much of a clash between medieval myth and modernism, Donner's work as a director was duly noted and praised apart from the slang, sentiment and score. Jack Kroll of *Newsweek* commented on Donner's "real feeling for the atmospherics of fable." The film chronicles the tale of Navarre (Rutger Hauer) and Isabeau (Michelle Pfeiffer), who have been cursed to be "always together, eternally apart." It is the Bishop of Aquila (John Wood), whose envious love of Isabeau caused him to doom Navarre to the form of a wolf by night, and she, to the form of a hawk by day. The lovers battle both the curse and some evil henchmen with the help of an urchin, Gaston (Matthew Broderick), and a priest, Imperius (Leo McKern). The lovers can be freed only during an eclipse and the film builds with suspense toward the climactic event. Richard Corliss in *Time* magazine was not as thrilled with Donner's visual work. He stated that Donner was "no spellbinder of medieval melancholy."

Leaving "medieval melancholy" behind, Donner made a switch to action adventure for kids, with *The Goonies,* which was produced by Steven Spielberg. The film follows the adventures of a group of children who are about to lose their homes to developers. They encounter visually exciting characters as they follow an old map with the promise of a buried treasure that will pay off the land developers and stop the foreclosure. Undoubtedly choosing Donner to direct the gooney adven-

A story of medieval myth, *Ladyhawke* starred Michelle Pfeiffer and was produced and directed by Donner.

ture because of his skill with action sequences, Spielberg seemed to take much of the heat for the criticism of the film.

Lethal Weapon

Luckily for Donner, his most notable and successful series of films would begin with his next project—the first of the *Lethal Weapon* series, with Mel Gibson and Danny Glover. The series introduced two homicide cops, Riggs (played by Mel Gibson) and Murtaugh (played by Danny Glover), who become partners and chase drug dealers all over California. Glover's character is a fifty-year-old family man readying for retirement, and Gibson's character is a depressed, wild rebel who is mourning the loss of his wife. Their two natures

are irreverently at odds as they endure moment after moment of life-threatening peril. The plot in each of the *Lethal Weapon* films is almost strictly formula. But viewers return to the series out of a sense of loyalty to the characters of Riggs and Murtaugh, and the visual excitement of Donner's expertly executed action sequences.

The first *Lethal Weapon* film was highly praised as entertaining, action-packed, and well paced, and Richard Donner was the motivation behind the film's punch and profits. Reviewer Roger Ebert of the *Chicago Sun-Times* wrote, "The movie's so tightly wound up, it's like a rubber band ready to snap. Richard Donner . . . throws action scenes at us like hardballs. . . . this movie thrilled me from beginning to end." Having also seen many of Donner's other films, he stated, "Richard Donner

The second in Donner's successful "Lethal Weapon" action series features Mel Gibson and Danny Glover.

has directed a lot of classy pictures. . . . This time he tops himself." Richard Harrington, a reviewer for the *Washington Post*, praised Donner's ability to "[keep] things moving along at such a scintillating pace. . . . Donner knows how to keep his film in motion and his actors on edge."

Lethal Weapon 2, the second installment in the series, was released in 1989 to mixed reviews. The film was popular with audiences, who packed the theaters, but critics seemed to have tired of the *Lethal Weapon* recipe. Peter Travers in *Rolling Stone* referred to *Lethal Weapon 2* as "business as usual," although Donner was again praised for his lively action sequence expertise. When *Lethal Weapon* 4 was released in 1998, critics referred to the final two films as lackluster, chaotic and loud. Film analysts have even compared the success formula of the Lethal Weapon series to James Bond films. In an interview with *Entertainment On-line*, Donner and the series' producers addressed the staying power of the *Lethal Weapon* series. Donner stated, "each picture is an entity. . . . we worked very hard to get a script that was driven by a good story and get good characters, and the evolution of the characters was fresh within it." Joel Silver, one of the film's producers spoke of Donner's penchant for safety when filming stunts, "he's . . . a stickler for safety and the sets that are in Dick's movies are extremely thorough in making sure no one ever gets hurt."

During the years spanning the *Lethal Weapon* series, Donner directed several other feature films as well as producing HBO's *Tales from the Crypt*. One of these films was the Dickens classic, *A Christmas Carol*, updated with a new title: *Scrooged*. In this version Bill Murray plays the main character, a TV executive named Frank Cross. The usual Dickens characters grace the plot: the mild executive who Frank fires, the phantom of Frank's old boss, the polite chairman of the board, and the "Ghost of Christmas Past." For his work on this film, Donner was praised by David Ansen in *Newsweek* as "a stylish technician," but criticized for his temperate sense of humor.

In 1992, after an intense bidding war between Warner Brothers and Columbia Pictures, Donner was enlisted to direct the childhood adventure drama, *Radio Flyer*. In an interview with Mimi Avins in *Premiere*, Donner states, "In a strange way, this picture is a good example of how I've always looked at life." The film is a tale of two young boys who

If you enjoy the works of Richard Donner, you may also want to check out the following films:

Die Hard, starring Bruce Willis and Alan Rickman, 1988.
Face/Off, directed by John Woo, starring Nicholas Cage and John Travolta, 1997.
Rush Hour, starring Jackie Chan and Chris Tucker, 1998.
The Professional, starring Jean Reno, Gary Oldman, and Natalie Portman, 1994.

fit a Radio Flyer Wagon with wings to escape their abusive stepfather. Initially, Donner was on the losing side of the bidding war for the script. But when screenwriter and director David Mickey Evans was unable to deliver, Donner was sought to replace him. Donner told Gregg Kilday in *Entertainment Weekly*, "I didn't think I could do it to David. . . . But . . . he asked if I'd do it. He was sincere and so I said I'd do it as long as (he) would stay with me on the movie." Michael Douglas, the film's producer said that Donner's "energy, enthusiasm, and warmth, was great." Though not as commercially successful as some of Donner's previous work, the movie accurately depicted childhood wonder and trauma on film.

The Gibson-Donner Connection

In 1994 Donner teamed up with Mel Gibson in the western, *Maverick*, and again in 1997 with *Conspiracy Theory*. In *Maverick*, a motion picture remake of the TV western series, Donner directs Mel Gibson as the title character, joined by Jodie Foster and James Garner. According to Fred Schruers of *Premiere*, the prevailing mood on the set was easy hominess and fun. Donner's amiable bossiness kept the production pace as entertaining as the film. The production crew even handed out T-shirts with "Donnerisms" stacked in a Top Ten List, from "Who's not ready? I want names!" to "Why are you looking at your watch? Are you a producer?" Critics considered the film solid entertainment. In Donner's own words to *Entertainment Weekly* writer Bruce Fretts, the film "is entertainment. We're not trying to upgrade anyone's intellectual level." Donner's cast was very enthusiastic about his work. James Garner

Gibson and Glover with Chris Rock and Rene Russo in *Lethal Weapon 4*.

said, "Dick just throws it all in, then gets out his scissors, and it comes out great." Jodie Foster stated, "With Donner, you get the feeling it's just haphazard, but he knows what he's doing better than anybody I've ever worked with." And Mel Gibson stated, "We had a blast."

Donner again teamed up with Gibson in 1997's *Conspiracy Theory* with Julia Roberts. Gibson plays Jerry Fletcher, a paranoid taxi driver opposite Roberts' Alice, a Justice Department attorney. Donner and writer Brian Helgeland serve up a buffet of conspiratorial elements. It was with this film that critics noticed a deviation from Donner's more commercial work, which unfortunately fell just short of the mark of a great film. A reviewer in *New York* magazine stated, "for the first time, Richard Donner . . . comes close to breaking into the clear and becoming a true film creator." And perhaps this is what awaits audiences of Donner's future films.

In all, strength, dependability, excellent pace, warmth, imagination and skilled technique,

though not artistically lauded, have characterized Richard Donner's work as a director. Donner, now an industry veteran has sought to entertain audiences with straightforward stories, plots, and characters. Ultimately, his diversity and adaptability have provided him the staying power necessary in an industry where commercial success can be erratic and elusive.

■ **Works Cited**

Ansen, David, "Curmudgeons and Cocoons," *Newsweek*, November 28, 1998, p. 87.

Avins, Mimi, "Shot by Shot," *Premiere*, April, 1992.

Canby, Vincent, "Hollywood Has an Appealing New Star—Old Gooseberry," *New York Times*, July 25, 1976, p. 13.

Canby, Vincent, "Screen: It's a Bird, It's a Plane, It's a Movie," *New York Times*, December 15, 1978, p. C15.

Clark, John, filmography of Richard Donner, *Premiere*, April, 1992, p. 136.

Review of *Conspiracy Theory*, *New York*, August 25, 1997, p. 148.

Corliss, Richard, review of *Ladyhawke*, *Time*, May 13, 1985, p. 69.

Donner, Richard, on-line discussion of *Lethal Weapon 4* with Jennifer Gwartz and Joel Silver, *Entertainment On-Line*, www.etonline.com, 1998.

Ebert, Roger, review of *Lethal Weapon*, *Chicago Sun-Times*, March 6, 1987.

Fretts, Bruce, "Funsmoke," *Entertainment Weekly*, May 6, 1994, pp. 26-29.

Harrington, Richard, review of *Lethal Weapon*, *Washington Post*, March 6, 1987.

Hatch, Robert, review of *Inside Moves*, *Nation*, February 21, 1981, pp. 219, 221.

"Here Comes Superman!!!," *Time*, November 27, 1978, pp. 59-61.

Kilday, Gregg, "Taking a 'Flyer,'" *Entertainment Weekly*, February 28, 1992, pp. 28-31.

Kroll, Jack, "Deviled Ham," *Newsweek*, July 12, 1976, pp. 69-70.

Kroll, Jack, "Max's Misfits," *Newsweek*, January 5, 1981, p. 55.

Kroll, Jack, "Fly-by-Knight Affair," *Newsweek*, April 22, 1985, p. 76.

Nash, Jay Robert, and Stanley Ralph Ross, *The Motion Picture Guide*, Volume N-R, Cinebooks, Inc., 1986, p. 2243.

Nash, Jay Robert, and Stanley Ralph Ross, *The Motion Picture Guide*, Volume S, Cinebooks, Inc., 1987, pp. 3221-22.

Sarris, Andrew, "The Kid from Krypton Makes Good," *Village Voice*, December 25, 1978, p. 46.

Schickel, Richard, "Bedeviled," *Time*, June 28, 1976, p. 46.

Schruers, Fred, "How the West was Fun," *Premiere*, June, 1994, pp. 46-53,

Travers, Peter, "Oh, No, Not Again," *Rolling Stone*, August 10, 1989, p. 31.

■ For More Information See

PERIODICALS

Entertainment Weekly, December 4, 1992, p. 68-70; June 3, 1994, p. 36; October 13, 1995, p. 55.

Newsweek, May 30, 1994, p. 64.

New Yorker, December 12, 1988, p. 114-117.

Rolling Stone, March 19, 1992, p. 104; August 21, 1997, p. 115-116.

Time, July 24, 1989, p. 53; August 18, 1997, p. 62.

Variety, February 24, 1992, p. 248; October 2-8, 1995, p. 39.

—Sketch by R. Darrow Bernick

Lois Duncan

ety of Children's Book Writers and Illustrators, Phi Beta Kappa.

Personal

Original name, Lois Duncan Steinmetz; born April 28, 1934, in Philadelphia, PA; daughter of Joseph Janney (a magazine photographer) and Lois (a magazine photographer; maiden name, Foley) Steinmetz; married second husband, Donald Wayne Arquette (an electrical engineer), July 15, 1965; children: (first marriage) Robin, Kerry, Brett; (second marriage) Donald Jr., Kaitlyn (deceased). *Education:* Attended Duke University, 1952-53; University of New Mexico, B.A. (cum laude), 1977.

Addresses

Agent—Claire Smith, Harold Ober Associates, 425 Madison Ave., New York, NY 10017.

Career

Writer; magazine photographer; instructor in department of journalism, University of New Mexico, 1971-82. Lecturer at writers' conferences. *Member:* National League of American Pen Women, Soci-

Awards, Honors

Three-time winner during high school years of *Seventeen* magazine's annual short story contest; Seventeenth Summer Literary Award, Dodd, Mead & Co., 1957, for *Debutante Hill;* Best Novel Award, National Press Women,1966, for *Point of Violence;* Edgar Allan Poe Award nominations, Mystery Writers of America, 1967, for *Ransom,* 1969, for *They Never Came Home,* 1985, for *The Third Eye,* 1986, for *Locked in Time,* and 1989, for *The Twisted Window;* Zia Award, New Mexico Press Women, 1969, for *Major Andre: Brave Enemy;* grand prize winner, Writer's Digest Creative Writing Contest, 1970, for short story; Theta Sigma Phi Headliner Award, 1971; Ethical Culture School Book Award, Library of Congress' Best Books citation, and *English Teacher's Journal* and University of Iowa's Best Books of the Year for Young Adults citation, all 1981, and Best Novel Award, National League of American Pen Women, 1982, all for *Stranger with My Face;* Notable Children's Trade Book in the Field of Social Studies, National Council for Social Studies and the Children's Book Council, 1982, for *Chapters: My Growth as a Writer;* Child Study Association of America's Children's Books of the Year citation, 1986, for *Locked in Time* and *The Third Eye;* Children's Book Award, National League of American Pen Women, 1987, for *Horses of Dreamland;* Margaret A. Edwards Award, 1991, *School Library Journal*/Young Adult Library Services Association, for body of work.

Duncan has also received several American Library Association Best Books for Young Adults citations and *New York Times* Best Books for Children citations, as well as numerous librarians', parents' and children's choice awards from organizations in the states of Alabama, Arizona, California, Colorado, Florida, Indiana, Iowa, Massachusetts, Nevada, New Mexico, Oklahoma, Tennessee, Texas, South Carolina, and Vermont, in addition togroups in England.

■ Writings

YOUNG ADULT NOVELS

Debutante Hill, Dodd, 1958.
(Under pseudonym Lois Kerry) *Love Song for Joyce,* Funk, 1958.
(Under pseudonym Lois Kerry) *A Promise for Joyce,* Funk, 1959.
The Middle Sister, Dodd, 1961.
Game of Danger, Dodd, 1962.
Season of the Two-Heart, Dodd, 1964.
Ransom, Doubleday, 1966, published as *Five Were Missing,* New American Library, 1972.
They Never Came Home, Doubleday, 1969.
I Know What You Did Last Summer, Little, Brown, 1973.
Down a Dark Hall, Little, Brown, 1974.
Summer of Fear, Little, Brown, 1976.
Killing Mr. Griffin, Little, Brown, 1978.
Daughters of Eve, Little, Brown, 1979.
Stranger with My Face, Little, Brown, 1981.
The Third Eye, Little, Brown, 1984, published in England as *The Eyes of Karen Connors,* Hamish Hamilton, 1985.
Locked in Time, Little, Brown, 1985.
The Twisted Window, Delacorte, 1987.
Don't Look Behind You, Delacorte, 1989.
Gallows Hill, Delacorte, 1997.
The Longest Hair in the World, Bantam Doubleday Dell Books for Young Readers, 1999.

JUVENILE

The Littlest One in the Family, illustrated by Suzanne K. Larsen, Dodd, 1960.
Silly Mother, illustrated by Larsen, Dial, 1962.

Giving Away Suzanne, illustrated by Leonard Weisgard, Dodd, 1963.
Hotel for Dogs, illustrated by Leonard Shortall, Houghton, 1971.
A Gift of Magic, illustrated by Arvis Stewart, Little, Brown, 1971.
From Spring to Spring: Poems and Photographs, photographs by the author, Westminster, 1982.
The Terrible Tales of Happy Days School (poetry), illustrated by Friso Henstra, Little, Brown, 1983.
Horses of Dreamland, illustrated by Donna Diamond, Little, Brown, 1985.
Wonder Kid Meets the Evil Lunch Snatcher, illustrated by Margaret Sanfilippo, Little, Brown, 1988.
The Birthday Moon (poetry), illustrated by Susan Davis, Viking, 1989.
Songs from Dreamland (poetry), illustrated by Kay Chorao, Knopf, 1989.
The Circus Comes Home, photographs by father, Joseph Janney Steinmetz, Delacorte, 1992.
The Magic of Spider Woman, illustrated by Shonto Begay, Scholastic, 1996.

OTHER

Point of Violence (adult), Doubleday, 1966.
Major Andre: Brave Enemy (young adult nonfiction), illustrated by Tran Mawicke, Putnam, 1969.
Peggy (young adult nonfiction), Little, Brown, 1970.
When the Bough Breaks (adult), Doubleday, 1974.
How to Write and Sell Your Personal Experiences (nonfiction), Writers Digest, 1979.
Chapters: My Growth as a Writer (autobiography), Little, Brown, 1982.
A Visit with Lois Duncan (videotape), RDA Enterprises, 1985.
Dream Songs from Yesterday (audio cassette), Silver Moon Productions, 1987.
Songs from Dreamland (audio cassette), Silver Moon Productions, 1987.
Our Beautiful Day (audio cassette), Silver Moon Productions, 1988.
The Story of Christmas (audio cassette), Silver Moon Productions, 1989.
Who Killed My Daughter?: The True Story of a Mother's Search for Her Daughter's Murderer, Delacorte, 1992.
Psychics in Action (audio cassette series), Silver Moon Productions, 1993.
(With William Roll) *Psychic Connections: A Journey into the Mysterious World of Psi,* Delacorte, 1995.

(Editor) *Night Terrors: Stories of Shadow and Substance,* Simon and Schuster, 1996.
(Editor) *Trapped! Cages of Mind and Body,* Simon and Schuster, 1998.
I Walk at Night, Viking Penguin, 2000.

Contributor of over five hundred articles and stories to periodicals, including *Good Housekeeping, Redbook, McCall's, Woman's Day, The Writer, Reader's Digest, Ladies' Home Journal, Saturday Evening Post,* and *Writer's Digest.* Contributing editor, *Woman's Day.*

■ Adaptations

Summer of Fear was made into the television movie *Strangers in Our House* by NBC-TV, 1978; Listening Library made cassettes of *Down a Dark Hall,* 1985, *Killing Mr. Griffin,* 1986, *Summer of Fear,* 1986, and *Stranger with My Face,* 1986; RDA Enterprises made cassettes of *Selling Personal Experiences to Magazines,* 1987, and *Songs from Dreamland,* 1987.

■ Sidelights

Lois Duncan writes macabre, suspenseful novels for young adults that have made her a favorite with teen readers and adult critics alike. Though her portrayals of average suburban high–school students and their encounters with the sociopathic or the paranormal have sometimes been faulted for various thematic flaws, her work has matured along with the readership she began writing for in the 1950s. Although some critics accuse Duncan of being melodramatic, she has found an eager audience of young adults. Through her use of action, deft characterization, and other-worldly elements, Duncan weaves stories that capture the reader's attention. In most of Duncan's books, her heroines—almost all of her lead characters have been high school females—are confronted with a dark event of somesort that unsettles their placid world. "It is a mark of Duncan's ability as a writer that the evils she describes are perfectly plausible and believable," noted an essay on the author for *St. James Guide to Young Adult Writers.* "As in her use of the occult, her use of warped human nature as a tool to move the plot along briskly never seems contrived or used solely for shock effect; it is integral to the story."

Duncan's road to her career as a successful novelist is an interesting tale in itself, one in which a belief in her own abilities and a courage to move forward into uncharted territories have brought her immeasurable rewards. The tangible returns on her efforts have been numerous—the list of honors her two dozen titles have earned is a long one, and includes several American Library Association citations for Best Book for Young Adults. Many of the events, characters, and plots in her books were drawn from actual events in her own life, or those of her children. But the intersection of Duncan's personal and professional life crossed a heartbreaking boundary when a 1989 novel eerily foreshadowed some circumstances surrounding the murder of her eighteen-year-old daughter.

Duncan was born in 1934 in Philadelphia, Pennsylvania to parents who were magazine photographers. Both were well educated: her father Joseph Steinmetz was a Princeton alumnus, while mother Lois had attended Smith College. Duncan—who borrowed her pen name from a grandmother rather than use the same name as her mother when her own career got underway—wasjoined by an infant brother a few years her junior, who arrived after the Steinmetzes had moved to Sarasota, Florida. There they lived near the ocean, and when school let out for the summer, the children embarked with their parents on long trips across the southeastern United States and into the Caribbean, for the Steinmetzes arranged the bulk of their work assignments during these months.

At heart, however, Duncan was a writer, not an adventurer. Reversing the standard story hour concept, she told her parents tales when she was a preschooler, which they then wrote down for her, since she could not yet write. In kindergarten, she recited a poem she had made up for show-and-tell one day, and her teacher accused her of memorizing it from another source. "It was years before I trusted a teacher again," Duncan recalled in an essay for *Something About the Author Autobiography Series.* With her love of books, she grew into an introspective, shy girl who from the age of seven wore braces on her teeth and eyeglasses; she was also overweight as a child. At the age of ten, she submitted a story to the popular women's magazine *Ladies' Home Journal,* and received a rejection letter that was so kindly worded that it gave her much positive reinforcement. "The warmth of the letter cushioned its impact," Duncan said in her 1982 book *Chapters: My Growth*

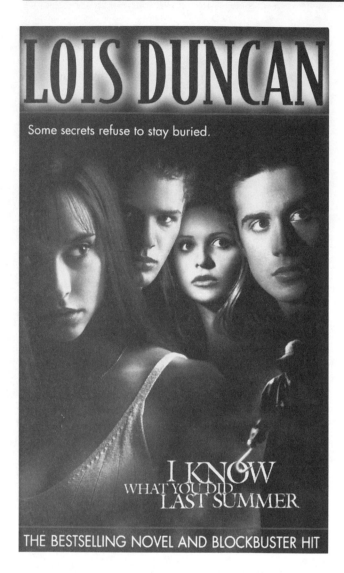

Some secrets refuse to stay buried.

I KNOW WHAT YOU DID LAST SUMMER

THE BESTSELLING NOVEL AND BLOCKBUSTER HIT

Duncan's bestselling 1973 thriller about a group of teenagers who share a dangerous secret spawned two popular feature films.

as a Writer. "I swallowed my disappointment and mailed the story off to another magazine."

A Turning Point

During her adolescent years, Duncan wrote an exhaustive number of stories of an ambitious sort: most were lurid tales of adventure, romance, and crime, all of which were met with rejection. "Each day when other, better-adjusted children were skipping rope and playing hopscotch and going over to play at each other's houses, I was rush-

ing home to check the mail and see which stories had come back from what magazines," she wrote in *Something About the Author Autobiography Series.* A turning point in her career came with the arrival of a new neighbor, MacKinlay Kantor, who was also a friend of the Steinmetzes. Kantor would go on to win the 1956 Pulitzer Prize for his novel of the Civil War era, *Andersonville.* When she brought her latest story to him and asked for his professional opinion, Kantor told Duncan that it was "trash." He instructed her that at the age of thirteen she was reaching beyond her creative energies, and should write what she knew, instead of the sensational, melodramatic shockers. "Later that week I did write a story about a fat, shy little girl with braces and glasses who covered her insecurity by writing stories about imaginary adventures," she recalled in the essay for *Something About the Author Autobiography Series.*

That story became the first that Duncan ever sold, and the day that she received the acceptance letter and $25 check from *Calling All Girls,* "was the most incredible moment of my life," Duncan told *Authors and Artists for Young Adults.* "Those were the days when teenagers babysat for thirty-five cents an hour, and twenty-five dollars seemed like a fortune." The milestone also coincided with less dramatic, but equally important changes in her life. The braces were finally removed, and her childhood pudginess suddenly disappeared. She began to earn some local notoriety as a published writer, but admitted to failure in another area: she earned poor grades in almost every subject outside of English class.

The rejection slips from the magazines still arrived with regularity. Though she was now trying to write about teenage subjects, a number of stories she sent to another popular magazine, *Senior Prom,* were rejected as contrived and overly dramatic as well. One rejection letter suggested that Duncan "reach into your own life," as the writer recalled in *Chapters.* She was flunking Home Economics, a required course for high-school females at the time that provided instruction in the household arts, so "the next thing I submitted was a short personal—experience piece called 'Home Economics Report,' and not only did *Senior Prom* buy it, they raised the purchase price to $50," Duncan recalled in *Chapters.* The first-person confession about her inability to sew even impressed Duncan's Home Economics teacher, who changed her grade from an F to a C. Duncan also received fan mail from other high-school girls across the country that also disliked the course.

At the age of sixteen, Duncan won second place in *Seventeen* magazine's annual fiction contest; the following year she took third, and at the age of eighteen won first prize with her story about a Korean War veteran adjusting to civilian life. Her own life was about to undergo a similar change of venue, though from Duncan's point of view, from the reverse standpoint. She enrolled in Duke University in 1952, and found it a tremendously difficult adjustment from her carefree home with

Bestselling author of *I Know What You Did Last Summer*

LOIS DUNCAN

Down a Dark Hall

At Blackwood School for Girls, the private lessons might kill you.

When famous ghosts invade the bodies of students at her school, Kit uses her special powers to discover what's behind the weird events.

her independent-minded parents. She found the lack of privacy disturbing: "If you were noncommunicative, two dozen well-meaning dorm mates asked anxiously what the matter was," Duncan remembered in her *Something About the Author Autobiography Series* essay. "If you closed yourself in your room for twenty minutes, people rapped on the door to find out if you were 'all right in there.'" Moreover, Duncan suffered from an extremely poor visual memory, which made it difficult to remember faces; thus meeting a large number of people in a short period of time was utterly overwhelming for her.

Duncan also felt her creative spirit founder, and stopped writing the stories that had become such a part of her daily life for years. At Christmas, she told her parents that she wanted to drop out, but she realized that her only option was to return to home. In the early 1950s, few jobs for women offered a solid income, and a young unmarried woman living in her own apartment was considered rather unusual at the time. Resolving to adjust to her situation, Duncan returned to Duke and began dating a senior. When he proposed a few months later, she accepted and dropped out of college after their 1953 wedding.

Contest Win Leads to Publishing Contract

After her husband earned his degree, he went on to serve in the U.S. Air Force for two years, during which time Duncan lived with him on a series of military bases across the country. She found herself a housewife at the age of nineteen, with few friends, no car of her own, and a husband who did not want her to work. She remembers this time as one of emptiness, and again, she could not find within herself the energy to write. Ironically, the birth of her first child, a daughter named Robin, energized Duncan, and she suddenly began writing again, though her time was far more constricted. By the time her second child was born, Duncan had written her first novel, *Debutante Hill*. She entered it in the Seventeenth Summer Literary contest from publisher Dodd, Mead, and it came back with a letter requesting that she make a change: on one page, a young man not yet of legal drinking age has a beer, and Duncan was asked to change this, since publishers of books for teens in the 1950s were extremely conservative. She changed it to a soda, and the manuscript won first prize: a thousand dollars and a publishing contract. Even more memorably for Duncan, she received a personal note from one of the judges, who had once been an intern at *Calling All Girls* and remembered Duncan's submissions.

Debutante Hill, published in 1958, fit into the era's typical fiction fare for teens with its chronicle of middle-class social angst. Duncan had been inspired to write it when she read a breathlessly worded newspaper article about the local high-school debutante season, which made her wonder how theteen girls who had not been designated "debutantes" dealt with the matter. The debutante year, typically when a girl was seventeen or eighteen, involved a "coming out" party at a country club or sponsored by a local charitable organization, as well as a prescribed whirl of parties and social engagements. The anti-elitist father of Duncan's lead character, high school senior Lynn Chambers, is opposed to the custom, and she so is unable to participate. All of her friends from school do, however, and Chambers undergoes a few rough months that in the end, offer her a series of opportunities for personal growth far more eventful than the debutante scene. "Duncan writes exceptionally well, and has the happy ability to make a reader care what happens to her characters," assessed a *Christian Science Monitor* review from 1959.

Duncan's own personal life was experiencing tough times by the time of *Debutante Hill,* however. Her husband, who had enrolled in law school, grew resentful that Duncan had so little attention left to devote to him now that she was mother to two—soon to be three—as well as an emerging writer of some success. The family was living in St. Petersburg, Florida, when the marriage disintegrated after her husband, by then an attorney, became involved with someone else. At a loss, Duncan moved to New Mexico, where her younger brother lived, and took her three children with her to start over.

Duncan's career as an author was well underway, but it was not yet a lucrative profession. Between the teen novels she continued to write for Dodd, Mead—*The Middle Sister* (1961), *Game of Danger* (1962), and *Season of the Two-Heart* (1964)—she was earning under $2,000 a year; she also had written several illustrated books for younger readers. The last of these three titles, however, revealed Duncan's nascent interest in tackling more serious

Bestselling author of *I Know What You Did Last Summer*

LOIS DUNCAN

Summer of Fear

Rachel's not jealous of her beautiful cousin. But she *is* afraid.

In this work, Rachel strives to discover the strange and deadly truth about her cousin Julia.

social issues for teens in its presentation of cultural conflicts in New Mexico. A Pueblo teen moves in with a non-Native family in order to attend high school in Albuquerque, and takes care of its small boys for their often absent mother. Martha Weekoty realizes that though aboriginal-heritage children are not blessed with material riches, they do receive an abundance of emotional nurturing. Martha also comes to see, however, that respect for the traditional ways sometimes hampers positive progress. In the end, she is torn between a marriage proposal and her desire for a college education. Ruth Hill Viguers, reviewing *Season of the Two-Heart* for *Horn Book,* commended

Duncan's handling of the themes. "The several threads of plot are woven together in a convincing and moving climax," declared the critic.

In Albuquerque, Duncan had found a job at an advertising agency that paid $275 a month, and supplemented her income by entering contests. After winning one call for a first-person account of "the most frightening event of your life," Duncan suddenly found herself a writer for true-confession magazines with the first-prize check for $500. She then bought a slew of these lurid magazines that were popular during the 1950s and '60s, and "by the time that I'd read each one from

cover to cover, I had a pretty good idea of how these stories were put together," Duncan wrote in *Something About the Author Autobiography Series.* "They were sensational dramas of sin and suffering, written in first person as though they were true, but since they bore no by-lines, it was obvious they were really fakes."

Duncan quit her secretarial job and began writing one story a week, nearly every one of which she sold. Soon, she was able to move her family out of their cheap apartment and into a home of their own, but she still spent twelve hours a day at the typewriter. Finally her brother, who worked for the government, took her to a work-related party one evening for some escape, and there she met an electrical engineer named Don Arquette, whom she married in 1965. Duncan and Arquette dated for two years, but Duncan later joked that he was wary about proposing because of the salacious "confessions" she wrote as a career.

Duncan heeded Arquette's suggestion that she try writing for more wholesome magazines, and sent a two-page story about the time she won a live porpoise in another one of her contests to *Good Housekeeping.* As she recalled in *Something About the Author Autobiography Series*, "Back came a check for three times the amount I was used to receiving for a sixteen-page confession story. I was incredulous. Somehow, during those years of sitting down every day and forcing out words, I had learned the professional way of telling a story, and those story-telling techniques could evidently betransferred over into other forms of writing."

New Wave of YA Literature

With this success Duncan became a regular contributor to an array of women's magazines, and both this income and her marriage freed her to return to writing teen fiction again. But it was now 1966, and sweeping changes were occurring in American society, and some of those issues were finding their way into young adult novels. "I immediately discovered that something had happened in the time that I had been away," Duncan wrote in *Something About the Author Autobiography Series.* "The world had changed, and so had the books that were considered acceptable reading for young people. No longer did any writer have to worry about getting a manuscript back because someone in it drank a beer."

Bestselling author of *I Know What You Did Last Summer*

LOIS DUNCAN

Killing Mr. Griffin

They only meant to scare him. . . .

A prank played by high school students to get back at a teacher goes terribly wrong in this 1978 novel.

Duncan found a host of books on library and bookstore shelves that explored the grittier side of life even in a seemingly pleasant, middle-class American suburbs. Family violence, teen pregnancy, counterculture pressures, and the growing generation gap were all topics under examination, but Dodd, Mead rejected her manuscript for her next novel, 1966's *Ransom,* as too abrupt a departure for her style as an already established author. The tale centers around a group of well-to-do Arizona high school students who are kidnapped by their bus driver and two accomplices, then hid on a mountain under harsh conditions; under duress, they each confront their own personal weaknesses. *Ransom* found a receptive publisher in Doubleday, and it became a runner-up for the Edgar Allan Poe Award from the Mystery Writers of America, a significant career triumph for Duncan.

Her next book, *They Never Came Home,* dealt with criminal intent on a more personal level. This 1969 novel follows the ruse of a sociopathic teen, Larry, who sells drugs and embezzles money, to take advantage of a fellow runaway who has amnesia. "Duncan writes well and simply on mature issues," declared Richard F. Shepard in the *New York Times Book Review,* who called the novel "a well-paced action story, with a full quota of heroes and villains, and a series of narrative hooks guaranteed to hold any reader."

Duncan had two children with Arquette by the early 1970s, but was unable to write about emotionally difficult themes for a time after the death of her mother, with whom she was very close. Instead, she returned to writing for very young children with *Hotel for Dogs,* published in 1971, and began teaching at the University of New Mexico that same year. While she taught what she knew—magazine writing—Duncan realized there was much more she would like to know, and so began taking courses to finish her degree. She graduated with a Bachelor's degree in English in 1977.

During her college years, Duncan returned to writing young adult novels with *I Know What You Did Last Summer.* The 1973 novel would become one of her most well known works, a perennial favorite for teen readers and the basis for a 1997 motion-picture film of the same name. The story revolves around a quartet of teens returning home from a party one evening; the driver of their car

hits a young bicyclist, and they panic. Julie, her boyfriend Ray, and Helen and Barry flee the scene and vow to keep the secret amongst them forever. Over the next year, their friendship disintegrates, and then each receive an anonymous letter stating, "I know what you did last summer." They begin to be tormented by mysterious phone calls, and for a time suspect that the culprit might even be one of their own. A series of incidents culminating in a fatal attack on the car's driver forces them to realize that someone does indeed know their secret, and that they are in far more danger than jail terms. At the time of its publication,

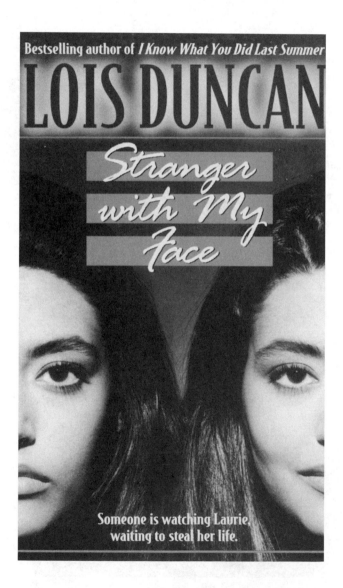

In this haunting, macabre tale, Laurie discovers she has a twin sister when the twin tries to take over Laurie's body.

Kirkus Reviews called *I Know What You Did Last Summer* "a high velocity chiller with a double identity twist," while Linda Silver, writing in *School Library Journal*, termed it "suspenseful to the end," though she found the quartet of teens "too vapid to merit any real concern." The work remained in print for several years—somewhat of a feat for the teen novel genre, since such books usually begin to show their age rather quickly.

Duncan began to explore the supernatural world that would become the mainstay of her work with the 1971 book *A Gift of Magic*. The novel presents the children of the fictional Garrett family—one is a dancer, the other musically gifted, but Nancy realizes that her gift of extrasensory perception is a far more unusual one. Duncan had long been fascinated by parapsychology: while a student at Duke in the early 1950s, she signed up to participate in an experiment conducted by researchers in the field. In the interim years, she had read extensively on the topic, and occasionally broached the idea of writing a book with this theme for teens, but publishers summarily rejected her suggestions. But *A Gift of Magic* did strike a chord with students and critics, with *School Library Journal* critic Peggy Sullivan remarking that "current interest in the occult and psychic phenomena will widen the audience for the book," the 1971 review stated.

Down a Dark Hall, Duncan's next novel for teens after *I Know What You Did Last Summer*, delved into the paranormal and offered readers a coming-of-age story, a literary lesson, and a good scare in the process. It centers around Kit, whose entrance examination for a new private academy for girls has revealed she possesses some degree of extrasensory perception. Soon she realizes that the school is haunted, and that its headmistress communes with the spirits who share the dormitories and classrooms of the uneasy students. The ghosts are some rather notable cultural figures, like Emily Brontë and landscape artist Thomas Cole, and begin to invade the bodies of students in a ruse by Madame Duret to create items of fake artistic value for her to sell. Kit, along with the headmistress's more scrupulous son, discovers the plot and they extricate themselves from the situation when tragedy is imminent. "Duncan's off-hand treatment of romance allows her to focus on the intelligence and rationality of her heroine," noted Gloria Levitas in a *New York Times Book Review* assessment.

Duncan's 1976 novel, *Summer of Fear*, continued along the same eerie, teen-in-danger path. The plot centers around teenage Rachael, who leads a pleasant life in Albuquerque. After the sudden death of distant relatives in the Ozark Mountains, their orphaned daughter Julia, who is near to Rachael's age, moves to New Mexico to live with them. Rachael is the only one to think Julia somewhat odd—everybody seems to love her. Julia summarily adopts Rachael's best friend as her own, transforms herself with Rachael's clothes, and then even lures her boyfriend away; Rachael even begins to believe that she is seducing her father. When Rachael realizes that her cousin cannot be photographed, she thinks Julia might be a witch. Enlisting the help of a local professor with an academic background on the occult, Rachael's suspicion begins to prove itself correct. The discovery of an odd wax doll, the death of the family dog, and the stroke that fells her academic advisor propel *Summer of Fear*'s plot along to a near-deadly crescendo. "Vigorous characterization, a neatly tailored plot, and a sense of foreboding," listed Ethel L. Heins as its charms in her *Horn Book* review of *Summer of Fear*, which she categorized as "a successful thriller." Though Julia Whedon, who evaluated it for the *New York Times Book Review*, termed Rachael and her family the standard "cut-outs, the story is well paced and decently suspenseful."

Pens Challenging Teen Works

Duncan entered a new phase of teen fiction only tentatively explored in *I Know What You Did Last Summer* with her 1978 novel, *Killing Mr. Griffin*. The themes of personal responsibility, peer pressure, and social ethics found ample ground with this tale about a group of high school students who loathe their tough, challenging English teacher. Complaining of too much homework, three students—athletic Jeff, senior-class president David, and spoiled cheerleader Betsy—willingly go along with their enigmatic friend Mark's idea to teach Mr. Griffin a lesson of their own. To carry out Mark's plan, they enlist a solid student, Susan, eager to hang out with this popular crowd. They kidnap their teacher, and tie him to a tree in the woods overnight; in the morning, they return to find Griffin dead; he suffered from chronic heart trouble, and did not have his medication with him. Mark convinces the others to hush up their involvement, but soon Susan begins to cave in emotionally as the events of *Killing Mr. Griffin* spiral out of the teens' control. "It is only when Mark begins to pressure the group to kill again that they recognize him for the evil person he his, but by then it's almost too late," assessed *St. James Guide to Young Adults Writers.* Mark, according to Richard Peck in his *New York Times Book Review,* is a boy whose "charisma and talent for delegating authority will make him the most familiar figure to young readers. This is a book for people who've learned in the schoolyard where nice guys finish."

Richard Peck commended Duncan for eschewing the usual teen-novel staples of sex or substance abuse in his *New York Times Book Review,* "But the taboo she tampers with is far more potent and pervasive: the unleashed fury of the permissively reared against any assault on their egos and authority. . . . The value of the book lies in the twisted logic of the teen-agers and how easily they can justify anything." But Duncan also began to draw some critical controversy at this point in her career. Some adults felt her works presented titillating messages for teens, and concluded without any redeeming merit. Hildagarde Gray, writing in *Best Sellers,* called *Killing Mr. Griffin* "a story that absolutely invites the borderline delinquent to branch out into areas of rebellion that horrify when their potential is considered."

Duncan's next work, *Daughters of Eve,* was met with similar criticism. The title of the 1979 novel is also the name of an exclusive service club for girls at a small-town Michigan high school. Their advisor is a new teacher with feminist beliefs, Irene Stark, but over the course of the book she emerges as a bitter, unbalanced woman. Initially, her efforts to educate the girls seem positive—she tries to encourage them to become more assertive, for instance—but it becomes apparent that she is coercing the naïve students into disobeying their families and taking vicious revenge upon the opposite sex. A student with ESP realizes that something is amiss, but not before an aggressive boy and an abusive father meet with harm. Critics found this harsh assessment of feminist principals far too heavy-handed, and Duncan also was faulted for allowing her villains to triumph. "The implication that sisterhood is not only powerful but downright dangerous is hardly a progressive message," remarked Cyrisse Jaffee in *School Library Journal.* Yet not all reviews assessed it in negative terms. "A savage novel," stated *New York Times*

Book Review writer Natalie Babbitt, who compared it to William Golding's classic *Lord of the Flies* and termed it "finely constructed and told. . . . this novel enables us to see ourselves as the barely civilized creatures we truly are."

Duncan continued to return to the occult-driven plot in her novels for teens. Her 1981 novel *Stranger with My Face* also proved popular with readers in its tale of Laurie, who learns during her senior year that she is one of twins who were adopted separately. Strange occurrences have begun to plague her life, and she discovers that her twin, Lia, is also on the remote New England island where Laurie lives. Laurie's adoptive parents tell her that both girls are half-Navaho, and when researching the group's spiritual beliefs, Laurie learns that the Navaho practice of astral projection—the ability to leave one's body—which helps to explain some of the odd events. Laurie realizes that her identical twin, who has endured an abusive childhood, is attempting to take over her body; a showdown at the ocean saves her from oblivion. "Professionally orchestrated suspense for the willingly susceptible," declared *Kirkus Reviews* in its critique of *Stranger with My Face.* Zena Sutherland, writing in *Bulletin of the Center of Children's Books,* granted that a certain suspension of belief is necessary on the part of readers, "but Duncan makes it possible and palatable by a deft twining of fantasy and reality."

Duncan continued to write suspense-filled novels during the 1980s. In *The Third Eye,* a teen realizes that she has the gift of foresight, and immediately finds herself a social outcast when her powers help solve a local mystery. But Karen is then plagued by chilling visions, and discovers that a local couple is kidnapping infants and selling them to childless couples. Nancy Palmer, reviewing it in *School Library Journal,* declared that this 1984 book "does not rank among Duncan's best"; Palmer's British counterpart, reviewing *The Third Eye* under its United Kingdom title, *The Eyes of Karen Connors,* agreed. Anthony Horowitz, writing in the *Times Literary Supplement,* conceded that "Duncan brings a freshness of writing and some chilling descriptions" to the table, but faulted the author for a plot that "collapses into patness and predictability."

The plot of Duncan's next title, *Locked in Time,* explored another facet of sorcery. Nore, the heroine of this 1985 novel, visits her father's new wife

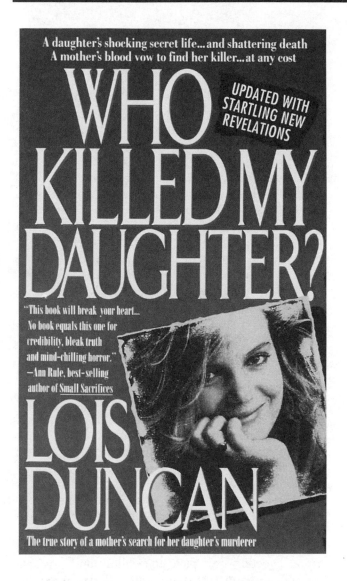

A daughter's shocking secret life...and shattering death
A mother's blood vow to find her killer...at any cost

UPDATED WITH STARTLING NEW REVELATIONS

WHO KILLED MY DAUGHTER?

"This book will break your heart... No book equals this one for credibility, bleak truth and mind-chilling horror."
—Ann Rule, best-selling author of Small Sacrifices

LOIS DUNCAN

The true story of a mother's search for her daughter's murderer

Duncan's quest to find the truth behind her daughter's death led her to discover the girl's shocking secret life.

and her children in Louisiana for the summer; "strange events and unlikely occurrences lead her to believe her new relatives are 'locked in time'— ageless—but her discovery of their secret leads to terrible danger for Nore," recapped *St. James Guide to Young Adults Writers*. The essay described the book as "one of Duncan's most exciting and sophisticated novels." The danger of the unknown sociopath returns as theme in Duncan's next work, *The Twisted Window*, published in 1987. Tracy Lloyd is lonely, left by her father with relatives after her mother dies, when she meets Brad Johnson; the young man asks for her help in res-

cuing his infant sister, who has been allegedly kidnapped by a stepparent. Tracy belatedly discovers the truth, while for readers, "the ground slips from beneath our feet," noted Sarah Hayes in her *Times Literary Supplement* review. Hayes commended the work, finding it in possession of "all of the Duncan hallmarks—the build-up of tension; the manipulation of our sympathies; and the dramatic climax."

When Duncan began writing for teens, her own youth was not far behind her as a housewife in Florida in the 1950s. Later, as her five children grew up, she came to find inspiration for characters in her own daughters and sons, as well as from their social circle. Mark, in *Killing Mr. Griffin*, for instance, was based on her oldest daughter's first real boyfriend, whom the author described as "a very sick young man, and he was the most charming young man you could ever meet," Duncan told *School Library Journal*'s Roger Sutton. "It wasn't until things got very bad that we discovered he was the kind of guy who would swerve in the road to run over a dog." In the same interview, Duncan used the anecdote to defend her books against charges that she gives teens negative role models. Her daughter Robin's bad experience caused Duncan to realize, as she put it, "'These people—they're *there*,'" she told Sutton.

Personal Tragedy

But drama intruded unexpectedly on Duncan's life in July of 1989, when she and her husband received a phone call in the middle of the night from a hospital. They rushed to the Albuquerque facility to learn that their youngest child, daughter Kaitlyn, had been shot in the head while driving. Only eighteen years old, Kait was on her way to college in a few weeks and the killing appeared at first to be a random, bizarre tragedy. Duncan and her family had faith in law-enforcement officials, but then began to feel frustration when some disturbing clues hinted that it was not a chance crime. The Duncans hired private investigators, and learned that Kait's boyfriend had been part of a crime ring involving insurance fraud. They suspected she learned of the scam, since they knew she was planning to break up with him; the Duncans surmise that others ordered her silenced. Three men were arrested, but charges were dropped due to lack of evidence.

If you enjoy the works of Lois Duncan, you may also want to check out the following books:

Gilbert B. Cross, *A Witch Across Time,* 1990.
Joan Lowery Nixon, *Whispers from the Dead,* 1989.
Barbara Abercrombie, *Run for Your Life,* 1984.

Compounding her grief was Duncan's realization that some of the circumstances surrounding Kait's murder had eerie parallels with her last novel. *Don't Look Behind You* had been published just a month before her daughter was killed, and centers around the threats encountered by a teenage girl, April, who is in a federal witness protection program after her family uncovers a ring of drug dealers and must flee for fear of retribution. In one scene, April is chased by contract killers in a Camaro; the lead that Albuquerque police had about Kaitlyn Arquette's murder was that the killers drove a Camaro. "It was as if these things I'd written about as fiction became hideous reality," she said in the *School Library Journal* interview with Sutton.

The coincidences led Duncan to contact Dr. William Roll, a professional colleague of the researcher who had conducted those Duke University ESP experiments that Duncan participated in as a student in the 1950s. Roll explained to her that "precognition is very much a proven reality, that it's also been proven that people who are creative individuals have much more psychical ability than others," Duncan told *School Library Journal.* "He said that very often, as far as writers go, future events will turn up in their fiction, especially if the situation has to do with violence."

The notes that Duncan took during this time, to help her sort out the details of her own investigation into the crime, became the basis for *Who Killed My Daughter?: The True Story of a Mother's Search for Her Daughter's Murderer,* her 1992 nonfiction book. Here, Duncan relates several threads of evidence that she was able to uncover, but ones that failed to help law-enforcement officials solve the case. A man at the crime scene was never questioned, for instance, and the note left in Kait's apartment, her mother believes, was forged. Her aim in writing the book, Duncan stated, was the hope that it might be read by someone with information who will be inspired to step forward; the case has been plagued by the recanting of several witnesses, who perhaps fear repercussion for cooperating with law-enforcement authorities.

Duncan's readers, declared Claire Rosser in *Kliatt,* "will find this tragedy all the more poignant simply because it is horrifyingly true," she noted inher review of *Who Killed My Daughter?* And though *Voice of Youth Advocates* reviewer Mary Jane Santos remarked that "the reader tends to get lost in the myriad of minutia presented here," citing the numerous transcripts and factual evidence presented, Santos nevertheless granted that "the strength and tenacity of Duncan is admirable."

Ten years later, the Kaitlyn Arquette case remained unsolved, and Duncan and her husband had relocated to the other side of the country in order to escape the painful memories. Her forays into teen fiction have been very few since. Instead, she teamed with Dr. Roll, director of projects for the Psychical Research Foundation, to write *Psychic Connections: A Journey into the Mysterious World of Psi.* This 1995 nonfiction work, aimed at junior high and high school readers, tries to explain various psychic phenomenon from a balanced perspective. Ghosts, telepathy, extrasensory perception, crime detection and psychic healing, and possible ties to accepted spirituality are all discussed, as is the demon of statistical interpretation; Duncan tries to show how data and facts can be misconstrued, and she also explores how the psychic interviewing process works. Through it all, she relates her own forays into the paranormal, and how inconclusive they ultimately proved. A *School Library Journal* review by Cathy Chauvette found that Duncan's "own experiences are compellingly related and she convincingly conveys her own sense of confusion as she finds herself backed into the corner of belief." Nancy Glass Wright, writing for *Voice of Youth Advocates,* praised Duncan's latest as "acomprehensive overview . . . that generally reads well and that is sometimes riveting." A review in *Bulletin of the Center of Children's Books* by Deborah Stevenson called it ambiguous in result, "successful neither as a collection of true mysterious tales nor as a science-based defense of a controversial subject."

Duncan's first work of fiction in eight years appeared with her 1997 novel, *Gallows Hill*. The story centers around Sarah Zoltanne, newcomer to a small Ozark town. Her new high school plans a Halloween carnival, and a well-liked, good-looking senior boy asks Sarah to run the fortune-telling booth. She brings her Hungarian grandmother's crystal paperweight for authenticity, but the prophecies she causally relates prove true, and students begin to turn on her. Once just an outsider, now she is openly derided as a witch, and Sarah worries about the strange dreams she now has about witch hunts in early seventeenth-century New England. Her only friend is also possessed by similar dreams, and in true Duncan fashion, they extricate themselves from catastrophe in the nick of time. *Voice of Youth Advocates* critic Delia A. Culberson commended the way in which Duncan blended historical fact with compelling drama, and found it "an unusual and intriguing tale peopled with believable characters. It also illustrates how ignorance and bigotry can prevail against fairness and common sense." Reviewing it for *School Library Journal*, Bruce Anne Shook faulted a hasty, somewhat formulaic finish, but concluded that "despite its weaknesses, this is still an exciting, suspenseful tale that will certainly be welcomed by Duncan's many fans."

Duncan was dismayed by the film version of *I Know What You Did Last Summer*, which launched the film career of Jennifer Love Hewitt and proved successful enough to merit a sequel. "They made it into a slasher film," Duncan told Susan Schindehette in *People*. "And I don't think murder is funny." She says she is still haunted in her sleep by her murdered daughter. "In dreams, Kaitlyn tells me, 'Don't give up, mother,'" Duncan told Schindehette. "It's not a matter of revenge. It's a matter of Kait being worth the truth."

■ Works Cited

Babbitt, Natalie, review of *Daughters of Eve*, *New York Times Book Review*, January 27, 1980, p. 24.

Chauvette, Cathy, review of *Psychic Connections*, *School Library Journal*, May, 1995, p. 125.

Culberson, Delia A., review of *Gallows Hill*, *Voice of Youth Advocates*, April, 1997, p. 28.

Review of *Debutante Hill*, *Christian Science Monitor*, February 5, 1959, p. 11.

Duncan, Lois, *Chapters: My Growth as a Writer*, Little, Brown, 1982.

Duncan, Lois, essay in *Something about the Author Autobiography Series*, Volume 2, Gale, 1986, pp. 67-79.

Eaglen, Audrey, "Lois Duncan," *St. James Guide to Young Adult Writers*, St. James Press, 1999, pp. 252-255.

Gray, Hildagarde, review of *Killing Mr. Griffin*, *Best Sellers*, August, 1978, pp. 154-155.

Hayes, Sarah, "Fatal Flaws," *Times Literary Supplement*, January 29-February 4, 1988, p. 119.

Heins, Ethel L., review of *Summer of Fear*, *Horn Book*, April, 1977, p. 167.

Horowitz, Anthony, "Parent Problems," *Times Literary Supplement*, February 22, 1985, p. 214.

Review of *I Know What You Did Last Summer*, *Kirkus Reviews*, September 1, 1973, p. 972.

Jaffee, Cyrisse, review of *Daughters of Eve*, *School Library Journal*, September, 1979, p. 155.

Levitas, Gloria, "Haunts and Hunts," *New York Times Book Review*, November 10, 1974, pp. 8, 10.

Peck, Richard, "Teaching Teacher a Lesson," *New York Times Book Review*, April 30, 1978, p. 54.

Rosser, Claire, review of *Who Killed My Daughter?*, *Kliatt*, May, 1994, p. 26.

Santos, Mary Jane, review of *Who Killed My Daughter?*, *Voice of Youth Advocates*, December, 1992, p. 304.

Schindehette, Susan, "Who Killed My Daughter? An Eight-Year-Old Unsolved Slaying Still Plagues Writer Lois Duncan," *People*, November 24, 1997, p. 103.

Shepard, Richard F., review of *They Never Came Home*, *New York Times Book Review*, June 8, 1969, p. 42.

Shook, Bruce Anne, review of *Gallows Hill*, *School Library Journal*, May, 1997, p. 132.

Silver, Linda, review of *I Know What You Did Last Summer*, *School Library Journal*, April, 1974, p. 64.

Stevenson, Deborah, review of *Psychic Connections*, *Bulletin of the Center of Children's Books*, September, 1995, pp. 12-13.

Review of *Stranger with My Face*, *Kirkus Reviews*, January 1, 1982, p. 11.

Sullivan, Peggy, review of *A Gift of Magic*, *School Library Journal*, November, 1971, p. 122.

Sutherland, Zena, review of *Stranger with My Face*, *Bulletin of the Center of Children's Books*, April, 1982, p. 146.

Sutton, Roger, interview with Lois Duncan, *School Library Journal*, June, 1992, pp. 20-24.

Viguers, Ruth Hill, review of *Season of the Two-Heart*, *Horn Book*, February, 1965, p. 59.

Whedon, Julia, "Witches and Werewolves," *New York Times Book Review*, March 6, 1977, p. 29.

Wright, Nancy Glass, review of *Psychic Connections*, *Voice of Youth Advocates*, August, 1995, p. 181.

■ For More Information See

BOOKS

Children's Literature Review, Volume 29, Gale, 1993.
Twentieth-Century Children's Writers, 3rd edition, St. James Press, 1989.

PERIODICALS

Booklist, April 15, 1992, p. 1482.
Bulletin of the Center of Children's Books, February, 1974; January, 1980, pp. 92-93; July-August, 1987; July/August, 1998, p. 393.
Children's Book Review Service, spring, 1982, p. 116.
Horn Book, February, 1982.
Interracial Books for Children Bulletin, Volume 11, number 6, 1980, pp. 17-18.
New York Times Book Review, August 16, 1998, p. 14.
Publishers Weekly, June 1, 1998, p. 48.
School Library Journal, November, 1981; July, 1989; August, 1992, p. 190.
Times Literary Supplement, March 26, 1982, p. 343.

—Sketch by Carol Brennan

Charles Frazier

■ Personal

Born in 1950, in Asheville, NC; son of a high school principal and librarian; married Katherine (an accounting professor), 1976; children: Annie. *Education:* University of North Carolina—Chapel Hill, B.A., 1973; University of South Carolina, Ph.D.

■ Addresses

Home—Raleigh, NC. *Agent*—Atlantic Monthly Press, 19 Union Square W., 11th floor, New York, NY 1003.

■ Career

Writer, university professor, and horse breeder. University of Colorado—Boulder, instructor in Early American Literature; taught literature at a the University of Colorado; nonfiction writer, 1985; freelance writer, 1990—. Raises horses on farm near Raleigh, NC.

■ Awards, Honors

National Book Award, 1997, for *Cold Mountain*.

■ Writings

(With Donald Secreast) *Adventuring in the Andes: The Sierra Club Travel Guide to Ecuador, Peru, Bolivia, the Amazon Basin, and the Galapagos Islands* (nonfiction), Sierra Club Books (San Francisco, CA), 1985.
Cold Mountain (novel), Atlantic Monthly Press (New York City), 1997.

■ Work in Progress

Another novel, about the "self-contained cultures" of summer resorts near the turn of the century in the North Carolina mountains.

■ Sidelights

Charles Frazier's first novel, *Cold Mountain*, stunned the literary world, becoming a best-seller and winning the 1997 National Book Award. The work also grabbed the hearts of readers by telling, as *People* contributor Michelle Green stated, "an eloquent and timeless love story." In *Cold*

Mountain Frazier was not only celebrating love but also "such old fashioned virtues as hard work and self-reliance," according to Malcolm Jones, Jr., in *Newsweek*. "He wanted to put readers in touch with their past."

"What interests me about historical fiction is, how do you, the reader, connect those characters and that situation to your own life? But at the same time, I want the diction of the book to make people understand this is a different world."

—Charles Frazier

Frazier was born in 1950 in Asheville, North Carolina. Frazier's father, Charles O., was his high school principal while his mother, Betty, was a school librarian and administrator. (As Frazier commented to Green: "just imagine high school with parental scrutiny added.") Frazier also told Green he was a "moderately" good student, adding that after graduation, "I thought I wanted to teach literature, probably, if I thought about it much at all." Even though he only had a vague idea about what he wanted to do with his life, Frazier attended the University of North Carolina and graduated with a Bachelor of Arts degree in 1973. He then enrolled in Appalachian State University's graduate program. It was there Frazier met a fellow student, Katherine. They married in 1976. For the next fifteen years, Frazier taught literature at the University of Colorado, earning a Ph.D. in English from the University of South Carolina as well, before returning to North Carolina.

During this time Frazier also traveled extensively in South America. In 1985, Frazier and coauthor Donald Secreast published *Adventuring in the Andes*. This nonfiction travel advice book featured information on native cuisine, hotels, and hiking trails, as well as warnings about possible island diseases. A reviewer in *Kliatt* called the book "excellent" and "invaluable," and Harold M. Otness, writing in *Library Journal*, felt it was "a fine choice for travel collections." Yet it wasn't a trip overseas that inspired Frazier's turn to fiction, but a

trip to his grandparents' home at Cold Mountain, North Carolina, where he learned a piece of family history.

Walking The Long Path to *Cold Mountain*

Frazier grew up in the rural culture of North Carolina. It wasn't until the mid-1980s when he returned to his grandparents that he began, as he told *People*, "a lot of note taking on . . . the folklore, the music, the Indian history, the natural history [of the area]. But I didn't know what I was going to do with it." Frazier was certain about one thing, though; as he remarked to Alexandra Jacobs in *Entertainment Weekly*: "I sure didn't want to write a battlefield kind of book. I wanted to

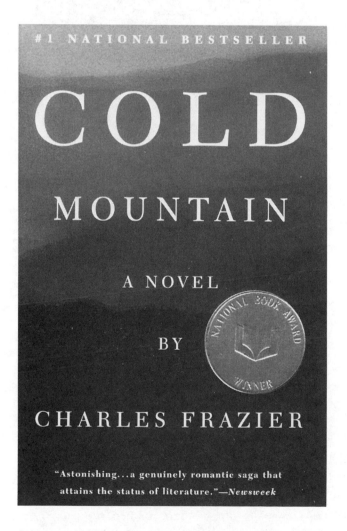

A visit to his grandparents' home in Southern Appalachia inspired Frazier's bestselling love story.

write about the old Southern Appalachian culture. Like watching somebody make molasses with a mule."

Frazier's ideas lacked focus, however. As he commented in *Salon Magazine* on-line, "I needed some point of access." This point of access came from the author's father. Charles O. had been researching his family history when he discovered the story of W. P. Inman, one of the Fraziers' ancestors. Inman, a Confederate soldier during the Civil War, deserted after being wounded in battle and walked back to his home at Cold Mountain. That bit of family history provided the spark Frazier needed. As he told Green, "It's like someone saying, 'Here's a brief outline for a book; what do you think?'"

> "I'm not sure we were ever on *the path*, that we're not always floundering off somewhere in the underbrush. . . . But we have this desire to look back and think that we were closer to it than we are now. How did we get where we are? A way to answer that question is to see where we've been."
>
> —Charles Frazier

Little did Frazier know that he would spend more than seven years writing *Cold Mountain*. He surrendered himself to a painstaking research process, "often declining all human companionship for weeks on end, the better to steep himself in arcane Southern folklore," according to Jacobs. During this time, his family's support proved invaluable. In fact, Frazier's wife, Katherine, convinced him to leave his teaching position to focus on his writing. "I don't know many wives," Frazier commented to Green, "who would have said to a 40-year-old man, 'Sure, honey, quit your job. Write that novel.'" For her part, Katherine didn't "see why it's exceptional to want your spouse to be happy doing what he does best." Frazier's daughter, Annie, helped her father by reading aloud chapters of the book. The author remarked to Green, "It really helped to hear it in somebody's else's voice and to see if she was getting the rhythm of the sentences."

In 1993 Frazier, prodded by his wife, turned over some 100 pages of his manuscript to novelist Kaye Gibbons, a mutual friend. Gibbons found the work enthralling; as she told Green, "I was so stunned that my left arm went numb. Outside of Eudora Welty and William Faulkner, I had never seen anything like it." In the fall of 1995, with Katherine and Annie's support, Gibbons' high praise, and his agent's persuasion, Frazier showed his manuscript to publishers. Within two months, Atlantic Monthly Press paid Frazier a six-figure sum for the publishing rights. Thus, the phenomenon of *Cold Mountain* had begun.

Popularity, Fame, and Writing

With the publication of *Cold Mountain*, Frazier—dubbed "a famously laconic loner" by Jones—became not only a best-selling, award-winning author but a bona fide celebrity. What was it about his work that captured so much attention? Critics often cite the emotion-filled narrative, which parallels Homer's *Odyssey*, the richness and authenticity of Frazier's language, and the strong, well-developed characters. *Cold Mountain* intertwines the story of Inman—his desertion from the Confederate army and his journey home—with the story of his Ada, his love. While Inman encounters danger and adventure on his trek, Ada struggles to survive on the family farm, joining forces with a local girl, Ruby, after Ada's father dies. "As the lovers' reunion approaches," stated Claire Messud in the *Washington Post Book World*, "both are aware of their internal (and external) transformations, irrevocable changes that reflect those of the country in which they live." A wealth of historical detail adds to the drama; *Library Journal* contributor David A. Berona called the work "a remarkable effort that opens up with a historical past that will enrich readers. . . ."

Reviewers also praised the author's use of an archaic narrative voice. In *Newsweek*, Jones remarked on the "pleasure of Frazier's language—forceful and perfectly cadenced to capture the flavor of a long-gone era. . . ." Messud noted that Frazier "has captured his characters' lost quotidian speech, and the novel's pages are peppered with words such as 'hinnies,' 'spavins,' and 'taliped.'" *Observer* critic Christina Patterson admitted that Frazier's style makes for slow going at first, but she also believed "the reader is forced to take it all at a slightly slower pace, to savour each episode of

If you enjoy the works of Charles Frazier, you may also want to check out the following books and films:

Stephen Crane, *The Red Badge of Courage*, 1895.
Jeff Shaara, *Gods and Generals*, 1996.
Michael Shaara, *The Killer Angels*, 1975.
Jane Smiley, *The All-True Travels and Adventures of Lidie Newton*, 1998.
Gone with the Wind, a film starring Clark Gable and Vivien Leigh, 1939.

this magnificent adventure story and to allow the magic of the prose to work in its own way."

Readers and critics alike were taken with the finely-drawn portraits of Inman and Ada. James Polk, writing in the *New York Times Book Review*, observed that both characters "are between their pasts and their futures, escaping the former and traveling toward the latter. Although Inman's journey . . . covers more physical distance and has more immediate drama, Ada's is richer and deeper; in the end, perhaps it is she who travels farther." Messud stated that "readers impatient with the relentless linearity of Inman's progress will find respite in Ada's concentric growth, and vice versa."

The success of *Cold Mountain* prompted some critics to call Frazier a natural-born storyteller; in *Newsweek*, Jones lauded his ability to "conjure war's horror with a poet's economy." Frazier, for his part, told *Newsweek* that he "worked hard" on creating "the physical texture of another time and place. What interests me about historical fiction is, how do you, the reader, connect those characters and that situation to your own life? But at the same time, I want the diction of the book to make people understand this is a different world." It seems that readers had no trouble connecting to Inman and Ada's story. In 1998, *Cold Mountain* spent over eighty weeks on the best-seller list and was optioned by Oscar-winning director Anthony Minghella (*The English Patient*), who will write and direct the film version of the book.

How has Frazier handled his newfound fame? After months of book tours, Frazier acknowledged

that he was exhausted but added, "When you think of the alternative—and that's nobody being interested—it doesn't seem that bad." Even his wife, Katherine, has welcomed Frazier's success, telling *People*, "He was my secret for so many years. I'm glad now other people are having achance to enjoy him." Yet it isn't fame, celebrity, or attention which Frazier craves, but a sense of home and community, things he believes are lacking in the modern world. The author told Jones that he had been struck by some album liner notes—written by Bob Dylan—that pondered "how far off the path we've come." "I'm not sure we were ever *on* the path," Frazier said, "that we're not always floundering off somewhere in the underbrush. . . . But we have this desire to look back and think that we were closer to it than we are now. How did we get where we are? A way to answer that question is to see where we've been."

■ Works Cited

Review of *Adventuring in the Andes, Kliatt*, fall, 1985, p. 57.

Berona, David A., review of *Cold Mountain, Library Journal*, May 15, 1997, p. 100.

Frazier, Charles, "*Cold Mountain* Diary," *Salon Magazine* on-line, located at www.salonmagazine. com, (July 9, 1997).

Green, Michelle, "Peak Performance: A Hot First Novel, Cold Mountain, Brings Charles Frazier Literary Stardom," *People*, February 23, 1998.

Jacobs, Alexandra, "'Mountain' Man," *Entertainment Weekly*, September 26, 1997, pp. 46-47.

Jones, Malcolm, Jr., "The Pinnacle of Success," *Newsweek*, April 6, 1998, pp. 62-65.

Messud, Claire, "Tried in the Fire," *Washington Post Book World*, July 6, 1997, p. 6.

Otness, Harold M., review of *Adventuring in the Andes, Library Journal*, June 1, 1985, p. 127.

Patterson, Christina, "Hope Is Where the Hearth Is," *Observer*, July 20, 1997, p. 17.

Polk, James, "American Odyssey," *New York Times Book Review*, July 13, 1997, p. 14.

■ For More Information See

PERIODICALS

Booklist, June 1-15, 1997, p. 1656.
Esquire, November, 1998, pp. 70-72.

People, July 21, 1997, p. 29.
Publishers Weekly, November 24, 1997, pp. 14-15.
School Library Journal, November, 1997, p. 146.

—*Sketch by Ann Schwalboski*

Kaye Gibbons

citation from Ernest Hemingway Foundation, both for *Ellen Foster*; National Endowment for the Arts fellowship, for *A Virtuous Woman*; Nelson Algren Heartland Award for Fiction, *Chicago Tribune*, 1991, PEN/Revson Foundation Fellowship, and North Carolina Sir Walter Raleigh Award, all for *A Cure for Dreams*; Chevalier de L'Ordre des Arts et des Lettres, 1996.

■ **Personal**

Born in 1960, Nash County, NC; married Frank Ward (an attorney); children: (from previous marriage) three daughters. *Education:* Attended North Carolina State University and the University of North Carolina at Chapel Hill.

■ **Addresses**

Home—Raleigh, NC.

■ **Career**

Novelist.

■ **Awards, Honors**

Sue Kaufman Prize for First Fiction, American Academy and Institute of Arts and Letters, and

■ **Writings**

NOVELS

Ellen Foster, Algonquin Books (Chapel Hill, NC), 1987.
A Virtuous Woman, Algonquin Books, 1989.
A Cure for Dreams, Algonquin Books, 1991.
Charms for the Easy Life, Putnam (New York City), 1993.
Sights Unseen, Putnam, 1995.
On the Occasion of My Last Afternoon, Putnam, 1998.

Contributor to the *New York Times Book Review*.

■ **Adaptations**

Ellen Foster was adapted for audiocassette by Simon and Schuster in 1996, and for a Hallmark Hall of Fame television movie in 1997; movie rights to *A Virtuous Woman* were bought by the Oprah Winfrey production company.

■ Sidelights

Kaye Gibbons burst upon the American literary scene at the age of twenty-seven with publication of her Southern coming-of-age novel, *Ellen Foster.* This short novel tells the story of plucky, spirited Ellen, eleven going on thirty, a survivor who faces the suicide of her abused mother, fends off the drunken advances of her father, and deals with the malignant neglect of aunts and a grandmother to finally find a family for her herself. Something of a female Huck Finn, Ellen Foster, both character and novel, won the hearts of readers and earned prestigious literary awards for its young Southern author. The novel became the first in a string of bestsellers for Gibbons, all set in the South and told in the simple vernacular of that region.

Resilient is a word often used to describe a typical Kaye Gibbons character. Her female protagonists are survivors, quiet domestic heroines in the conflict between the sexes. Her male characters are mostly '3-D': the men in a Gibbons novel can usually be counted on to "disappoint, disappear and die," as Stephen McCauley pointed out in a critical appraisal of *A Cure for Dreams* in the *New York Times Book Review.* But her women persevere and more. There is Ellen of course, and then comes Ruby in *A Virtuous Woman*, Lottie in *A Cure for Dreams*, Charlie in *Charms for the Easy Life*, Hattie in *Sights Unseen*, and Emma in Gibbons's sixth novel, *On the Occasion of My Last Afternoon.* Often these narrators are young: Ellen is eleven, Hattie twelve, and Emma an adolescent throughout much of the action of the last-named novel. Gibbons's trademark heroine is, as Kathryn Harrison noted in the *New York Times Book Review,* "a girl who, having lost her mother—having lost all comfort and safety—attacks the chaos of her life with heartbreaking bravery. For this girl, assuming blame is less terrifying than perceiving herself a victim of an impossibly cruel fate. Focused on the frailty or absence of her mother, the vigilant heroine misses out on childhood."

Gibbons's female characters do not go softly into that good night. They fight what others might term fate; they wage quiet wars against sexist inequity, against racism, against buttons that refuse to close properly, for Gibbons's characters do not exist on the abstract plane. One of her great strengths as a writer is her use of concrete detail. "When I talk and when I write," Gibbons told a chat room sponsored by Barnes and Noble, "I try to avoid the abstract. I am drawn to detail in writing as a way of offering density and showing rather than telling. I couldn't imagine something more unbearable than having somebody asking me to write about an abstract like tenderness, with no examples of it, with no examples of chimps picking lice out of a little chimp's head. I would have to show examples of an emotion."

Like her own female protagonists, Gibbons does not beat her own drum too loudly. "Soft-spoken and self-deprecating, Kay Gibbons is the stealth candidate among Southern writers," James Wolcott remarked in *The New Yorker.* "She has produced a handful of seriocomic studies of female coping and comradeship which may someday lodge on the permanent shelf."

Being Ellen Foster

While being lovingly thorough about every aspect of the history of her fictional characters, Gibbons has long maintained a reticence about her own past. In fact, there are parallels in Gibbons's early life and to that of the fictional life of her first female protagonist, Ellen Foster. Born in Nash County, North Carolina, in 1960, Gibbons grew up in the South with all its prejudices and pride. Gibbons's own mother committed suicide when the author was ten, and this occasioned the break up of her family, including her alcoholic father. Gibbons thereafter lived with a couple of aunts before finally moving in with an older brother. But of this she has little to say, not wishing it to be the focus of critical analysis or gossip. "I had read enough Thomas Wolfe to know what would happen if that occurred," Gibbons told Bob Summer in an interview for *Publishers Weekly.* "I didn't want the publicity hook to be my miserable childhood." Gibbons went on to say, however, the "the years between 10 and 13 were pretty hard." And in the Barnes and Noble chat room, she commented: "I knew as a child that I had a gift that the other children didn't get, and because I was born dirt-poor with a suicidal mother and alcoholic father, I feel like I deserved to have that present in my cradle. I thought I would grow up and teach literature. I didn't think that people made livings at being writers unless they were dead or from Mississippi. But I have always used books as a haven."

An avid reader as a child, Gibbons was a constant patron of the local library, as the books at home consisted mainly of a Bible and a set of encyclopedias. She graduated from Rocky Mount High School and then went on to North Carolina State University on a scholarship, intending, as she noted, to go into teaching. But her interest in writing led her to change school; attending the University of North Carolina at Chapel Hill, she became fascinated with the writings of James Weldon Johnson, an African American poet of the turn of the twentieth century. "He seemed to me to be the first poet in the South—not the first writer, since Twain had already done it—to make art out of everyday language," Gibbons told Summer. "Inspired by him, I wanted to see if I could have a child use her voice to talk about life, death, art, eternity—big things from a little person."

In 1985, Gibbons began writing a poem from the point of view of a young black girl, Starletta, but soon the poem turned into a novel narrated by a young white girl, Ellen, a friend of Starletta's. Gibbons was still taking classes at Chapel Hill at the time, with Louis Rubin, who founded the Algonquin Press at the university. Rubin looked at the book Gibbons came up with, and showed it to some influential literary friends as well, Walker Percy and Eudora Welty among them, and decided to publish this first novel. For Gibbons, still without a degree, married and with two children, this was a life-altering event.

A Southern Author

"When I was little I would think of ways to kill my daddy. I would figure out this way or that way and run it through my head until it got easy.

"The way I liked best was letting go a poisonous spider in his bed, it would bite him and he'd be dead and swollen up and I would shudder to find him . . .

"But I did not kill my daddy, He drank his own self to death the year after the County moved me out. I heard how they found him shut up in the house dead and everything. Next thing I know he's in the ground and the house is rented out to a family of four."

So begins Gibbons's first novel, *Ellen Foster,* and the reader is immediately presented with a narrator who is a female equivalent of Holden Caulfield and Huck Finn. The book that follows is a narrative mix of flashback memories of Ellen's abused childhood and current scenes of her life in a foster family. Ellen's mother is the daughter of a well-to-do family who never forgave her for marrying beneath herself. Sickly, she still must take care of her brutish husband. Young Ellen tries to protect her mother from her father, but finally her mother opts out by taking an overdose of pills. Ellen's father refuses to allow her to get help for her dying mother. After Ellen's mother dies, her drunken father becomes even worse, signing over the farm for a monthly remittance which he promptly drinks up. Ellen's only friends are a black family and their mute daughter Starletta who live nearby. Despite her liking for these people, Ellen is still stuck with blind prejudice, a result of her Southern upbringing.

When Ellen's father makes drunken advances toward her, she runs off to Starletta's house and then to an aunt's. However, when the aunt learns that Ellen hopes to make the move permanent, she sends the girl back to her abusive parent. Finally, discovering bruises on the young girl, a teacher intervenes and takes Ellen in for a time, until the court awards custody to her maternal grandmother, a woman still bitter about her daughter's marriage. Ellen is put to work in the fields where the work is hard, but where she begins to learn about the realities of her family and families in general from some of the field hands. Ellen's father drinks himself to death and then her grandmother too falls ill. When she dies, Ellen is sent to other aunts, and while in their reluctant care, she spies a single woman at church with a bevy of children and is informed this is the local foster family. Ellen decides she wants to be part of Mrs. Foster's family, confusing the adjective for a name, and offers the woman all the money she has saved if she can only be part of her family. Refusing the money, the woman happily takes the love-starved youth in. Ellen has finally found a home.

Baldly told, the novel has melodramatic overtones. As *Publishers Weekly* noted, "this slim first novel . . . [does] resemble a Victorian tearjerker, transplanted to the South." But as Alice Hoffman commented in *New York Times Book Review,* "What might have been grim, melodramatic material in

Kaye Gibbons
author of *A Virtuous Woman*

Ellen Foster

"Ellen Foster is a southern Holden Caulfield, tougher perhaps, as funny....A breathtaking first novel."
—Walker Percy

Vintage Contemporaries

Set in the rural south, this 1987 novel describes the coming of age of a spirited young woman in a dysfunctional family.

the hands of a less talented author is instead filled with lively humor . . . compassion and intimacy. This short novel focuses on Ellen's strengths rather than her victimization, presenting a memorable heroine who rescues herself." *Booklist*'s Brad Hooper noted that this "commendable first novel" is "humorous and unsentimental . . . never weepy or grim, despite the subject matter."

Other reviewers commended Gibbons's use of language and her willingness to tackle large themes. *Kirkus Reviews* drew attention to the "laconic and telegraph-style voice" of the youthful narrator, while Pearl K. Bell, writing in *New Republic*, noted that "Gibbons never allows us to feel the slightest doubt that [Ellen] is only 11. Nor does she

ever lapse into the condescending cuteness that afflicts so many stories about precocious children." Bell went on to note that "the voice of this resourceful child is mesmerizing because we are right inside her head. The words are always flawlessly right." Bell also praised Gibbons for the fact that she "doesn't evade the racism of Southern life, which she subtly reveals through the tenacious child's mind." Linda Taylor, reviewing the novel in *Sunday Times,* felt that *Ellen Foster* "is one of those novels that you feel compelled to read from cover to cover in one sitting. . . . [I]t is a novel about sexism, racism, family rancor and child abuse, issues that are dealt with through revelation rather than moral axe-grinding."

Still other reviewers remarked on the literary tradition into which *Ellen Foster* fits, drawing comparisons to both *Huck Finn* and *Catcher in the Rye.* *Kirkus Reviews* noted that "Ellen Foster is a kind of Huck Finn," while her father, "like Huck's Pap, is a piece of mean, worthless, lecherous, drunken white trash." Expanding on this theme, Veronica Makowsky commented in *Southern Quarterly* that "*Ellen Foster* is Gibbons's attempt to rewrite the saga of the American hero by changing 'him' to 'her' and to rewrite the southern female *bildungsroman* by changing its privileged, sheltered, upper-class heroine to a poor, abused outcast." But Makowsky further noted that "although [Ellen's] gutsy, vernacular voice recalls Huck Finn, she does not light out for the territories" as did Huck. Rather, Ellen finds strength in "the female tradition of community and nurturance."

Awards committees agreed with the reviewers: Gibbons's debut novel won the Sue Kaufman Prize for First Fiction from the American Academy and Institute of Arts and Letters as well as a citation from the Ernest Hemingway Foundation. Gibbons's literary career was solidly launched.

A Bounty of Female Protagonists

Gibbons is best known for her strong female characters, and in her second novel, *A Virtuous Woman,* she presents Ruby, a woman who never made headlines but whose quiet, determined, virtuous life resounds in the telling. Set again in the rural South and employing the idiomatic vernacular of the region, *A Virtuous Woman* is told from the dual viewpoints of Ruby, as she lays dying from lung cancer, and from that of her second husband, Jack

Julie Harris and Jena Malone starred in the 1997 Hallmark Hall of Fame adaptation of *Ellen Foster*.

Stokes, several months after Ruby's death. By this time Jack has worked through all the meals in the freezer that Ruby has lovingly prepared for him before dying. The novel has little plot; its strength lies in the retelling of an ordinary life made extraordinary by such details. And it is also the story of how Jack finally must get on with his life after losing Ruby.

"The story, which is a pleasure to read," wrote Deanna D'Errico in *Belles Lettres,* "evokes subtly and lovingly the bond that has united Jack and Ruby through life and beyond." Roz Kavaney, writing in *Times literary Supplement,* also remarked on the novel's readability: "Kaye Gibbons's second novel . . . has the simplicity of a good Country-and-Western song . . . here she shows us two adults for whom extremity has revealed the bare bones of life." Kavaney concluded, "A *Virtuous Woman* dares to do the ordinary thing, to transfigure the commonplace into a plain language that speaks with as much complexity as the rococo might, but with more appropriateness." Not all reviewers agreed with such an assessment on Gibbons's use of the vernacular, however. Padgett Powell, writing in *New York Times Book Review,* felt that "Jack and Ruby speak in a kind of standard somewhat-low-white-South idiom that is not off the beam enough to be interesting in itself, that is rarely (to its benefit) 'poetic' and that calls attention mostly to its own ordinariness." Powell felt, however that there "is guile in this pedestrianness. In the absence of verbal or dramatic fireworks . . . structure stands in." Powell thought that "the architecture of this novel is remarkable," terming this "compact, complex novel . . . somewhat stripped-down descendant of Faulkner's *As I Lay Dying.*"

Writing about the Family

With her third novel, *A Cure for Dreams,* and fourth, *Charms for the Easy Life,* Gibbons wrote a pair of multigenerational family sagas. *Charms,* in fact, was initially intended as a sequel to *A Cure for Dreams,* but Gibbons later decided against such a course. In the first-named novel, the main characters are Lottie, her daughter Betty, and granddaughter Marjorie. While Lottie is the focus protagonist, much of the story is told through the narrative voice of Betty; this technique, as Gibbons has pointed out, prevents strong characters from completely running away with the story.

Betty tells the story of her mother, Lottie, and her difficult life in rural Kentucky in the late nineteenth century. Lottie finally escaped such a life by marrying and moving to North Carolina, though in the event such an escape proved only another imprisonment as her workaholic husband kept her emotionally isolated. This changed, however, with the birth of Betty. Betty becomes Lottie's focus and begins to alarm her as she grows up and is in turn attracted to the wrong kind of men. Lottie, settled in North Carolina, becomes something of the leader of the local women, organizing card parties, imparting wisdom, and even helping a friend who shoots her abusive husband.

"That's about all," noted Rhoda Koenig in *New York* magazine, "but a lot goes on in this little

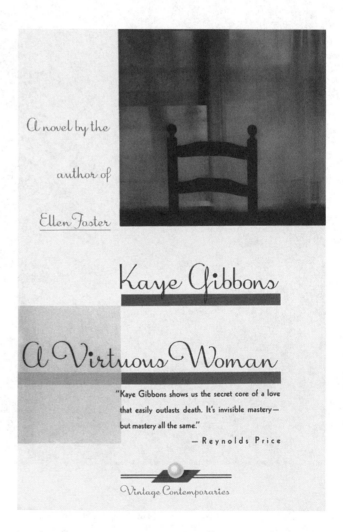

Gibbons' 1989 novel explores the marriage between two people who seem to have nothing in common.

mill town of neglected women and taciturn, sometimes brutal men." Koenig called Gibbons's story an "absolutely darling novel," without meaning belittling the novel. "I suppose if there is a platonic perky, plucky, and dear, though—ones that have resisted the gunky accretions of self-dramatizing cuteness—it's here that they apply." Benedict Cosgrove, writing in *San Francisco Review of Books*, called the novel "a celebration of the spoken word, of family history verbally constructed and passed on," while *New York Times Book Review* critic James Wilcox pointed to the well chosen details "like the proverbial picture worth a thousand words." Josephine Humphreys, writing in the *Los Angeles Times Book Review*, declared: "Full of unforgettable scenes and observations, characters drawn surely and sharply, and writing that is both lyrical [and] lightning-keen, this is a novel of vision and grace. It *shines.*"

Three generations of women are also at the heart of *Charms for the Easy Life*, the story of Charlie (Clarissa) Kate, a midwife with a charismatic personality, her daughter, Sophie, and Sophie's daughter, Margaret, who narrates the novel. Spanning forty years, the novel takes its name from a rabbit's foot "easy-life charm" given to Charlie by a black man whom she saves from a lynching. The novel focuses on the activities of Charlie, a folk healer with subscriptions to magazines such as the *New England Journal of Medicine* and *Saturday Review of Literature* which enable him to keep up with the intellectual and medical world from her home in rural North Carolina. The character of Charlie originally took form in *A Cure for Dreams* as the African American midwife who was Lottie's best friend. Initially intended as a sequel to that novel, *Charms for the easy Life* soon took on its own life, and Charlie outgrew the constraints of the former character.

Charlie is abandoned by her husband; her daughter is, as well. The three generations of women ultimately live together; only at the end of the novel does it appear Margaret may have a happy relationship, with Tom Hawkins, a sympathetically drawn male character. Set partly during World War Two, the novel owes a debt to two other writers, according to Gibbons: Studs Terkel, whose writings about the Second World War allowed Gibbons to understand the common people during that conflict, and Gabriel Garcia Marquez, whose *One Hundred Years of Solitude* showed her how to include history in the narrative.

Writing about Charlie in *New York Times Book Review,* Stephen McCauley called her "an implacable force of nature, a pillar of intellect, with insight and powers of intuition so acute as to seem nearly supernatural." Reviewing the novel in *Time* magazine, Amelia Weiss also commented on Charlie's character, noting that "her best healing power lies in her self. . . . and it is her 'winning streak' of a life that she passes on to her daughter Sophie and to Margaret." Weiss also noted that "[s]ome people might give up their second-born to write as well as Kaye Gibbons, so graceful and spirited are her fictional histories of North Carolina women."

Gibbons's fifth novel, *Sights Unseen,* came out in 1995, a novel that took seven rewrites to tell the story of a girl who nearly loses her mother to insanity. Writing it, Gibbons was in part exorcising her own fears of manic-depression, a condition she has been diagnosed with. Hattie, twelve years old, is another youthful narrator like Ellen Foster, which attracts young readers to Gibbons's ranks of loyal fans. Through her observations the reader follows the roller coaster ride of the mother's battle with mental illness and its effects on her family.

Hattie states at the outset: "Had I known my mother was being given electroconvulsive therapy while I was dressing for school on eight consecutive Monday mornings, I do not think I could have buttoned my blouses or tied my shoes or located my homework." From there, the narrative takes off to explore the mostly painful but sometimes humorous world in which Hattie is growing up. Gibbons's subject matter here is, as Jacqueline Carey pointed out in *New York Times Book Review*, "a manic-depressive mother and the havoc she wreaks in her family." Carey went on to comment, "Hattie's sights are always set at a delicate intersection of the ordinary and the horrific." Carey concluded that she found *Sights Unseen* "even better" than *Charms for the Easy Life.* "It is more intense, more vibrant, both richer and stranger." *Booklist*'s Donna Seaman remarked that "Gibbons writes seamless and resonant novels, the sort of fiction that wins hearts as well as awards," and further noted that *Sights Unseen* "is a novel that deserves unwavering attention from start to finish, like a symphony or a sunset." And Rebecca Ascher-Walsh concluded in *Entertainment Weekly,* this "is another chance to read what is surely one of the most lyrical voices writing today."

If you enjoy the works of Kaye Gibbons, you may also want to check out the following books:

Dori Sanders, *Clover,* 1990.
Betty Smith, *A Tree Grows in Brooklyn,* 1943.
Russell Banks, *Cloudsplitter,* 1998.

A New Direction

Gibbon's career was given a huge boost in 1997 with production of her first novel, *Ellen Foster,* as a television movie, and the selection of both that novel and *A Virtuous Woman* for Oprah's Book Club. The first novel to appear after these life-changing events mapped new fictional territory for the North Carolina author. *On the Occasion of My Last Afternoon* is the story of another strong female protagonist, but this time with a historical perspective. Emma Garnet Tate Lowell is a Southerner who comes of age in the years leading up to the Civil War. Using the occasion of her seventieth birthday, Emma makes a clean breast of her life. She was born to privilege on a Southern plantation, but grows up with an increasing awareness of the inequity inherent in the slave system that supports her life and that of others in the South. The book, indeed, opens with her witnessing the aftermath of a senseless killing of a slave by her brutish father. Emma ultimately flees the family home and sets up house in Raleigh, North Carolina with her new husband, Quincy Lowell, a product of the Boston Lowells and a skilled surgeon. With the coming of war, Emma works alongside her husband, treats wounded soldiers, and sees firsthand the horrors of the conflict. Throw in an indomitable family servant, Clarice, and a guilty family secret, and there are the makings of a Southern epic on the grand scale.

Writing in *School Library Journal,* Molly Connally noted, "YAs will find Emma . . . and Quincy to be fascinating and endearing characters whose flaws as well as strengths are revealed as the story unfolds." Connally also mentioned that the "author's picture of life in the Civil War South is vivid and unsentimental, and her characters are drawn with clarity and sympathy." Other critics were less enthusiastic about this new direction in Gibbons's fiction, however. *Kirkus Reviews* called the novel "a Civil War tale that's historically researched to a fault but psychologically the stuff of melodrama," and concluded that it is "a book of saints, sinners, and sorrows offering much pleasure for history-snoopers (hospital scenes among the best) but finding no new ground for the saga of the South." Somewhat echoing this sentiment, the reviewer for *People* praised Gibbons's efforts at telling two stories at once, both Emma's personal history as well as the larger story of the antebellum South. However, this reviewer felt that the author's attempt "to find an authentic historical tone results in a vocabulary and style . . . [that is] stilted and eccentric." Despite this drawback, *People* concluded that Gibbons's sixth novel was "a nicely detailed portrait of the Old South."

Other reviewers applauded the early parts of the book, narrated by the youthful Emma. *Publishers Weekly* commented that "Emma . . . is far more interesting as a rebellious child than as a stoic grown woman. One finishes the novel admiring Emma and Clarice but missing the compelling narrative voice that might have made their story truly moving." Harrison, writing in *New York Times Book Review* added to this assessment, finding the book something of a "disappointment," with "its stark early chapters fizzling in the more generic horrors of the Civil War, a literary landscape many timesmapped. In fact, the farther Emma travels from the outspoken, defiant child she was at 12, the less interesting she becomes." But if finding fault in the structure, most reviewers again praised Gibbons's use of detail. Harrison noted the "psychic burn" imparted by one such "lovely moment" when Emma realizes someone has moved her Faberge egg, a wedding gift from Quincy, "in the same way a child knows another has ridden her cart even though the seat has not been moved, in the same way Clarice could lay hand on the copper bow . . . and know by feel, by the supernatural touch shared by women and children, than an unauthorized user had whipped cream in it."

Gibbons, who was knighted by the French government in 1996 for her contributions to literature, takes such criticism in stride. This author, for whom "writing is a metaphor for life," as she told the Barnes and Noble chat room, is content to work on her novels, producing one every two years or so, and leave the reviewing to others. As she told Summer in *Publisher Weekly,* "Nobody ever told me [the writing life] was going to be easy. . . . I wouldn't want to do anything easy, and I *chose* to be a writer. . . . It's working with that element of fear that keeps a book going." And fans hope Gibbons keeps going.

■ Works Cited

Ascher-Walsh, Rebecca, review of *Sights Unseen, Entertainment Weekly,* April 4, 1995, p. 53.

Bell, Pearl K., "Southern Discomfort," *New Republic,* February 29, 1988, pp.38-41.

Carey, Jacqueline, "Mommy Direst," *New York Times Book Review,* September 24, 1995, p. 30.

Connally, Molly, review of *On the Occasion of My Last Afternoon, School Library Journal,* September, 1998, p. 229.

Cosgrove, Benedict, review of *A Cure for Dreams, San Francisco Review of Books,* spring, 1991, pp. 31-32.

D'Errico, Deanna, "Two Timers," *Belles Lettres,* summer, 1989, p. 7.

Review of *Ellen Foster, Kirkus Reviews,* March 15, 1987, p. 404.

Review of *Ellen Foster, Publishers Weekly,* March 20, 1987, p. 70.

Gibbons, Kaye, *Ellen Foster,* Algonquin Books, 1987.

Gibbons, Kaye, *Sights Unseen,* Putnam, 1995.

Gibbons, Kaye, *On the Occasion of My Last Afternoon,* Putnam, 1998.

Gibbons, Kaye, "Author Interview," Barnes and Noble chat room, located at http://shop.barnesandnoble.com.

Harrison, Kathryn, "Tara It Ain't," *New York Times Book Review,* July 19, 1988, p. 12.

Hoffman, Alice, "Shopping for a New Family," *New York Times Book Review,* May 31, 1987, p. 13.

Hooper, Brad, review of *Ellen Foster, Booklist,* September 1, 1987, p. 27.

Humphreys, Josephine, review of *A Cure for Dreams, Los Angeles Times Book Review,* May 19, 1991, p. 13.

Kavaney, Roz, "Making Themselves Over," *Times Literary Supplement,* September 15, 1989, p. 998.

Koenig, Rhoda, "Southern Comfort," *New York,* April 1, 1991, p. 63.

Makowsky, Veronica, "The Only Hard Part Was the Food: Recipes for Self-Nurture in Kaye Gibbons's Novels," *Southern Quarterly,* winter-spring, 1992, pp. 103-12.

McCauley, Stephen, "He's Gone, Go Start the Coffee," *New York Times Book Review,* April 11, 1993, pp. 9-10.

Review of *On the Occasion of My Last Afternoon, Kirkus Reviews,* May 1, 1998, p. 602.

Review of *On the Occasion of My Last Afternoon, People,* June 15, 1998, p. 49.

Review of *On the Occasion of My Last Afternoon, Publishers Weekly,* April 20, 1998, p. 43.

Powell, Padgett, "As Ruby Lay Dying," *New York Times Book Review,* April 30, 1989, pp. 12-13.

Seaman, Donna, review of *Sights Unseen, Booklist,* June 1, 1995, p. 1683.

Summer, Bob, "Kaye Gibbons," *Publishers Weekly,* February 8, 1993, pp. 60-61.

Taylor, Linda, "A Kind of Primitive Charm," *Sunday Times,* May 8, 1988, p. G6.

Weiss, Amelia, "Medicine Woman," *Time,* April 12, 1993, pp. 77-78.

Wilcox, James, review of *A Cure for Dreams, New York Times Book Review,* May 12, 1991, pp. 13-14.

Wolcott, James, "Crazy for You," *New Yorker,* August 24, 1995, pp. 115-116.

■ For More Information See

BOOKS

Contemporary Fiction Writers of the South: A Bio-bibliographical Sourcebook, edited by Joseph M. Flora and Robert Bain, Greenwood Press, 1993.

Novels for Students, Volume 3, edited by Diane Telgen and Kevin Hile, Gale, 1998.

Sternburg, Janet, editor, *The Writer and Her Work, Volume II,* Norton, 1991.

Watkins, James, editor, *Southern Selves, from Mark Twain and Eudora Welty to Maya Angelou and Kaye Gibbons: A Collection of Autobiographical Writing,* Vintage, 1998.

PERIODICALS

Belles Lettres, winter 1993-94, pp. 16-18.

Kliatt, September, 1997, p. 4; September, 1998, pp. 4, 61.

Library Journal, June 1, 1998, p. 150; September 15, 1998, p. 129.

Los Angeles Times Book Review, June 11, 1989, p. 15.

New Yorker, June 21, 1993, p. 101.

Publishers Weekly, June 5, 1995, p. 48.

School Library Journal, September, 1993, p. 260; December, 1993, p. 29.

Tribune Books (Chicago), September 15, 1991, p. 7.

Washington Post Book World, July 12, 1998, p. 9.

—Sketch by J. Sydney Jones

Matt Groening

■ Personal

Surname is pronounced "*gray*-ning" (rhymes with "raining"); born February 15, 1954, in Portland, OR; son of Homer (a filmmaker) and Margaret (a teacher) Groening; married Deborah Caplan (his manager and business partner), October 29, 1986; children: two. *Education:* Evergreen State College, B.A., 1977. *Hobbies and other interests:* Watching badly translated foreign films; nurturing ducks.

■ Addresses

Home—Los Angeles, CA. *Office*—Twentieth Century-Fox, 10201 West Pico Blvd., Los Angeles, CA 90035. *Agent*—c/o Susan A. Grode, 1999 Avenue of the Stars, Suite 1600, Los Angeles, CA 90067.

■ Career

Writer, cartoonist, and business executive. Held numerous odd jobs in Los Angeles, CA, including cemetery landscaper, dishwasher in a nursing home, clerk in recording and copy shops, and ghostwriter/chauffeur to an elderly filmmaker, 1977-79; *Los Angeles Reader,* Los Angeles, worked variously as circulation manager, editor, writer, cartoonist, and author of "Sound Mix" music column, 1979-84; cofounder and partner with Deborah Caplan, Life in Hell Cartoon Co. and Acme Features Syndicate, beginning in 1980s; Twentieth Century-Fox Television, Los Angeles, creator, developer, animator, director, and producer of "The Simpsons" episodes for *The TracyUllman Show,* 1987-89; Twentieth Century-Fox Television, Los Angeles, creator, developer, animator, and executive producer with James L. Brooks and Sam Simon, *The Simpsons* television series, 1989—, director of voice recording sessions, 1990--, and creator and executive producer of *Futurama,* 1999—; publisher, Bongo Comics Group, 1993—, and Zongo Comics, 1994—.

■ Awards, Honors

Won short story contest, *Jack and Jill,* 1962; Emmy Award nominations, Academy of Television Arts and Sciences, for outstanding writing in a variety program, 1987, 1988, and 1989, for *The Tracey Ullman Show,* and for outstanding animated program, 1990, for Christmas program *The Simpsons Roasting on an Open Fire; The Simpsons* television program has won ten Emmy Awards, including Outstanding Animated Program in 1990, 1991, and 1995, a Peabody Award in 1997, seven Annie Awards, three Genesis Awards, three International Monitor Awards, and three Environmental Media Awards, among others.

■ Writings

"LIFE IN HELL"

Love Is Hell, privately printed, 1984, revised edition, Pantheon, 1985.
Work Is Hell, Pantheon, 1986.
School Is Hell, Pantheon, 1987.
Childhood Is Hell, Pantheon, 1988.
Akbar and Jeff's Guide to Life, Pantheon, 1989.
Greetings from Hell, Pantheon, 1989.
The Big Book of Hell, Pantheon, 1990.
With Love from Hell: A Postcard Book, HarperCollins, 1991.
How to Go to Hell, HarperCollins, 1991.
The Road to Hell, HarperCollins, 1992.
Binky's Guide to Love, HarperCollins, 1994.
Love Is Still Hell: Special Ultra-Jumbo 10th Anniversary Edition, Random House, 1994.
The Huge Book of Hell, Penguin, 1997.

The *Life in Hell* comic strip was privately printed, beginning in late 1970s, appeared in *Wet,* 1978, *Los Angeles Reader,* 1980-86, and *L.A. Weekly,* 1984—, and has been syndicated by Groening and Caplan to over two hundred periodicals worldwide through Acme Features Syndicate, 1980—. Also creator of "The Life in Hell Fun Calendars."

"THE SIMPSONS"

The Simpsons Xmas Book (adapted from a screenplay by Mimi Pond), HarperCollins, 1990.
Greetings from the Simpsons, HarperCollins, 1990.
The Simpsons Rainy Day Fun Book, HarperCollins, 1991.
(With sister, Maggie Groening) *Maggie Simpson's Alphabet Book,* HarperCollins, 1991.
(With Maggie Groening) *Maggie Simpson's Book of Animals,* HarperCollins, 1991.
(With Maggie Groening) *Maggie Simpson's Book of Colors and Shapes,* HarperCollins, 1991.
(With Maggie Groening) *Maggie Simpson's Counting Book,* HarperCollins, 1991.
The Simpsons Uncensored Family Album, HarperCollins, 1991.
The Simpsons Fun in the Sun Book, HarperCollins, 1992.

Making Faces with the Simpsons: A Book of Ready-to-Wear Masks, HarperCollins, 1992.
The Simpsons Ultra-Jumbo Rain-or-Shine Fun Book, HarperCollins, 1993.
Cartooning with the Simpsons, HarperCollins, 1993.
Bart Simpson's Guide to Life, HarperCollins, 1993.
Simpsons Comics Extravaganza, HarperCollins, 1994.
Simpson's Comics Spectacular, HarperPerennial, 1995.
Bartman: The Best of the Best!, HarperPerennial, 1995.
Simpsons Comics Simps-O-Rama, HarperCollins, 1996.
Simpsons Comics Stike Back, HarperPerennial, 1996.
The Simpsons: A Complete Guide to Our Favorite Family, edited by Ray Richmond and Anonia Coffman, HarperPerennial, 1997.
Simpsons Comics Wingding, HarperCollins, 1997.
Simpsons Comics Big Bonanza, HarperPerennial, 1998.
Simpsons Comics on Parade, Bongo Comics Group, 1998.
The Simpsons Guide to Springfield, HarperCollins, 1998.
Bart Simpson's Treehouse of Horror: Heebie-Jeebie Hullabaloo, HarperPerennial, 1999.
Homer's Guide to Being a Man, HarperCollins, 2000.

Creator of Simpsons calendars published by Random House and HarperCollins; creator, *Simpsons Illustrated Magazine,* 1991-93; creator, "Simpsons Trading Cards," SkyBox, Series I, spring, 1994, Series II, fall, 1994.

TELEVISION SCRIPTS

(Contributor of fifty "Simpsons" segments) *The Tracy Ullman Show,* broadcast on Fox-TV, 1987-89.
(With others) *The Simpsons,* broadcast on Fox-TV, 1990—.
(Contributor of animated character dialogue) *The Ice Capades Fiftieth Anniversary Special,* broadcast on ABC-TV, 1990.
(With others) *Futurama,* broadcast on Fox-TV, 1999—.

OTHER

(With Steve Vance) *Postcards That Ate My Brain,* Pantheon, 1990.

Also creator, with Steve Vance, of "Postcards That Ate My Brain" calendars, Portal, 1990, and *Futurama Y2Kalender,* HarperCollins, 1999.

■ Sidelights

"I had a very typical childhood," said Matt Groening in a *San Jose Mercury News* article by Michael Oricchio. "The only difference was that I took notes and vowed never to forget what it was like." Groening's vow helped drive him into cartooning, where he has been taking revenge on his childhood tormentors and a lot of other pretentious people for most of his adult life. In his *Life in Hell* comic strip and *The Simpsons* animated television series, Groening lampoons authority figures from playground bullies to classroom and office tyrants, viewing life through the eyes of children and adults who feel doomed, overpowered, or defiantly obnoxious. His best-known creation is Bart Simpson, who has his adventures chronicled on the most successful prime-time animated series since *The Flintstones.* *The Simpsons* went on to win ten Emmy and a slew of other awards, earn $500 million in merchandising, air in over 70 countries, become America's longest-running sitcom, and is set to star in a feature film, *The Simpsons Movie,* in 2000. For a time, students across America shocked their teachers by wearing T-shirts that display the Bart attitude: "'Underachiever'—And proud of it, man!" *Futurama,* Groening's futuristic series that debuted on Fox in 1999, was a gauge of the cartoonist's success—he was allowed to indulge his long-time dream of creating a science-fiction show and air it on Fox television, part of one of the most known entertainment networks in the world, Twentieth Century Fox.

Groening was born and raised in Portland, Oregon. Strangely, the names of his family resemble those of the Simpson clan, including father Homer, mother Margaret, and sisters Lisa and Maggie. Groening now suggests that the coincidence was an inside joke that got out of hand. "My whole family was smart and funny," he told Jim Sullivan in the *Boston Globe,* "where the Simpsons are stupid and funny." Unlike Bart Simpson's condescending attitude towards Homer, Groening considered his father the "hippest" dad in the neighborhood: a man who, during the conformist 1950s, sought out such unusual jobs as cartoonist and creator of short films. Because

Created and produced by Groening, *The Simpsons* won ten Emmy Awards and became the longest-running and most successful animated television series ever.

of his work, Homer Groening subscribed to a huge range of general-interest magazines; accordingly, Matt was gazing at the cartoons in the *New Yorker* and *Punch* even before he could read. Soon he was doodling like his dad.

The closest resemblance between the Simpsons and the Groenings lies in the bickering between siblings. As the third child of five, Matt was picked on by an older brother and sister, and he, in turn, picked on his two younger sisters. For Groening such childhood memories are amazingly vivid—even intense. "I really do remember being in my crib and being bathed in the sink," he declared in the *Los Angeles Times*. "I remember being that small. At the time, I thought everything was dramatic. . . . Adults have forgotten how scary it is."

Tough Times in School

Scariest of all for Groening was elementary school. He found it a rigid, humorless, uncreative place that had no use for a child whose talent was doodling. "I could understand getting sent to the principal's office for dropping an encyclopedia out the window, but I couldn't understand them ripping my cartoons up," he continued. To console himself Groening started keeping a diary in the fifth grade. That way, in years to come, he could examine the record and decide if he'd been right to rebel.

Resisting all threats and pleas, Groening remained a nonconformist. He became a fan of satirical comics like Walt Kelly's *Pogo* and the notorious *Mad* magazine. When *Jack and Jill* magazine invited readers to submit their own ending to a Halloween story, Groening won a prize for his morbid finale: a boy dies from a bump on the head and swoops down from the attic once a year to join his family for dinner. By high school Groening began to hit his stride. He wrote and cartooned for the school newspaper, hung out with antiwar students from a nearby college, and, with fellow misfits from his high school, formed a sarcastic political party called Teens for Decency and got himself elected student body president. "You are what you are," Groeing once said in the *Los Angeles Times*, "basically despite school."

When it came time for college, Groening applied to only two: far-off Harvard University (he didn't make it) and nearby Evergreen State in Olympia, Washington. Founded in the late 1960s, Evergreen was a classic hippie school with no tests, no grades, and no classes (they were called seminars). Groening, who was really too conservative to be a hippie, responded to the freedom of Evergreen with a burst of self-discipline. Since he didn't see cartooning as a viable career, he decided to be a writer and soon became editor of the student newspaper. There he met Lynda Barry, an aspiring artist who cartooned on the side and who later created the best-selling strip *Ernie Pook's Comeek*. "I had been trying to

make other people laugh and I found out by looking at Lynda's cartoons that if you make yourself laugh, it's generally good for other people as well," Groening told Richard Harrington in the *Washington Post*. He decided to publish some of Barry's cartoons in the paper and, inspired by her example, published some of his own as well. This didn't change Groening's plans, however: "I didn't expect there to be an audience for what I was drawing because I didn't see anything drawn that crummy. There was nothing else as crude."

Eager for a writing job after graduation, Groening moved to an apartment in Los Angeles, but noth-

In this popular 1993 title, Groening gives readers a self-help manual Bart Simpson-style.

ing went right for him. The only writing job that materialized was as ghostwriter/chauffeur to a forgotten, eighty-eight-year-old Hollywood filmmaker who was trying to compose his memoirs. Other memorable jobs included record-store clerk, copy-shop clerk, graveyard landscaper, and dishwasher in a convalescent home. Faced with the prospect of explaining his lack of success to folks back home, Groening decided to entertain them with his cartoons instead. His life in Los Angeles was thus reborn as *Life in Hell*, the chronicle of a frustrated, harassed-looking rabbit named Binky. The first *Life in Hell* comic strips were run off on photocopiers, stapled into booklets, and mailed by Groening to old friends. Soon he tried selling some of the booklets to punk patrons of the record store where he worked. "The punks' reactions were pretty much either they liked it or they tore it up," he told *Newsweek* contributor Jennifer Foote, "which could have meant they liked it too."

Life in Hell Takes Off

Wet magazine, a pioneer of off-the-wall New Wave graphics, liked the strip enough to run several installments in 1978. Groening also tried to interest both of Los Angeles's alternative weeklies in his work, and in 1979 he landed a job with the *Los Angeles Reader*. Within a year *Life in Hell* was a weekly feature of the *Reader*, and Groening's job soon expanded into editor and rock music columnist. As originally seen in the *Reader, Life in Hell* was different from the comic strip now popularized in books and calendars; Binky the rabbit "was really hostile, ranting and raving, the way I felt," Groening explained in a *Rolling Stone* article by Tish Hamilton. "After a year of doing the comic strip and not getting much response, I decided to make the rabbit a victim instead of an aggressor. And the second I made the rabbit a victim, people started liking the comic strip. The more tragedies that befell this poor little rodent, the more positive response I got."

Binky took his present-day form: a lonely, beleaguered office worker with a nightmarish love life that results in his having an illegitimate son. The son, Bongo, is a troubled school-aged rabbit with only one ear. With the addition of Sheba, Binky's girlfriend (and not Bongo's mother), Groening had a cast of characters on whom he could in-

flict the humiliations of everyday life, including love, work, and childhood. When a girlfriend dumped him, for instance, he responded with "Love Is Hell," a thirteen-part comic-strip miniseries that told readers about the nine types of boyfriends (such as Old Man Grumpus), nine types of girlfriends (Ms. Vaguely Dissatisfied), and nine types of relationships (Sourballs vs. The World). He also wrote about a more pressing frustration: having an office job. "Isn't It About Time You Quit Your Lousy Job?" asked one of Groening's favorite strips. "Wake up, chumply. You're not getting any younger. The clock is ticking. You can't just sit there in your cubbyhole while life passes you by."

Groening might still be writing for the *Reader* if not for Deborah Caplan, who worked in the advertising department and was quick to see his potential. "It didn't take many sales calls before I realized that Groening's comic strip was the major drawing card of the newspaper," she told Joanne Kaufman in *People* magazine. Caplan fell in love with Groening, and, as an added bonus, she helped organize his life. In the mid-1980s Groening and Caplan quit their jobs and formed the Life in Hell Cartoon Company and Acme Features Syndicate, which syndicated the comic strip and sold all kinds of hell-related products, from posters to T-shirts to coffee mugs. Even before *The Simpsons* became a mass-market phenomenon, the Life in Hell Cartoon Company was pulling down a six-figure income. "Everyone I know goes, 'Well, if I had a Deborah, I could be a success, too,'" he said in the *Los Angeles Times*. "And they're right." The pair was married in 1986, and figurines of Binky and Sheba topped the wedding cake.

The boom in hell made Groening more ambitious, leading to a string of comic miniseries and cartoon books. The first book, *Love Is Hell*, was privately published by Caplan in 1984 and sold more than twenty thousand copies; subsequent books are titled *Work Is Hell, School Is Hell,* and *Childhood Is Hell*. To gear up for the *School Is Hell* series, Groening ransacked high school dumpsters for the notebooks and papers that students toss out at the end of the year. The final product surveyed such topics as "Trouble: Getting In and Weaseling Your Way Out" and "How to Drive a Deserving Teacher Crazy." *Childhood Is Hell*, based in part on Groening's fifth-grade diary, included a "Childhood Trauma Checklist" and a tribute to "Your Pal the TV Set." For variety Groening gave an increasing role in *Life in Hell* to gay entrepreneurs Akbar and Jeff, whose empty grins were somehow as creepy as Binky and Bongo's frowns. *Los Angeles Times Book Review* critic Charles Solomon noted that while Groening's artwork is not great in the traditional sense, it serves as a vehicle for good writing and sharp wit. "Groening," Solomon declared, "is one of the funniest and most original cartoonists working in the comics today."

The increasing popularity of Groening's "Hell" cartoon led to inquiries from the television industry, which found him a tough bargainer. When asked about potential projects, he told Sullivan, "I'd talk about how bad TV cartoons were and that I'd like to do something with the same standards as [the 1960s cult favorite] 'Rocky and Bullwinkle'—great writing, great voices, great music. They got all cold and distant after that and claimed that 'Rocky and Bullwinkle' was a failure because it only appealed to smart kids." Groening, who felt that TV viewers were ready again for something like smart animation, stood fast. Finally he got an offer from James L. Brooks, the noted producer and writer for such television programs as *The Mary Tyler Moore Show* and *Taxi* and movies like *Terms of Endearment* who was now at the adventurous new Fox television network. At first the pair planned to do an animated version of the comic strip, but then Fox laid down its terms: Groening must surrender all legal rights to the characters. Instead Groening sold Fox the concept for a whole new animated show, with human characters who were nearly as frazzled as his rabbits—"a messed-up American family," as he put it. The Simpsons were born.

Scores Big with *The Simpsons*

The Simpsons are a blue-collar clan who live in the mythical town of Springfield—the same hometown as the Andersons, the well-adjusted television family of the 1950s comedy *Father Knows Best*. The Simpsons, however, look like somebody's parody of a happy television family. Ten-year-old Bart is irreverent, irrepressible, and usually in trouble. He cheats on tests, sneaks into movies, and never misses a chance to one-up his father. Homer is fat, bald, stupid, and often grumpy—just a regular guy. He works at a

nuclear power plant, where his blunders often put Springfield on the edge of annihilation. Marge Simpson, wife and mother, is crowned by an enormous blue beehive hairdo. She holds the family together with kindhearted wisdom, although sometimes her advice is a little off target. Lisa is an eight-year-old genius who's full of common sense, but vaguely smug. And Baby Maggie "isn't TV-baby-cute; she's just there, all wide eyes and sucking noises," wrote Ken Tucker in *Entertainment Weekly*. "At its heart this is guerrilla TV," said Tucker's colleague Joe Rhodes—"a wicked satire masquerading as a prime-time cartoon."

As a television series, *The Simpsons* started small: it was a supplement to another prime-time series, *The Tracey Ullman Show*. At first the animation spots—written, directed, and produced by Groening—were used as fifteen-second lead-ins to commercial breaks; finally it got its own ninety-second segment. There was just enough time for a joke, but the Simpsons characters were clearly established. In one segment, for instance, Marge blithely sings "Rock-a-Bye Baby" to little Maggie, who takes the words literally and imagines herself cradled in a treetop and crashing to the ground. Going to a full-length series, however, was by no means a foregone conclusion. Because animation is generally drawn by hand, it requires a lot of time and money. But an advance screening of the show impressed Fox chairman Barry Diller, and a commitment for a series was approved. After the full-length program debuted on Fox in January of 1990, it was soon one of the fifteen most-watched shows on American television—an amazing feat for a fledgling network that had yet to reach one-fifth of the country. "*The Simpsons* kept Fox in business in the early years," *Futurama* animation director Claudia Katz told writer Alex Needham for *Face*. Needham also commented about the effect *The Simpson* had on American TV culture. "In America, TV used to be so diffuse: There was no country-unifying soap, no one show watched by the whole family. *The Simpsons* had become this show." *The Simpsons* became America's longest-running sitcom.

Named one of three executive producers of *The Simpsons*, Groening aimed for quality. He wanted animation with enough depth to appeal to grown-ups, animation with characters so vivid that people would forget it was animation, and

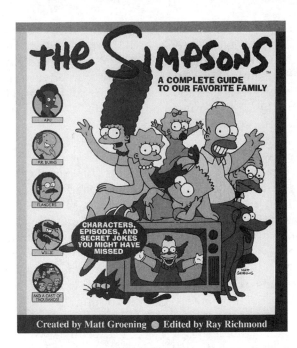

Groening wrote the introduction to this 1997 guide to the first eight seasons of *The Simpsons*.

a situation comedy that would transcend the old sitcom formula of one-liners and easy sentiment. But beyond production values—as everyone from TV critics to sociologists agreed—*The Simpsons* clicked because the audience was ready for it. The show was seen as a revolt against decades of happy family sitcoms, from *Father Knows Best* to *The Cosby Show*, which projected a world that was too good to be real. As America faced a long list of stubborn social and economic woes, many of which took a toll on family life, the "messed-up" Simpsons looked surprisingly realistic.

Like many people in the audience, the Simpsons weren't fulfilled in life; they were lucky to survive it. In one episode Homer is treated like a hero for preventing a nuclear explosion, then has to admit that he pushed the right button by accident. In another episode playground bullies menace Bart, who instead of taking the high road teams up with a local gun nut and fights dirty. When he's threatened with flunking out of fourth grade, he studies pathetically hard, and he is delighted to scrape by with a "D." And when Lisa suffers from childhood depression, an old musician teaches her how to survive by playing the blues: "The blues isn't about feeling better," he confides, "it's about making other people feel

worse." Yet despite all their flaws, bickering, and money troubles, the Simpsons still manage—just barely—to love each other. "Part of the Simpson appeal," Groening said in a *Chicago Sun-Times* article by Earnest Tucker, "is the acknowledgement that you can still love the people who drive you crazy."

The popularity of *The Simpsons* created a marketing tidal wave as fans scooped up as many as one million Simpsons products a day, including T-shirts, caps, bubble gum, boxer shorts, and a talking Bart doll. Not surprisingly, some authority figures did not find the Simpsons funny at all. Across America various principals, teachers, and child psychologists warned that Bart was providing a bad example to the young. Bart's foes included United States drug enforcement chief William Bennett, who backed off on his attack when he was forced to admit that he had never watched the show. Many blasted the notorious "Underachiever" T-shirt, which was banned from some classrooms. "If you read the T-shirt, it says, 'Bart Simpson, quote, underachiever, unquote,'" Groening commented to Dave Rhein in the *Des Moines Register*. "[Bart] has been labeled an underachiever and his response to that is that he's proud of it. He didn't call himself an underachiever. He does not aspire to be an underachiever." Besides, as the author told *Mother Jones* contributor Sean Elder, "Kids are smarter than alot of adults give them credit for. I feel sorry for authority figures who are troubled by kids having fun."

Continued success for Groening came in 1993 with the founding of the comic book company Bongo Comics Group, for which he serves as publisher. The company's first titles were *Simpsons Comics*, *Radioactive Man*, *Itchy & Scratchy*, *Bartman*, and *Krusty Comics*. During Bongo Comics' first year of publication, the company was honored with a Diamond Gem Award for best new publisher of the year and the Will Eisner Award for best short story for "The Amazing Colossal Homer." The success of Bongo Comics ultimately led to the creation of Zongo Comics in 1994.

Introduces *Futurama*

By the late 1990s, with the success of *The Simpsons*, the door was opened to many other animated shows not necessarily made for kids.

If you enjoy the works of Matt Groening, you may also want to check out the following:

King of the Hill, an animated television show on FOX, created by Mike Judge.
South Park, an animated television show on Comedy Central, created by Trey Parker and Matt Stone.

The raucous *South Park* debuted on Comedy Central and was wildly received, spinning off into a full-length film. MTV had a hit with *Beavis and Butthead,* two animated teenage losers who made rude and lewd comments over music videos, and who also starred in a feature film. Fox produced *King of the Hill,* yet another animated dysfunctional family somehow keeping it together while audiences laughed at their expense. So, based on his success with *The Simpsons,* Groening decided to indulge a long-time fantasy—he wanted to produce a science-fiction show. In 1997, he teamed up with David X. Cohen, a fellow sci-fi buff and a scriptwriter for *The Simpsons* who'd worked on *Beavis and Butthead.* The two conspired over sci-fi movies, sci-fi books by writers like Isaac Asimov and Phillip K. Dick, 1980s computer games, vintage sci-fi magazines, and old TV shows like *Lost in Space* and *Doctor Who.* What they came up with was *Futurama.*

"Matt Groening has seen the future, and, quite frankly," wrote Dan Snierson in *Entertainment Weekly,* "it looks ridiculous." A pizza delivery boy inadvertently gets frozen in 1999 and wakes up 1,000 years later. Set in the year 3000, Groening's take on the future included one-eyed and lobster-clawed aliens, jet-powered scooters, evil mega-corporations, robots and spaceships, and mobile phones implanted directly into thumbs. While Groening was inspired by sci-fi classics, *Futurama* also poked fun at them. The *Futurama* world featured Stop'n'Drop (25¢ suicide booths), coin-operated prostitutes, and a state motto of, "You gotta do what you gotta do," which means doing a state-assigned job. In Groening's year 3000, people still watched *The Simpsons.* Like *The Simpsons, Futurama* featured a host of celebrity cameo appearances, only in *Futurama,* stars like Pamela Anderson, Dennis Rodman, Leonard

Nimoy and the Beastie Boys gave voices to animated versions of their own heads, kept in jars in the "Head Museum." Its star was a lazy, lying, stealing, beer-drinking robot named Bender. "Bender gets around the censor problems. He can't be a bad role model for kids," Groening said in *Face,* "[h]e's a robot."

"The way I sold them the show," Groening said in *Face,* "was by saying,'This is *The Simpsons* in the future,' and the dollar signs danced in front of their eyes." When Fox executives saw the first episode of *Futurama,* the dollar signs stopped dancing. *Futurama,* they complained, was nothing like *The Simpsons.* "Yes it is," Groening replied. "It's new and original." There was no way Groening could outdo *The Simpsons,* Groening told Snierson. "I won't. I can't. Nothing can. I just hope every review isn't '*Futurama* is no *Simpsons.*' It's not a horse race." Despite executive worries, 19 million people watched the first episode.

More than anyone Groening was having fun. "Everybody's got a fantasy of watching television and getting annoyed with it and saying, 'Boy, if I had my own TV show, this is what I would do.' And in an extremely easy way, I have arrived at that," he told *Philadelphia Inquirer* writer Rip Rense. "We lucked out. I'm real comfortable now. I'm real lucky." He even has plans for a theme park, his answer to Disneyland. "It'd be great!" he told *Face,* "You'd have Simpsons island with a 600ft statue of Homer. They'd sell donuts and beer in his head." As happy as anyone who lives in hell can expect to be, Groening and Caplan remodeled their house near the ocean and began raising their children. He remains friends with Lynda Barry, and in many papers their comic strips run side by side. And, most of all, he has learned the true meaning of success. "It means," he told Earnest Tucker, "that people who used to beat me up in high school call me up and want to be friends."

■ Works Cited

Elder, Sean, "The Rehabilitation of Bart Simpson," *Mother Jones,* January, 1991, p. 13.
Foote, Jennifer, "A Doodle God Makes Good," *Newsweek,* September 28, 1987, pp. 70-71.
Groening, Matt, *The Big Book of Hell,* Pantheon, 1990.

Hamilton, Tish, "Rabbit Punch," *Rolling Stone,* September 22, 1988, p. 81.

Harrington, Richard, "Drawing on the Humor in Life's Little Horrors," *Washington Post,* December 18, 1988.

Kaufman, Joanne, *"Life in Hell's* Matt Groening Goes Overboard to Make *The Simpsons* the First Family of TV 'Toons," *People,* December 18, 1989, p. 108.

Krier, Beth Ann, "An Alternative Cartoonist Who Draws the Line," *Los Angeles Times,* August 23, 1987.

Morgenstern, Joe, "Bart Simpson's Real Father," *Los Angeles Times,* April 29, 1990.

Needham, Alex, "Nice Planet . . . We'll Take It!", *Face,* October, 1999, pp. 70-78, 209.

Oricchio, Michael, "Hell Ain't So Bad," *San Jose Mercury News,* November 8, 1988.

Rense, Rip, "The American Family (Cartoon-Style)," *Philadelphia Inquirer,* February 11, 1990.

Rhein, Dave, "Bart's Philosophy Concerns Some Teachers," *Des Moines Register,* August 26, 1990.

Rhodes, Joe, "The Making of 'The Simpsons,'" *Entertainment Weekly,* May 18, 1990, p. 36.

Snierson, Dan, "Space Case," *Entertainment Weekly,* March 26, 1999, p. 46.

Solomon, Charles, review of *Love Is Hell, Los Angeles Times Book Review,* June 29, 1986, p. 2.

Sullivan, Jim, "Animation's Answer to the Bundys," *Boston Globe,* January 14, 1990.

Tucker, Ernest, "Success of 'Simpsons' Overwhelms Creator," *Chicago Sun-Times,* April 15, 1990.

Tucker, Ken, review of *The Simpsons, Entertainment Weekly,* May 18, 1990, p. 43.

■ For More Information See

PERIODICALS

American Film, October, 1989, p. 112.
Animation, fall, 1989, p. 22.
Entertainment Weekly, May 18, 1990, p. 36; February 21, 1992, p. 9; August 7, 1992, p. 70; March 12, 1993, p. 48; May 28, 1993, p. 73; December 9, 1994, p. 68; April 2, 1999, p. 73.
Esquire, July 1999, p. 32.
Los Angeles Times, February 23, 1990.
Los Angeles Times Book Review, December 1, 1991; June 6, 1993, p. 15.
Mother Jones, December, 1989, p. 28; March, 1999, p. 34.
Newsweek, December 25, 1989, p. 70; April 23, 1990, pp. 58, 64; March 29, 1999, pp. 70-71.
New York Times, February 21, 1990; July 14, 1991.
People, October 30, 1995, p. 17.
Publishers Weekly, August 10, 1992, p. 72; September 14, 1992, p. 127.
Rolling Stone, June 28, 1990, p. 40.
San Francisco Examiner, November 16, 1988; January 21, 1990.
School Library Journal, September, 1991, p. 298.
Village Voice, February 2, 1988.
Washington Post Book World, September 22, 1991.

ON-LINE

Futurama Web site, located at http://www.fox.com/futurama/index.html (October 29, 1999).
The Simpsons Web site, located at http://www.foxworld.com/simpsons/simpsons.htm (October 29, 1999).

Thomas Harris

■ Personal

Born c. 1940 in Jackson, TN (some sources say Jackson, MS); son of William Thomas (an electrical engineer and farmer) and Polly (a high-school teacher) Harris; children: Anne. *Education:* Baylor University, B.A., 1964.

■ Career

Worked as a reporter for the Waco *News-Tribune; Associated Press,* New York City, general assignment reporter and night editor, 1968-74; freelance writer, 1968—.

■ Writings

Black Sunday, Putnam, 1975.
Red Dragon, Putnam, 1981, published as *Manhunter,* Bantam, 1986.
The Silence of the Lambs, St. Martin's, 1988.
Hannibal, Delacorte, 1999.

■ Adaptations

Black Sunday was filmed by John Frankenheimer for Paramount, 1977; *Red Dragon* was filmed as *Manhunter* by Michael Mann for De Laurentiis Entertainment Group, 1986; *The Silence of the Lambs* was filmed by Jonathan Demme for Orion, 1991.

■ Sidelights

Described by those close to him as a Southern gentleman with a knack for whipping up gourmet meals and entertaining friends with good conversation packed with trivia tidbits, Thomas Harris might be regarded as too nice to dream up a character as frightening as Dr. Hannibal "the Cannibal" Lecter. Harris's imagination brought readers a villain capable of committing some of the most gruesome deeds portrayed in fiction. Stephen King dubbed Harris's Hannibal as "the great fictional monster of our time" in a *New York Times* book review of *Hannibal,* Harris's long-anticipated third novel starring the cannibal with good diction, learning, and etiquette.

Harris's years as a crime reporter in Waco, Texas, and New York City perhaps formed an integral part of his ability to imagine horror as he experienced and communicated stories of evil permeating in real life. Perhaps professional circumstances forced him to analyze and evaluate the roots and extremes of

FROM THE AUTHOR OF HANNIBAL AND THE SILENCE OF THE LAMBS

THOMAS HARRIS

"Frighteningly believable." —*Chicago Tribune*

BLACK SUNDAY

THE *NEW YORK TIMES* BESTSELLER

International terrorists plot to bomb the Super Bowl and kill the President of the United States in this 1975 thriller.

evil in humans. Since Harris has a blanket policy of not giving interviews, reviewers and fans can only guess about what he draws from in creating allusions of evil and judgments regarding what spawns it and drives it. To individuals inquiring about the motivation for his work, Harris points to the work itself, maintaining that it should speak for itself.

Harris was born in Jackson, Tennessee (some sources say Mississippi), in 1940. His father, William Thomas Harris, Jr., was an electrical engineer, and his mother, Polly, was a high school science teacher. When his father decided to take up farm-

ing for a living, Thomas moved with his family as a small child to Rich, Mississippi, where he spent the rest of his youth. Harris's mother described him as a gentle boy who had a voracious appetite for reading and learning. Harris pursued his enjoyment of the written word in college as an English major in college, graduating with a bachelor's degree from Baylor University in 1964. While in college, he married a Baylor co-ed, with whom he had a daughter, Anne, in 1962. Although his marriage did not make it into the 1970s, he maintained a closeness with his daughter, who went to work in publishing as an adult. During his studies, Harris took a job at the Waco *News-Tribune* covering crime reports. A major story Harris covered was a criminal investigation into a child prostitution ring in Mexico. Several of the children were murdered. According to a Waco *News* colleague and college friend, interviewed by Phoebe Hoban from *New York,* Harris was extremely meticulous in his research and thorough in his description of the events and investigation surrounding them. Harris also dabbled in writing for magazines during that period, enjoyed the writings of Thomas Wolfe, and covered his beat on his motorcycle.

After earning his degree, Harris spent some time traveling in Europe before settling in a position with the *Associated Press* in New York, where he worked as a general-assignment reporter and night editor from 1968 to 1974. Harris still moved around by motorcycle in New York and enjoyed having a beer with friends from *AP* at Tweeds, Teacher's, and the Lions Head. Harris and *AP* colleagues, Sam Maull and Dick Riley, decided to tap from their experiences as journalists and think of a clever plot for a novel. The result was Harris's 1975 thriller *Black Sunday.* The advance from Harris's publisher Putnam was split among the three men. Harris quit journalism and devoted his professional life to writing suspense novels.

In *Black Sunday* a Vietnam veteran-gone-bad plots to destroy an American football stadium with 80,000 spectators, among them the President of the United States, on Super Bowl Sunday. He appeals to the Palestinian terrorist group known as Black September to obtain explosives, which he plans to launch from the Goodyear Blimp. The American sociopath, named Lander, successfully hijacks and pilots the blimp over the stadium with a crew of Palestinian terrorists on board. Israeli Secret Service agent Major Kabakov is the man at the center of the team of

FBI and Israeli agents set into motion to stop the terrorists. The novel grapples with the question of whether madness is born of violence. The interplay between the Palestinian terrorists and the American veteran is not only critical to the plot's terrorist mission and outcome, but also to the theme of the novel, which examines psychological motivations for acts of terror committed against humanity.

Introducing Dr. Hannibal Lecter

Harris' second novel, *Red Dragon* (1981), introduced readers to one of the most memorable and disturbing characters ever to appear in popular literature, Dr. Hannibal Lecter. Many critics have compared Hannibal's impact on late twentieth-century American popular culture with the effect Frankenstein's monster and Dracula had in earlier times. The difference between Hannibal and the supernatural monsters of horror-show fame is as simple as it is terrifying: Hannibal Lecter is all too human. Indeed, according to *Entertainment Weekly*, Harris told Thomas McCormack, his editor at St. Martin's, which published Harris second novel starring Hannibal, *The Silence of the Lambs*, that "I can't write it until I believe it." McCormick admitted, "For most writers this would be an unexceptional remark, but considering the book Tom was talking about . . ." Considering the character of Hannibal, it would be disturbing to think that reality could potentially give rise to a human capable of the degree of wickedness and horror that Hannibal Lecter is.

The complexity of the Hannibal character makes him engrossing to the reader and engaging to his co-characters. He is thought-provoking, and a point of departure for discussions about the nature of evil and the motivation necessary to carry it out. The fact that Hannibal only cannibalizes individuals he perceives as rude—what he calls "free-range rude"—may hauntingly even endear him to readers (or viewers of films based on Harris's books) in a eerie way. Stephen King wrote of Harris's grip over audiences via Hannibal in the *New York Times Book Review*, "In a late-century literary landscape where most psycho-villains are little fellows in rubber masks, armed with knives and burdened with cumbersome sexual kinks, Dr. Lecter casts a long shadow indeed." Reviewing Harris's third novel, *Hannibal,* King stated in the same article, "*Hannibal* is a balloon Harris bats steadily onward, probably with a grin on his face. The balloon happens to be full of poison gas and bad dreams, true, but . . . Harris is not writing for everyone." Harris's Hannibal novels would probably not be described as gratuitous horror, however. In other words, many readers and viewers intrigued by the complexities of Hannibal are not the same folks among the loyal flock of fans at Freddy Krueger movies. Hannibal's entertainment value and effect on culture is more cerebral than merely thrill-based. Harris's prose, which is clinical and thorough, could be regarded as fascinating by those who value detail and trivia and tedious and dull by those abhorring such chronicling in entertainment-oriented works.

MEET HANNIBAL LECTER FOR THE VERY FIRST TIME
FROM THE AUTHOR OF HANNIBAL AND THE SILENCE OF THE LAMBS
THOMAS HARRIS
RED DRAGON
THE *NEW YORK TIMES* BESTSELLER

In his second novel, Harris introduced readers to Dr. Hannibal Lecter.

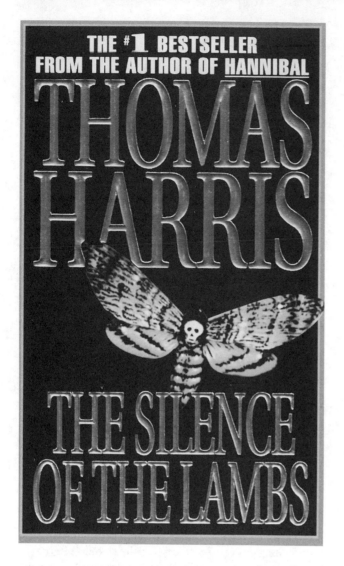

THE #**1** BESTSELLER
FROM THE AUTHOR OF HANNIBAL

THOMAS HARRIS

THE SILENCE OF THE LAMBS

The gruesome, cannibalistic Hannibal Lecter, a former psychiatrist, helps FBI Agent-in-training Clarice Starling capture a serial killer in this famous 1988 thriller.

Dr. Hannibal Lecter first appears in *Red Dragon* to offer clues to investigator Will Graham, who is assigned to solve the murders of two families. Concluding that the slayings are the work of a serial killer, Graham consults with the imprisoned serial killer/cannibal to get at the mindset of serial killers so that he may narrow in on clues more easily. Graham's interaction with Hannibal, a former prominent psychiatrist before he was caught by Graham and locked away, leads Graham to face his own inner demons and to recognize his own propensity for evil. The killer he must hunt down, called the "tooth fairy" by the

FBI, is Francis Dolarhyde, a delusional, psychotic man with a cleft palate who as a child was abandoned and raised by an abusive grandmother. He believes that he will be transformed into the Red Dragon of the Apocalypse if he slays families. During his murderous rampage, Dolarhyde becomes romantically involved with a blind woman and is, in his mind, egged on to murder her by the spirit of his dead grandmother, whom he imagines as speaking to him. The blind woman's perilous love for Dolarhyde is integral to the thrill and suspense of the plot, while Hannibal's insight into the essence of evil and his instruction to Graham about how to capture a serial killer adds psychological and philosophical depth to the novel as a whole.

Hannibal reprises his disturbing role as mentor in Harris's third novel, *The Silence of the Lambs* (1988). This time his protege is Clarice Starling, a student at the FBI training academy assigned to conduct a psychological evaluation of Dr. Hannibal Lecter. Despite horrifying accounts of Hannibal's behavior—including an incident where he chewed off and swallowed the tongue of a nurse attempting to give him an electrocardiogram—Starling treats Hannibal with common courtesy when she first finds him in his cell reading an Italian magazine. He baits her with an opportunity for her to learn about what makes a serial killer tick. In return, but in advance of his instruction, he wants to delve into her psyche. He wrestles out of her an account of her most traumatic life experience: while staying on a relative's farm as a child she heard the screams of spring lambs being slain.

As Starling's interplay with Hannibal develops and matures into a strange, mutually respectful relationship, Hannibal offers her clues that set her on the trail of a serial killer known as Buffalo Bill. Later revealed as Jame Gumb, Buffalo Bill preys on overweight women, whom he skins alive. Having lived a troubled childhood, Gumb developed a curious sexual disorder that put him on a quest to create a "women's suit" from women's skin. His last potential victim is the missing daughter of a United States Senator. Starling, with Hannibal's assistance, is on a mission to save her. Hannibal's motivation in helping Starling can be rationalized differently by Harris's readers. Whether Hannibal sincerely liked Starling or that he only sought to increase her vulnerability to him is an open question. What is clear is that Hannibal is a character with a deep and vast intellect and a complex persona.

Books Hit the Big Screen

Both *Red Dragon* and *Silence of the Lambs* were scripted for film adaptations. The former was directed by Michael Mann and released in 1986 as *Manhunter,* but failed to draw a satisfactory appeal among audiences at the box office. Reportedly, through comments made by Harris's uncle in various articles about his nephew, Harris was not pleased with the film adaptation of his novel either. Harris and the viewing public, however, were impressed with the film version of *Silence of the Lambs.* Directed by Jonathan Demme and starring Jodie Foster as Clarice and Anthony Hopkins as Hannibal, the film won five Oscars.

The great success of the movie also boosted sales of copies of the novel, as well as its print predecessor, *Red Dragon.*

Hannibal, the sequel to *Silence of the Lambs,* was contracted as part of a two-book deal worth $5.2 million. *Hannibal* was initially expected to be in possession of the publisher, Delacorte, a few years earlier than its March of 1999 manuscript delivery date. Delacorte quickly got the manuscript to press and released it in June of 1999, with an initial printing of 1.2 million copies. Harris opposition to editorial alterations of his content, perhaps, assisted in hastening the process to publication.

The story begins with updates on the lives of both Clarice and Hannibal, the former struggling as an FBI agent and the latter living a life of

Jodie Foster as Clarice Starling and Anthony Hopkins as Hannibal Lecter in the 1991 film version of *Silence of the Lambs,* which received five Academy Awards, including Best Actor for Hopkins, Best Actress for Foster, and Best Picture.

haute culture in Italy. A survivor of one of Hannibal's escapades of torture, Mason Verger, who is dependant on a respirator and who must cope with the torment of living without a face, is on Hannibal's trail and much closer to nailing him than the FBI, who has been searching for him since his escape from detention seven years ago. Verger, who had been abducted, drugged, and hideously maimed by Hannibal years earlier, is the wealthy heir to his family's meatpacking business. Obsessed with revenge, Verger secretly offers underground thugs three million dollars for Hannibal's seizure. His aim is to put Hannibal through a torturous bout of having his flesh eaten alive by vicious trained pigs.Verger hopes to be entertained by Hannibal's agony as an onlooker, for this would be poetic justice in his view. As wicked and dangerous as Hannibal seems to readers, Verger, a former hench-

Hannibal Lecter and Clarice Starling return in this much-anticipated 1999 novel.

If you enjoy the works of Thomas Harris, you may also want to check out the following books:

Jeffrey Wilds Deaver, *The Bone Collector*, 1997.
Joyce Carol Oates, *Zombie*, 1995.
Tom Clancy, *The Sum of All Fears*, 1991.

man of Idi Amin and a child molester, is most likely perceived as even more thoroughly evil. Moreover, Harris draws readers into Hannibal's weakness, passion, and prime source for his emotional dysfunction and angst: his memory of his beloved sister, who as a child, was murdered and cannibalized. Hannibal's grief over his sister and his relationship with Clarice, which intensifies and is integral to the movement of the plot, causes readers to perhaps think of Hannibal as at best emotionally scarred and tormented and at worst not quite a manifestation of pure evil. Certainly readers can be expected to be perplexed by Hannibal.

A movie deal for *Hannibal* was in the early stages of negotiations even before the book hit bookstores, partly in the form of a dispute over who controlled the movie rights—MGM, who bought Orion, the studio that made *Silence of the Lambs,* or Universal, who cited a deal with producer Dino De Laurentiis to share his negotiation rights over the film. Jonathan Demme turned down opportunity to direct the film. At about the same time the book was reaching the public, De Laurentiis was making offers to Hopkins and Foster to star, respectively, as Hannibal and Clarice again. After paying for Oscar-winning talent to make another box-office success like *Silence of the Lambs,* the budget for *Hannibal* could reach $100 million, according Corie Brown of *Newsweek.*

As to what many reviewers noted as a more intensive look into evil's ultimate brutality, grotesqueness, and injustice, writer Paul Gray of *Time,* opined "*Hannibal* displays a disquieting streak of sadism that Harris' two previous novels involving Lecter largely avoided." Indeed Harris himself stressed in an aside within the novel's text, "Now that ceaseless exposure has calloused us to the lewd and the vulgar, it is instructive to see what still seems wicked to us."

Readers may wonder if these words equal a challenge to other authors or to himself to delve even further into the vile unthinkable.

Harris lives with his girlfriend, Pace Barnes, and his pets in the Hamptons' Sag Harbor and Miami's artsy district. Friends of Harris's maintain that, although he may not speak with the press, he is not a recluse. He responds to fan mail and poses for photos. A talented gourmet cook, he enjoys having friends for dinner—well, certainly not in the same sense that Dr. Hannibal Lecter may dine with "friends."

■ Works Cited

Gray, Paul, "Dessert, Anyone?", *Time*, June 21, 1999, p. 72.

Review of *Hannibal*, *Entertainment Weekly*, May 7, 1999, p. 22.

Hoban, Phoebe, "The Silence of the Writer," *New York*, April 15, 1991, pp. 48-50.

King, Stephen, "Hannibal the Cannibal," *New York Times Book Review*, June 13, 1999, p. 4.

■ For More Information See

BOOKS

Contemporary Popular Writers, St. James Press, 1997.

St. James Guide to Horror, Ghost and Gothic Writers, St. James Press, 1998.

PERIODICALS

Best Sellers, March 1, 1975, p. 525.

Booklist, February 1, 1975, p. 544; October 1, 1981, p. 138.

Entertainment Weekly, June 26, 1992, p. 58; May 7, 1999; June 25, 1999, p. 123.

Library Journal, April 1, 1975, p. 693; November 1, 1981, p. 2153.

Los Angeles Times Book Review, July 7, 1988, pp. 8, 12.

Newsweek, November 9, 1981; June 7, 1999, pp. 72-73.

New York Times, August 15, 1988, p. C16; March 25, 1990.

New York Times Book Review, February 2, 1975, p. 14; November 15, 1981, p. 14.

People, July 12, 1999.

Publishers Weekly, November 4, 1974, pp. 62-63; September 25, 1981, p. 76; June 14, 1999, p. 46; July 12, 1999, p. 45.

Saturday Review, November, 1981.

Time, May 26, 1975, pp. 81-82.

Times (London), May 25, 1991.

Tribune Books (Chicago), August 14, 1988, p. 7.

Washington Post Book World, August 21, 1988; May 21, 1989, p. 12.

—Sketch by Melissa Walsh Doig

Sheila Solomon Klass

■ Personal

Born November 6, 1927, in Brooklyn, NY; daughter of Abraham Louis (a presser) and Virginia (Glatter) Solomon; married Morton Klass (a professor of anthropology), May 2, 1953; children: Perri Elizabeth, David Arnold, Judith Alexandra. *Education:* Brooklyn College (now Brooklyn College of the City University of New York), B.A., 1949; University of Iowa, M.A., 1951, M.F.A., 1953. *Religion:* Jewish.

■ Addresses

Home—900 West 190th St., Apt. 2-0, New York, NY 10040. *Office*—Department of English, Manhattan Community College of the City University of New York, 199 Chambers St., New York, NY 10007. *Agent*—Ruth Cohen, P.O. Box 7626, Menlo Park, CA 94025.

■ Career

Writer, 1960—. Worked as an aide in a psychopathic hospital in Iowa City, IA, 1949-51; Julia Ward Howe Junior High School, New York City,

English teacher, 1951-57; Manhattan Community College of the City University of New York, began as an assistant professor, currently professor of English, 1965—. Guest at Yaddo colony, 1974. *Member:* International PEN.

■ Awards, Honors

Bicentennial Prize, Leonia Drama Guild, 1976, for one-act play, *Otherwise It Only Makes One Hundred Ninety-Nine;* New Jersey Institute of Technology children's literature award, 1983, for *Alive and Starting Over,* and 1988, for *The Bennington Stitch.*

■ Writings

FOR YOUNG ADULTS

To See My Mother Dance, Scribner, 1981.
Alive and Starting Over, Scribner, 1983.
The Bennington Stitch, Scribner, 1985.
Page Four, Scribner, 1986.
Credit-Card Carole, Scribner, 1987.
Rhino, Scholastic, 1993.
Next Stop: Nowhere, Scholastic, 1995.

FOR MIDDLE GRADE READERS

Nobody Knows Me in Miami, Scribner, 1981.
Kool Ada, Scholastic, 1991.
A Shooting Star: A Novel about Annie Oakley, Holiday House, 1996.
The Uncivil War, Holiday House, 1997.

FOR ADULTS

Come Back on Monday, Abelard-Schuman, 1960.
Everyone in This House Makes Babies, Doubleday, 1964.
Bahadur Means Hero, Gambit, 1969.
A Perpetual Surprise, Apple-Wood, 1991.
In a Cold Open Field, Black Heron, 1997.

Also author of one-act play, *Otherwise It Only Makes One Hundred Ninety-Nine.* Contributor of short stories and humorous articles to *Ms., Hadassah, Bergen Record, New York Times, Manhattan Mind,* and other publications.

■ Work in Progress

Louey in Paradise, a young adult novel about "one strange summer" in the life of author Louisa May Alcott.

■ Sidelights

Sheila Solomon Klass writes novels for middle readers and young adults that are largely character-driven, and which are often told in the first person. Usually domestic in setting, Klass's books speak of family relations—of learning to cope with inflated parental expectations, or of dealing with a new stepmother or a distant, noncustodial parent. Loosely labeled 'problem novels', such books as *To See My Mother Dance, The Bennington Stitch, Alive and Starting Over,* and *Next Stop: Nowhere* often feature youthful female narrators whose distinctive voices Klass manages to capture on paper. Klass writes of issues central to adolescents: self-image and self-worth, abandonment, death of a parent, friendship values, and the moral costs of materialism. A more recent departure in her fiction has been historical novels about Annie Oakley and Louisa May Alcott. In these books, as in her other works, Klass manages to reproduce the unique voice of her female protagonist, and it is this voice and the development of character that are at the heart of a Klass novel.

As Klass once stated, "My life and what happens around me, what I hear about and read about—these are the sources that initiate the act of writing. But almost immediately, imagination takes over and the story acquires its own energy and direction. What *really* happened is not pertinent.

It's forgotten. Fiction is not autobiography. It is experience transmuted by the imagination in inexplicable ways. It has its own truth and its own life." It is this transmutation that makes Klass's novels come to life, and her years of experience of not only writing but also teaching writing come to play in all her books.

Klass was an early writer. She once declared, "I've been a writer since adolescence. I write because writing is a supreme pleasure." Born in 1927, she was the second of three children born to Orthodox Jewish parents in New York City who struggled financially for much of their life. Her father, Abraham Solomon, was a Hungarian immigrant who worked in Manhattan's garment district as a clothes presser, one of the industry's lowest-paying jobs. From her mother Klass inherited a love of reading. "Her books had a special place on bookshelves wherever we lived, no matter how run down the apartment," Klass wrote in *Something About the Author Autobiography Series.*

The Solomon family lived in the Williamsburg section of Brooklyn, and at times during the tough years of the Great Depression, their situation was so precarious that they had to apply for Home Relief, a localized welfare program of the era. During the winter months, their apartment was warmed by a single kerosene heater, the fuel for which Klass's mother deemed a luxury, so she often spent time reading in warmth at the local library. Tension and worries over finances were a constant feature of Klass's home life—especially since her mother hailed from a family of far more assimilated Jews, who looked down upon Regina Solomon for marrying an immigrant who seemed unable to support his family. This situation provided the inspiration for Klass's first book for children, *Nobody Knows Me in Miami,* published in 1981.

With this novel, Klass established the basic formula she would continue to work with throughout her writing career: a young female protagonist learns basic values about family and friendships by making difficult decisions. Set in Brooklyn in 1937, *Nobody Knows Me in Miami* features ten-year-old Miriam, who is faced with a choice between staying with her poor family and assuming a richer material life with relatives in Miami. Uncle Mac and Aunt Lili (they were once simply Max and Lily) want to take Miriam—whom they call Mimi, as "it's more American"—back with

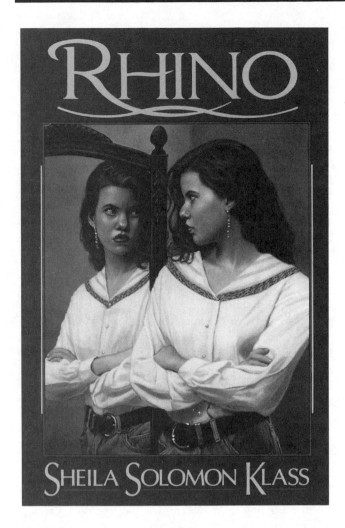

SHEILA SOLOMON KLASS

In this 1993 work, Annie learns an important lesson when she attempts to convince those closest to her that she needs a nose job.

them to Florida as their adopted daughter. At first this looks pretty good to Miriam, whose family is poor and who is tormented in her school. Eventually, however, Miriam sees her aunt for the snob she is, and opts to stay with her close-knit Jewish family that is not ashamed of its ethnic roots. As a critic in *Bulletin of the Center for Children's Books* stated, "Miriam decides to stay in Brooklyn, a rich little poor girl. . . . [The novel] has a convincing first-person style and some flavorful dialogue." A contributor in *Kirkus Reviews*, while noting the obvious snobbishness of Aunt Lili, also concluded that "this is a full enough story so that children who are inclined toward such ethnic nostalgia and old-timey values will take to Miriam, her loving family, and her clearly projected Brooklyn neighbors."

Blazing Her Own Path

As an adolescent, Klass began to find satisfaction not just in reading, but in writing as well. She was even named editor of her school magazine's graduation issue in the eighth grade. "So I felt very early the bliss that comes from making up an original story which others read and enjoy, no matter where it is printed or how few readers there are," Klass wrote in *Something About the Author Autobiography Series*. The public high schools in New York of the 1940s offered students a choice of either a college-preparatory course, or a commercial one that stressed bookkeeping and secretarial skills. Klass chose the academic one, against her parents' vehement wishes.

During her teen years, Klass baby-sat and took summer jobs for income, though she was still an avid reader and burgeoning writer. Secondhand clothes were the bane of Klass's youth: "My high school yearbook picture still makes me cringe," she wrote in *Something About the Author Autobiography Series*, "as editor on the frontispiece, I am wearing someone's discarded housedress." The Solomons lived in just a three-room apartment, and she often did her homework in the bathroom, the only relatively quiet spot in the house. When she learned that Brooklyn College administered an entrance exam for enrollment at this government-subsidized, tuition-free institution, she was ecstatic. Her parents, however, objected strenuously, urging her to instead find a job after receiving her high school diploma and begin to contribute to income to the household. As she wrote in *Something About the Author Autobiography Series*, her parents felt that college was a waste of time for a female, telling her that she "was too smart already. I had a big mouth. No man would ever marry me. Men did not like smart women."

Klass passed the Brooklyn College entrance exam, and moved out of her parents' home. She traded room and board for a live-in baby-sitting job for a kindly, well-to-do family in Flatbush, and lived in their attic for four years. She continued to write during college, finding success once more on the staff of the campus newspaper, and graduated with a degree and teaching credentials. After a brief stint as a secretary—a job at which she was admittedly inept—she and a friend from Brooklyn College applied, and were both accepted, into the University of Iowa M.F.A. program for writing, a great achievement.

A SHOOTING STAR

A Novel about Annie Oakley

Sheila Solomon Klass

Klass's first historical novel deals with the world's best sharpshooter at the end of the nineteenth century.

Klass finished her first year in Iowa with academic honors, but her seventeen-year-old brother—who had lied about his age to join the United States Army to escape the poverty and strife at home in Brooklyn—was declared missing in action during the first months of the Korean War in 1950. Klass's older sister, worried about their mother's odd behavior the following summer, summoned her back to New York. There, Klass learned that her mother had been giving her precious meager savings away to a fortune-teller who promised to return her son home safely "by burning her 'dirty money,' her life's savings," Klass wrote in *Something About the Author Autobiography Series*, "the pitiful few thousand dollars she had scrimped and struggled to save so she would never again have to be on Relief." This tragic in-

cident became the basis for Klass's 1997 novel for adults, *In a Cold Open Field*. She had actually written the manuscript in the 1950s, but even after numerous revisions publishers rejected it forty-five times.

Klass eventually earned two degrees from the University of Iowa, and began teaching at a junior high school in Harlem. She married editor and writer Mort Klass in 1953, the same year her collection of short fiction was published, *The Village Harlot and Other Stories*. Her husband's first job was at a progressive liberal arts school in Vermont, Bennington College, which later gave Klass gave her the idea behind the plot of her 1985 novel for young adults, *The Bennington Stitch*. By this time she had written both *To See My Mother Dance*, published in 1981, and *Alive and Starting Over*, which followed two year later.

Strong Female Protagonists

These last two works both featured Jessica Van Norden. In *To See My Mother Dance*, Klass deals with issues of abandonment by a parent and the acceptance of a stepparent. Jess is thirteen years old and resents her new stepmother, Martha. She dreams of seeing her mother again—the woman who abandoned her when she was one year old to pursue her own dreams of becoming a professional dancer. Martha, however, is not to be put off by her stepdaughter and locates Karen, the absent mother, in a religious commune in San Francisco. The subsequent visit with the burnt-out, abstracted Karen is enough to make Jess lose any illusions she may have had about her mother and ultimately brings her closer to Martha who wants the new family to work. A *Publishers Weekly* critic felt that "Klass captures the flippant, disdainful levity typical of wounded young adolescents" in Jess's speech, while *Booklist*'s Ilene Cooper concluded "the book is well crafted and has sufficient character and plot appeal for a junior high audience." A reviewer in the *Bulletin of the Center for Children's Books* felt that the book was "sad" rather than tragic, and "the story [is] strong in its characters, relationships, and dialogue." The award-winning *Alive and Starting Over* picks up Jess's story a couple of years later when a mysterious new boy at school, an illness in her family, and the loss of a friend bring both unsettling and challenging changes into her life. Diane Gersoni Edelman, writing in the *New York Times Book Re-*

view, noted that the premise of the book was "that it's . . . never too late to take your life in hand, to make constructive changes, to come to terms with circumstances not likely to change. . . . What readers will like best about this book is its message of realistic hope. It's palatably inspirational and upbeat without being saccharine."

The Bennington Stitch, Klass's award-winning 1985 novel for young adults, is cleverly named after the college which Amy's mother wants her to attend and the handicraft for which Amy seems better suited than an academic career. Low SAT scores make it virtually impossible for Amy to attend Bennington, and she does not want to anyway. Instead, she apprentices with a skilled quilt-maker while her mother achieves the dream of Bennington herself. Amy's situation is echoed in a subplot involving her boyfriend Rob, who wants to go to art school instead of medical school as his doctor father wishes. "This is ably written," commented a reviewer in the *Bulletin of the Center for Children's Books,* "has believable characters, and should appeal to readers who are facing the terrors of PSAT and SAT." Writing in the *New York Times Book Review,* Meg Wolitzer observed that in spite of some flaws in the work, "it is still rewarding to read a novel about young adults who have minds and ambitions of their own, and whose lives extend beyond the parameters of their families."

Another novel with a subtext of college application is *Page Four,* which takes its title from the fourth page of college application forms in which the applicant writes a personal essay. The novel also deals with a recurring theme in Klass' novels of an absent parent, in this case Dave's father who has run off to Alaska with a new wife, leaving behind a mother "paralyzed by her husband's sudden desertion," according to Roger Sutton in the *Bulletin of the Center for Children's Books.* Sutton went on to note that the "first-person, present-tense narrative . . . is nicely balanced between Dave's hurt at what his father has done and his attempts to move on. . . ." In *Credit-Card Carole,* a father once again initiates changes in a child's life; in this case not by running away but by making a career move from successful dentist to aspiring actor. The subsequent loss of income makes the daughter, Carole, change her shopping ways and learn "about real values through the experiences of good friends and her parents' struggle to realize a dream," according to a *Pub-*

lishers Weekly contributor. That same reviewer concluded that the book was a "meaty story about likable people" and that it was "fun to applaud [the parents'] small victory and Carole as she grows from a mall groupie into a person." Bonnie L. Raasch, writing in *School Library Journal,* noted that dialogue in the book was "realistic, and so are the characters." Betsy Hearne concluded in *Bulletin of the Center for Children's Books* that "this is a light-hearted book despite the weighty theme."

Troubles in suburbia are left behind with Klass's next work, *Kool Ada,* about the difficulties of adjustment after the loss of one's family. Eleven-year-old Ada adjusts initially by becoming silent. As Ada says to herself in the book: "I took shelter

An overweight girl struggles with her mother's attempts to overfeed her in this 1997 work.

in the cave of my mind where it is warm and safe. I just sat and sucked my thumb and bit my cuticles until they bled. I stopped talking and I lived back inside my head where I was a little bit protected." Sent to live with an aunt in Chicago after the death of her entire family, her one means of communication with new schoolmates is her feisty nature and ready fists. Ada, however, slowly comes out of her self-imposed shell through the intervention of an understanding teacher, neighbors, and her aunt. Katherine Bruner in *School Library Journal* thought the book was "Simple, but effective," and Frances Bradburn in the *Wilson Library Bulletin* observed that the "portrait Klass paints of Ada is a classic one. . . . Ada is a lovable, gutsy kid, one worthy of the special attention she receives. . . ."

With *Rhino,* Klass tackled a seemingly much less vital theme, that of self-image and cosmetic surgery. Yet Klass imbued this story with more than skin-deep detail. "This could be a shallow book, but it's not," noted Deborah Stevenson in the *Bulletin of the Center for Children's Books.* "Klass takes on images of self-worth and cosmetic adjustments honestly," Stevenson went on to observe, making Annie's quest for a nose job, or rhinoplasty, represent a process of growth and acceptance of change. In *Next Stop: Nowhere,* Klass returned to the theme of an absent parent, when fourteen-year-old Beth is sent by her wealthy mother to live with her divorced father in Vermont. The theme of materialism versus deeper values comes to play when Beth slowly learns to respect her ceramist father's less lavish style of life. A *Publishers Weekly* reviewer commented that "Beth's first-person narration contains insightful gems," while *Booklist's* Jeanne Triner noted that this "is a light, humorous story with a sweet romantic subplot." Susan Ackler in *Voice of Youth Advocates* concluded that "The warm cast of characters longs for another appearance, so I hope there is a sequel where we find out how Beth grows up."

Pens Fictional Biographies

Instead of a sequel, however, Klass made an abrupt departure with her next novel, *A Shooting Star.* As Klass once remarked, "I have become interested in writing novels based on the lives of real people—historical novels. I wrote *A Shooting Star* about the childhood of Annie Oakley, the best

---

If you enjoy the works of Sheila Solomon Klass, you may also want to check out the following books:

Lila Perl, *Fat Glenda Turns Fourteen,* 1991.
Sherry Garland, *The Last Rainmaker,* 1997.
Claudia Mills, *After Fifth Grade, the World!,* 1989.

---

sharpshooter in the world at the end of the nineteenth century, and I had such a good time doing that research that I went on to do a book about one strange summer in the life of Louisa May Alcott, the author of *Little Women.* That book, *Louey in Paradise,* is still in manuscript, but will be published soon."

The genesis of her first fictional biography of a real-life figure, *A Shooting Star: A Novel about Annie Oakley,* occurred one day when she heard a radio program about the celebrity riflewoman. Klass learned that Oakley, whose father had died when she was a very young girl, grew up in dire poverty on the Ohio prairie; one day, too hungry to consider the ramifications, she took his rifle down from the wall, went outside, and shot a rabbit for dinner. She was just eight years old. "Since I hate guns and anything to do with shooting, I'm not sure why Annie Oakley's life fascinated me so," Klass wrote in *Something About the Author Autobiography Series.* "Was it because I, too, grew up in a poor home?"

Reviewers responded warmly to Klass's story of Annie Oakley. A *Kirkus Reviews* critic dubbed it a "fast-moving first-person narration" with an "inventive plot . . . and a great happy ending." A contributor in *Publishers Weekly* noted that "Klass's portrayal of Oakley's courageous individualism makes this tale hit the mark," and Roger Sutton, writing in *Horn Book,* observed that "Annie Oakley shoots straight from the page in this fictionalized biography," and that "the real triumph of the book is its sure assumption of Annie Oakley's narrative voice. . . ."

Sandwiched between *A Shooting Star* and *Louey in Paradise,* Klass's *The Uncivil War* brings twelve-year-old Asa to do battle with her overprotective mother. The conflict rises when Asa's mother keeps trying to overfeed Asa, who is overweight and wants to lose some pounds. A cute new boy in class compounds her frustration when he calls her "Fatso." A writer in *Publishers Weekly* called the novel a "down-to-earth narrative" but noted that eating "smart" is more difficult for young people than the story suggests. Yet the critic goes on to claim Asa as a "worthy role model" because of her "self-determination" and "honesty." Deborah Stevenson, critiquing the work in *Bulletin of the Center for Children's Books,* stated that "several strands of the story don't always fit together as well as they might" but added, "the charm and credibility of the characters pull things together." After writing novels for over three decades, Klass—whose three children are also successful writers—still finds enjoyment in the craft. "Creating a story on paper is a peculiar joy unlike any other," she once explained. "Just the writing itself is the first reward. . . . Writing books for young people is a particular pleasure; I regularly go into the New York City public schools to talk to students about writing and to hear their opinions on my books. Often they are very honest and outspoken, and I learn much." In her capacity as an English professor, she also teaches writing, "the most pleasurable of jobs," according to Klass. "What I do in my classrooms is introduce my students to the highest high in the whole world—the high that is achieved by creating marvelous original works from their own imaginations."

All three of Klass's children are also professional writers. "While it's a great joy, I take no credit for it," wrote Klass in *Something About the Author Autobiography Series.* "I never urged it on them as a profession. I think it means that they saw how much pleasure I get from my writing, they tried it, and it worked for them, too."

■ Works Cited

Ackler, Susan, review of *Next Stop: Nowhere, Voice of Youth Advocates,* February, 1995, pp. 339-40.

Review of *The Bennington Stitch, Bulletin of the Center for Children's Books,* January, 1986, p. 89.

Bradburn, Frances, review of *Kool Ada, Wilson Library Bulletin,* June, 1992, p. 122.

Bruner, Katherine, review of *Kool Ada, School Library Journal,* August, 1991, p. 168.

Cooper, Ilene, review of *To See My Mother Dance, Booklist,* December 1, 1981, p. 499.

Review of *Credit-Card Carole, Publishers Weekly,* July 10, 1987, p. 72.

Edelman, Diane Gersoni, review of *Alive and Starting Over, New York Times Book Review,* December 11, 1983, p. 44.

Hearne, Betsy, review of *Credit-Card Carole, Bulletin of the Center for Children's Books,* October, 1987, pp. 32-33.

Klass, Sheila Solomon, *Nobody Knows Me in Miami,* Scribner, 1981.

Klass, Sheila Solomon, *Kool Ada,* Scholastic, 1991.

Klass, Sheila Solomon, essay in *Something About the Author Autobiography Series,* Volume 26, Gale, 1998, pp. 99-116.

Review of *Next Stop: Nowhere, Publishers Weekly,* December 19, 1994, p. 55.

Review of *Nobody Knows Me in Miami, Bulletin of the Center for Children's Books,* November, 1981, pp. 47-48.

Review of *Nobody Knows Me in Miami, Kirkus Reviews,* August 1, 1981, p. 935.

Raasch, Bonnie L., review of *Credit-Card Carole, School Library Journal,* October, 1987, p. 140.

Review of *A Shooting Star, Kirkus Reviews,* November 15, 1996, p. 1671.

Review of *A Shooting Star, Publishers Weekly,* December 2, 1996, p. 61.

Stevenson, Deborah, review of *Rhino, Bulletin of the Center for Children's Books,* November, 1993, p. 87.

Stevenson, Deborah, review of *The Uncivil War, Bulletin of the Center for Children's Books,* February, 1998, pp. 209-10.

Sutton, Roger, review of *Page Four, Bulletin of the Center for Children's Books,* March, 1987, p. 128.

Sutton, Roger, review of *A Shooting Star, Horn Book,* May-June, 1997, p. 323.

Review of *To See My Mother Dance, Bulletin of the Center for Children's Books,* May, 1982.

Review of *To See My Mother Dance, Publishers Weekly,* December 18, 1981, p. 71.

Triner, Jeanne, review of *Next Stop: Nowhere, Booklist,* January 15, 1995, p. 912.

Review of *The Uncivil War, Publishers Weekly,* December 22, 1997, p. 60.

Wolitzer, Meg, review of *The Bennington Stitch, New York Times Book Review,* October 27, 1985, p. 37.

■ For More Information See

BOOKS

St. James Guide to Young Adult Writers, second edition, St. James Press, 1999.

PERIODICALS

Booklist, September 15, 1985, p. 125.
Bulletin of the Center for Children's Books, February, 1984, p. 110; February, 1995, p. 203.
Horn Book, January-February, 1994, p. 74.
Kirkus Reviews, July 15, 1991, p. 932; December 1, 1993, p. 1525; April 1, 1998, p. 497.
School Library Journal, January, 1982, p. 88; April, 1982, p. 71; December, 1983, p. 75; October, 1985, pp. 182-83; February, 1987, p. 91; November, 1993, p. 125; April, 1995, p. 134.

—Sketch by J. Sydney Jones, updated by Carol Brennan

Henri Matisse

■ Personal

Born December 31, 1869, in Le Cateau-Cambresis, France; died November 3, 1954, in Nice, France; son of Emile and Gerard Matisse (store owners); married Amelie Noemie Alexandrine Parayre, 1898; children: one daughter, two sons. *Education:* Studied law at the Sorbonne, Paris, 1887-88; studied drawing under Bouguereau at the Academie Julian, Paris, 1892-93, and with Gustave Moreau from 1893-97, first unofficially, then, after 1895, as a student of the Ecole des Beaux-Arts; studied sculpture with Bourdelle, 1900-03.

■ Career

Associated at the Salon d'Autumn of 1905 with group known thereafter as Fauves; ran an art school, Paris, France, 1908-11; settled in Nice, France, 1917, and lived in Nice and Paris from 1922; stage and costume designs for Diaghilev ballet *Le Chant du Rossignol*, 1920, and for *Rouge et Noir* (also know as *L'Etrange Farandole*), 1939; trip around the world, 1930; painted mural for Barnes Foundation, Merion, PA, 1931-33; first "cut-

outs," 1938; deisgned and illustrated books during 1930s and 1940s; lived in Vence, France, 1943-48; decorated Chapel of the Rosary, Vence, 1948-51; worked in Nice on large decorative commissions based on paper cutouts until his death. Major paintings include *Woman With the Hat*, 1905, *Joie de Vivre*, 1906, *Blue Nude* (*Souvenir of Biskra*), 1907, *Harmony in Red*, 1908, *La Danse*, 1909, *The Painter's Family*, 1911, *Odalisques*, 1928, *Decorative Figure on an Ornamental Background*, 1925, *Polynesia, the Sea*, 1946, and *Large Red Interior*, 1948. Major sculptures include *Reclining Nude I*, 1907, and *The Back* (four-sculpture series), 1909-27. Work can be found in several permanent collections in museums in several European and U.S. cities, including Leningrad, Moscow, Paris, Copenhagen, New York, and Chicago.

■ Awards, Honors

First Prize, Carnegie International Exhibition of 1927; Legion of Honor, France.

■ Writings

(And illustrator) *Jazz*, Triade (Paris), 1947, reprinted, Braziller (New York), 1983.
Portraits, [Monte Carlo], 1954.
Ecrits et propos sur l'art, edited by Dominique Fourcade, [Paris], 1972.
Matisse on Art, Phaidon, 1973.

Also illustrator of books, including *Poesies de Stephane Mallarme,* 1932, *Ulysses,* by James Joyce, Limited Editions Club, 1935, and *Poemes de Charles d'Orleans,* 1950.

■ Sidelights

Henri Matisse ranks among the most acclaimed and imitated of modern artists, but his innovations shocked many of his contemporaries and only gained widespread acceptance after generating substantial controversy. By the late twentieth century, however, the influence of his bold style can be observed not only in the so-called fine arts but in virtually every facet of popular culture.

Born in Le Cateau-Cambresis, France, on December 31, 1869, Matisse was raised in northern France. His parents, Emile and Gerard Matisse, ran a kind of grocery store. Unlike many artists, he did not spend time drawing or painting as a child. He was expected to take over the family business or, with luck, become a lawyer. Matisse did study law in Paris for two years; but he unwittingly doomed his legal career when, in 1890 while working as a law clerk, he began attending early morning drawing classes meant for curtain designers. While recovering from appendicitis that year, Matisse received a box of paints from his mother and soon thereafter decided topursue a career in art. He was twenty years old.

Matisse studied for several years in Paris with traditional painters. To earn money he made copies of famous works at the French national museum, the Louvre. At the time Paris was the center of a revolution in the visual arts. Besides im-

The 1908 painting *Harmony in Red* reflects the artist's interest in design.

pressionism, other new ideas were being introduced by painters like Frenchmen Paul Cézanne and Georges Seurat and Vincent van Gogh of the Netherlands. At the Louvre Matisse was attracted to the passion of Spanish artist Francisco Goya. He also admired the work of his countryman Henri Toulouse-Lautrec and, like numerous artists of the time, was fascinated by the woodblock prints of Japan. Matisse experimented with ideas from all these sources; by 1897 he was on his way to finding his own style.

Paints A Blue Figure

The first results of his experimentation were revealed in 1898 when he painted a male nude—not in the usual flesh tones, but all in blue. This unorthodox choice reflected his conviction that color should be used to express emotion. By 1905 Matisse had become the leader of a group of artists called "Les Fauves," the wild beasts, after their exhibit shocked the public. Fauvism, as their style became known, is characterized by broad strokes of very bright, often clashing color. The heightened hues and dark borders defining shapes invested their work with tremendous energy. A noteworthy example from this time is Matisse's *Woman with the Hat,* a portrait of the artist's wife, Amelie Parayre—whom he'd married in 1898—in a very large *chapeau.* Although compositionally a traditional rendering of an elegant lady, the painting's use of color—the dress, hat, and even the face are painted in patches of green, red, orange, and blue—was scandalous for the time. Matisse gained some fame when American writer Gertrude Stein and her brother Michael Stein bought the painting. Over the years, the two bought many of his works.

Except for the Steins, however, Matisse attracted few buyers of his paintings and found it difficult to support his family. He and Amelie had two sons and a daughter. Amelie Matisse set up a hat shop in Paris to earn income for the family. She continued to serve frequently as a model for her husband.

Begins Romance With Color

In 1906 Matisse traveled to Italy and North Africa, both of which strongly influenced his style. In Italy he admired the frescoes of the pre-Renais-

If you enjoy the works of Henri Matisse, you may also want to check out the following:

The paintings of the French late Impressionist Pierre Bonnard.
The works of the great Dutch painter Vincent van Gogh.

sance Italian artist Giotto, with their simple, monumental style. In North Africa he was drawn to the brilliant colors and decorative patterns of Islamic art. He brought back from this trip pottery, cloths, carpets, and other items, which he often used in his paintings. His *Blue Nude (Souvenir of Biskra)* reflects these influences and his love of the human figure. Yet anatomy would ultimately take a back seat to design; in the next few years, rich colors and decorative patterns, including those of vines and flowers, seemed to overrun his paintings; in *Harmony in Red,* the pattern of the wallpaper and tablecloth leave little space in the painting for the woman standing at the table.

Matisse is also notable for repeating parts of previous paintings in newer works. For instance, in a still life from 1909, the viewer can see a section of his earlier painting *La Danse. La Danse,* along with a companion painting, *La Musique,* was commissioned by a Russian businessman named Sergei Shchukin, a great supporter of Matisse in these years. Matisse visited him in Moscow several times, and Shchukin eventually owned thirty-seven of his paintings. In 1923 Shchukin and another Russian collector opened the first museum of contemporary Western art in Moscow, including forty-eight of Matisse's works. Matisse also used the freedom of fauvism in his early sculptures. He worked with sculpture throughout his career, adapting for the medium his many concepts of form and space.

Incorporates Other Styles Into His Own

Around 1910 Matisse's style underwent another transformation. He delved into approaches derived from cubism and began using subtler colors, more simplified figures, and a greater number of geometric shapes. Matisse was never a cubist, but as with impressionism, he was able to incorporate

Matisse's exuberant style can be seen in the well-known 1909 work *La danse.*

many of the school's ideas and theories into his own style. This is evident in his 1911 painting *The Painter's Family,* in which the space is divided into multiple rectangular areas covered with decorative patterns of wallpaper, oriental rug designs, and upholstery prints.

After World War I Matisse began spending a substantial portion of each year in the south of France and eventually settled there permanently. Under the influence of the south's warm, sunny weather, his colors brightened again, and patterns and decorations became more prominent. He wrote that after many years of exploration, his art finally "had established a new clarity and simplicity of its own." Toward the end of the 1920s, Matisse took a trip around the world, spending six months in Tahiti, where Frenchman Paul Gauguin had done so much of his painting, and also traveling to the United States.

Soon after this visit, he received a commission from the Barnes Foundation in Pennsylvania to paint a mural in their museum, which contained many impressionist and post-impressionist works. This was the first of several interior design commissions Matisse accepted in the ensuing years. The largest project, often considered the masterpiece of his career, was the design of a chapel in the French town of Vence. Matisse created the stained-glass windows, interior decor, devotional objects, and clothing for the clergy. The chapel was dedicated in 1951.

Experiments with Paper

During the 1930s Matisse turned to designing and illustrating books. He began working with geometric and abstract shapes cut out of colored paper, silhouetting these against multihued backgrounds. Matisse's most famous book, *Jazz,* dates from 1947. The vivid colors, flowing shapes, and rhythmic feel evoke the qualities of that musical form. Matisse's works were exhibited often during the 1930s in major cities across Europe and the United

States. At a large exhibition in Paris in 1936, an entire room was devoted to his paintings.

In the 1940s and 1950s Matisse became increasingly handicapped due to illness. During the World War II years, he was often confined to his bed. His works from this period are smaller and include numerous book illustrations. These creations have a pronounced serenity about them, all the more remarkable since both Matisse's wife and daughter were arrested by the Nazis during this time. Amelie Matisse suffered two three-month

Painted the year before Matisse's death, *The Snail* illustrated the artist's revolutionary use of color.

prison sentences, and Marguerite Matisse was placed in solitary confinement, charged with resistance activities.

A Maverick To The End

War's end saw an increase in Matisse's activity. He often worked from a wheelchair or in bed, sketching designs on the wall with a piece of charcoal attached to a long pole. His last paintings recalled his favorite themes of female figures and interiors and include *Large Red Interior* from 1948. He spent many hours directing his assistants to find the perfect arrangements of his paper cutouts. Matisse passed the last years of his life designing the chapel at Vence and working on his cutouts. These free-form shapes brought together all of Matisse's ideas, from painting, sculpture, and the decorative arts. Despite his infirmities, he continued working until his death in Nice, France, on November 3, 1954, at the age of eighty-four, a maverick to the end.

■ For More Information See

BOOKS

Elderfield, John, *Henri Matisse: A Retrospective,* Museum of Modern Art, 1992.

Essers, Volkmar, *Henri Matisse, 1869-1954: Master of Colour,* Taschen, 1987.

Girard, Xavier, *Matisse: The Wonder of Color,* translated by I. Mark Paris, Abrams, 1994.

Herrera, Hayden, *Matisse: A Portrait,* Harcourt, Brace, 1993.

International Dictionary of Art and Artists, edited by James Vinson, St. James Press, 1990.

Kostenevich, Albert, *Henri Matisse,* Abrams, 1997.

Raboff, Ernest Lloyd, *Henri Matisse,* Lippincott, 1988.

Wilson, Sarah, *Matisse,* Rizzoli, 1992.

Anne McCaffrey

■ Personal

Born April 1, 1926, in Cambridge, MA; daughter of George Herbert (a city administrator and U.S. Army colonel) and Anne D. (maiden name, McElroy) McCaffrey; married H. Wright Johnson, January 14, 1950 (divorced, 1970); children: Alec Anthony, Todd, Georgeanne. *Education:* Radcliffe College, B.A. (cum laude), 1947; graduate study in meteorology, University of City of Dublin; also studied voice for nine years. *Politics:* Democrat. *Religion:* Presbyterian. *Hobbies and other interests:* Singing, opera directing, riding and horse care.

■ Addresses

Home—Dragonhold, Kilquade, Greystones, County Wicklow, Ireland. *Agent*—Virginia Kidd, Box 278, Milford, PA 18337.

■ Career

Liberty Music Shops, New York City, copywriter and layout designer, 1948-50; Helena Rubinstein, New York City, copywriter and secretary, 1950-52; author. Director of Fin Film Productions, 1979—, and Dragonhold, Ltd. Former professional stage director for several groups in Wilmington, DE. *Member:* Science Fiction Writers of America (secretary-treasurer, 1968-70), Mystery Writers of America, Authors Guild, Novelists' Ink, PEN (Ireland).

■ Awards, Honors

Hugo Award for best novella, World Science Fiction Society, 1968, for "Weyr Search"; Nebula Award for best novella, Science Fiction Writers of America, 1969, for "Dragonrider"; E. E. Smith Award for fantasy, 1975; American Library Association notable book citations, 1976, for *Dragonsong,* and 1977, for *Dragonsinger; Horn Book* Fanfare Citation, 1977, for *Dragonsong;* Ditmar Award (Australia), Gandalf Award, and Eurocon/Streso Award, all 1979, all for *The White Dragon;* Balrog citation, 1980, for *Dragondrums;* Golden Pen Award, 1981; Science Fiction Book Club Awards, 1986, for *Killashandra,* 1989, for *Dragonsdawn,* and 1990, for *The Renegades of Pern* (first place) and *The Rowan* (third place); Margaret A. Edwards Lifetime Achievement Award for Outstanding Literature for Young Adults, American Library Association's Young Adult Library Services and *School Library Journal,* 1999.

■ Writings

SCIENCE FICTION/FANTASY

Restoree, Ballantine, 1967.

(Editor) *Alchemy and Academe*, Doubleday, 1970.

To Ride Pegasus, Ballantine, 1973.

Get Off the Unicorn (short stories), Del Rey, 1977.

The Worlds of Anne McCaffrey (stories), Deutsch, 1981.

The Coelura, Underwood-Miller, 1983.

Stitch in Snow, Del Rey, 1984.

Pegasus in Flight, Del Rey, 1990.

Three Women, Tor Books, 1992.

(With Elizabeth A. Scarborough) *Powers That Be*, Del Rey, 1993.

Lyon's Pride (limited edition), Putnam, 1993.

(With Scarborough) *Power Lines* (sequel to *Powers That Be*), Del Rey, 1994.

The Girl Who Heard Dragons (story collection; includes *The Girl Who Heard Dragons*; also see below), Tor Books, 1994.

An Exchange of Gifts, illustrated by Pat Morrissey, ROC, 1995.

Freedom's Landing, Putnam, 1995.

(With Scarborough) *Power Play*, Del Rey, 1995.

No One Noticed the Cat, ROC, 1996.

(Editor with Scarborough) *Space Opera*, DAW Books, 1996.

(With Margaret Ball) *Acorna: The Unicorn Girl*, HarperPrism, 1997.

(With Ball) *Acorna's Quest*, HarperPrism, 1998.

If Wishes Were Horses, ROC, 1998.

Nimisha's Ship, Ballantine, 1999.

The Tower and the Hive, Putnam, 1999.

(With Scarborough) *Acorna's People*, HarperPrism, 1999.

"DRAGONRIDERS OF PERN" SERIES; SCIENCE FICTION

Dragonflight, Ballantine, 1968, hardcover edition, Walker & Co., 1969.

Dragonquest: Being the Further Adventures of the Dragonriders of Pern, Ballantine, 1971.

A Time When, Being a Tale of Young Lord Jaxom, His White Dragon, Ruth, and Various Fire-Lizards (short story), NESFA Press, 1975.

The White Dragon, Del Rey, 1978.

The Dragonriders of Pern (contains *Dragonflight*, *Dragonquest*, and *The White Dragon*), Doubleday, 1978.

Moreta: Dragonlady of Pern, Del Rey, 1983.

The Girl Who Heard Dragons (for children), Cheap Street, 1985.

Nerilka's Story, Del Rey, 1986.

Dragonsdawn, Del Rey, 1988.

The Renegades of Pern, Del Rey, 1989.

All the Weyrs of Pern, Del Rey, 1991.

The Chronicles of Pern: First Fall, Del Rey, 1992.

The Dolphins of Pern, Del Rey, 1994.

Dragonseye, Del Rey, 1997.

The Masterharper of Pern, Del Rey, 1998.

"HARPER HALL" SERIES; SCIENCE FICTION

Dragonsong, Atheneum, 1976.

Dragonsinger, Atheneum, 1977.

Dragondrums, Atheneum, 1979.

The Harper Hall of Pern (contains *Dragonsong*, *Dragonsinger*, and *Dragondrums*), Doubleday, 1979.

"FREEDOM" SERIES; SCIENCE FICTION

Freedom's Landing, Putnam, 1995.

Freedom's Choice, Putnam, 1997.

Freedom's Challenge, Putnam, 1998.

"DOONA" SERIES; SCIENCE FICTION

Decision at Doona, Ballantine, 1969.

(With Jody Lynn Nye) *Crisis on Doona*, Ace, 1992.

(With Nye) *Treaty at Doona*, Ace, 1994.

"SHIP WHO SANG" SERIES; SCIENCE FICTION

The Ship Who Sang, Walker & Co., 1969.

(With Mercedes Lackey) *The Ship Who Searched*, Baen Books, 1992.

(With Margaret Ball) *PartnerShip*, Baen Books, 1992.

(With S. M. Stirling) *The City Who Fought*, Baen Books, 1993.

(With Nye) *The Ship Who Won*, Baen Books, 1994.

(With S. M. Stirling) *The Ship Avenged*, Baen Books, 1997.

"DINOSAUR PLANET" SERIES; SCIENCE FICTION

Dinosaur Planet, Futura, 1977, Del Rey, 1978.

The Dinosaur Planet Survivors, Del Rey, 1984.

The Ireta Adventure (contains *Dinosaur Planet* and *Dinosaur Planet Survivors*), Doubleday, 1985.

"CRYSTAL SINGER" SERIES; SCIENCE FICTION

Crystal Singer, Del Rey, 1981.

Killashandra, Del Rey, 1985.

Crystal Line, Del Rey, 1992.

Crystal Singer Trilogy (contains *Crystal Singer*, *Killashandra*, and *Crystal Line*), Del Rey, 1996.

"PLANET PIRATE" SERIES; SCIENCE FICTION

(With Elizabeth Moon) *Sassinak*, Baen Books, 1990.

(With Nye) *The Death of Sleep,* Baen Books, 1990.
Generation Warriors, Baen Books, 1991.
(With Moon and Nye) *The Planet Pirates,* Baen Books, 1993.

"ROWAN" SERIES; SCIENCE FICTION

The Rowan, Berkley Publishing, 1990.
Damia, Ace, 1993.
Damia's Children, Putnam, 1993.

OTHER

The Mark of Merlin, Dell, 1971.
The Ring of Fear, Dell, 1971.
(Editor) *Cooking Out of This World,* Ballantine, 1973.
The Kilternan Legacy, Dell, 1975.
Habit Is an Old Horse, Dryad Press, 1986.
The Year of the Lucy (novel), Tor Books, 1986.
The Lady (novel), Ballantine, 1987, published in England as *The Carradyne Touch,* Futura/ Macdonald, 1988.
(Author of text) Robin Wood, *The People of Pern,* Donning, 1988.
(With Nye) *The Dragonlover's Guide to Pern,* Del Rey, 1989.
Three Gothic Novels: The Ring of Fear, The Mark of Merlin, The Kilternan Legacy, Underwood-Miller, 1990.
Dragonflight Graphic Novel, HarperCollins, 1993.
Black Horses for the King (juvenile historical fiction), Harcourt, 1996.
(Editor with John Betancourt) *Serve It Forth: Cooking with Anne McCaffrey,* Warner Books, 1996.
Dragon, HarperCollins Juvenile, 1996.
(With Richard Woods) *A Diversity of Dragons,* illustrated by John Howe, HarperPrism, 1997.

Contributor to anthologies, including *Infinity One,* 1970, *Future Love,* 1977, and *Once Upon a Time,* 1991, and to magazines, including *Analog, Galaxy,* and *Magazine of Fantasy and Science Fiction.*

Collections of McCaffrey's manuscripts are housed at Syracuse University, Syracuse, NY, and in the Kerlan Collection, University of Minnesota, Minneapolis, MN.

■ Adaptations

Dragonsong and *Dragonsinger* have been adapted as children's stage plays by Irene Elliott and produced in Baltimore, MD; the "Pern" books have also inspired a cassette of music, *Dragonsongs,* a board game, and two computer games. *The White Dragon, Moreta, Dragonlady of Pern, Nerilka's Story,* and *The Rowan* are all available on cassette, as is the 1999 *Nimisha's Ship;* a television series, *The Dragonriders of Pern,* premiered internationally in January, 2000.

■ Sidelights

Anne McCaffrey is a writer of many firsts: the first woman to win science fiction's coveted Hugo and Nebula Awards; the first sci-fi writer to break into the *New York Times* bestseller lists; and the first sci fi writer to be awarded the prestigious Margaret A. Edwards Award for lifetime achievement in young adult literature. Her award-winning "Dragonriders of Pern" series, fifteen strong and growing, rank, as James and Eugene Sloan noted in the *Chicago Tribune Book World,* as "the most enduring serial in the history of science fantasy." The series has proved so popular, with each new volume hitting the bestseller lists, "that it has almost transcended genre categorization," Gary K. Reynolds asserted in the *Science Fiction and Fantasy Book Review.* There are fan clubs galore, several Web sites, reference books that delineate the geography of McCaffrey's fanciful planet, Pern, other reference works that deal with all the characters in the richly textured series, board games, computer games, and television shows. McCaffrey's dragons are very busy critters.

The prolific American writer who makes her home in Ireland is far from being a one-trick pony, however. She has written over sixty books both in series and stand-alones translated into twenty-one languages in a career spanning over three decades. In addition to the "Dragonriders," McCaffrey has penned multi-volume adventures such as "The Ship Who Sang" series, "Crystal Singer" series, "Planet Pirate" series, "Rowan" series, and "Freedom" series, among others.

Noted for her well-developed characters and emphasis on emotion over science in her fictions, McCaffrey is often labeled a fantasy writer rather than a sci fi novelist. Michael Cart put the question to her in a *School Library Journal* interview in celebration of the Margaret A. Edwards Award. Science fiction or fantasy author? "We keep having to settle that question," McCaffrey replied. "*I write science fiction.* It may seem fantasy because I

McCaffrey's 1973 novel concerns the Talented, a group of girls and women, each of whom possesses an extraordinary gift.

the determined young musician of *Crystal Singer* and *Killashandra;* the talented psychics of *To Ride Pegasus* and the "Raven Women" series; and Helva, the independent starship "brain" of *The Ship Who Sang.* Through these works, Bogle indicated, "McCaffrey has brought delineations of active women into prominence in science fiction." Such considerations have won her a wide readership across gender and generations, making McCaffrey one of the most popular and prolific sci fi writers of her generation.

A Matter of Upbringing

McCaffrey was born on April Fools' Day, 1926, in Cambridge, Massachusetts. "I've tried hard to live up to being an April-firster," McCaffrey told Cart in her interview, but in fact there was not much room for levity in her early years. The daughter of a U.S. Army colonel father and a successful real estate agent mother, McCaffrey had a lot to live up to. Her father was "a grand figure—not very approachable, though," she told Cart. His children called him "The Colonel," and though he appeared more interested in his garden than offspring, he instilled in McCaffrey a desire to excel. He also gave her the gift of a love for riding, something the author has kept with her all her life. McCaffrey's mother, unlike other women of her generation, was not only a homemaker but a successful career woman, and she shared a secret with her daughter: as expected of her she would probably grow up, go to college, marry, and have children. But then what would she do with the rest of her life? "My parents gave me ambition and motivation to go do it," McCaffrey commented to Cart.

"It" in this case was to become a writer, something she knew she wanted to be from an early age. "When I was a very young girl, I promised myself fervently (usually after I'd lost another battle with one of my brothers) that I would become a famous author and I'd own my own horse," McCaffrey commented in her *Something about the Author Autobiography Series (SAAS)* essay. "Few women during my adolescence were encouraged to think of having independent careers, or careers at all: marriage was considered quite enough to occupy most women's lives. That's where I . . . lucked out: being subtly conditioned to have marriage, motherhood, AND self-fulfillment."

use dragons, but mine were biogenetically engineered; ergo the story is science fiction." McCaffrey's character-driven and emotion-filled approach to sci fi allows her to weave serious social commentary into her work, according to Edra C. Bogle in the *Dictionary of Literary Biography.* "Most of McCaffrey's protagonists are women or children, whom she treats with understanding and sympathy," Bogle commented. The injustices these characters suffer, brought about by a sometimes-stifling social system, "are at the heart of most of McCaffrey's books." In fact, the majority of McCaffrey's novels feature strong heroines: the ruling Weyrwomen of the "Dragonrider" books;

Books became, in addition to horses, early friends to McCaffrey. "I was not a popular child—being domineering, opinionated, disruptive, hyper," McCaffrey noted in her Edwards Award acceptance speech published in *JOYS*. "Reading so much while other girls played with dolls reinforced the notion that I was 'different'. . . . I pretended to glory in being 'different.' But, Gawd, I was a brat!" Her reading was wide and all-encompassing, but she especially loved utopian and dystopian literature. Tarzan's adventures were early favorites, as were the tales of Kipling."When I was 14, I read *Islandia* by Austin Tappan Wright, and it blew my mind, absolutely blew my mind," McCaffrey noted in a *Booklist* interview with Pat Monaghan. She began writing short stories by the age of eight, yet she did not have many best friends in those years. McCaffrey's self-esteem was given a boost, if one was needed, by attending Radcliffe, the sister college to Harvard at the time. "We were enjoined when I graduated to be first in whatever field of endeavor we chose to enter," McCaffrey remarked to Cart. "No one thought science fiction would be a proper venue. So, typically, I did what no one expected me to do."

Trailbreaker in Sci Fi

Out of college, McCaffrey took several copywriting jobs, and then, as prophesied by her mother, married. During one of her occasional bouts of bronchitis, she was stuck in her apartment and the only thing left to read was a pulp publication, *Amazing Stories*. Quickly she saw that she could produce such stories, and from there it was not a long jump to writing for science fiction magazines, a field not over-populated with women writers. Andre Norton was perhaps the one pre-eminent female writer in the genre when McCaffrey started out, and she was a great influence on McCaffrey. Since that time, women have become a strong presence in both science fiction and fantasy, but at the outset of McCaffrey's career, she was something of an anomaly, a pioneer.

McCaffrey's first novel, the 1967 work *Restoree,* announced some of her major themes: the use of a strong female protagonist and a blend of science and fiction in which the latter takes prominence. Sara is snatched from Central Park by a low flying space ship in what a reviewer for *Publishers Weekly* termed a "well-written and carefully plotted story," and is spirited away to "a fasci-

nating world that is technologically sophisticated, but culturally quaint and archaic," as the same reviewer noted. There Sara comes out of a sort of amnesia and discovers she is encased in a new body; she has become a "restoree."

In May 1967, with her children expected home from school any moment, McCaffrey came up with the idea of a land called Pern populated by symbiotic, biogenetically engineered, fire-breathing, telepathic dragons. Remembering what Andre Norton once said about dragons—that they had bad press—McCaffrey decided to make them a

Forbidden to play her music because she is a girl, Menolly runs away and attempts to survive on her own in this 1976 novel.

major character in what was intended as a short story. In the event, she created a major cottage industry with that one afternoon's thoughts.

"Dragonriders of Pern"

McCaffrey's short story ultimately turned into the 1968 novel *Dragonflight*, the work that introduces the Terran-populated planet of Pern and its knight-like Dragonmen and Weyrwomen who fly telepathic dragons in defense of their planet against the scourge of life-destroying Thread. Thread infests Pern every 200 years when the planet passes close to the Red Star which attempts to colonize Pern. Now, however, the ranks of the defenders have been thinned and they must battle a new onslaught of Thread.

Reviews of this first book in the Pern cycle often pointed out the fantasy elements in the book. A reviewer for the *Junior Bookshelf*, for example, noted that Pern and its Weyr satellite "is Tolkein-land rather than futuristic space-world," and *Publishers Weekly*, in its review of *Dragonflight*, felt that "readers surfeited with gadget-ridden supermodernistic space epics will welcome" this "science-fantasy." In the subsequent two books of the initial Pern trilogy, *Dragonquest* and *The White Dragon*, McCaffrey continued the saga of Pern, a former colony of Earth which has lost much of its scientific and historical knowledge. Hundreds of years after its founding, Pern is divided into a near-feudal society of landholders who often work against the less rigid communities of dragonriders, called Weyrs. McCaffrey's emphasis on the conflicts between individuals, the fight against Thread, and the unique telepathic relationship between dragon and rider made these early works popular withreaders of all ages, and led to *The White Dragon* becoming, in 1978, the first hardcover sci fi novel to reach the *New York Times* bestseller list.

To entice young female readers to the pages of science fiction, McCaffrey's editor prompted her to write a trilogy of Pern novels directed at young adults and featuring a female protagonist. Thus was born the "Harper Hall" series, which follows a teenage girl who comes from a very different situation than the robust dragonriders. In *Dragonsong*, the first book, Menolly has been forbidden to play or sing her music solely because she is a girl and "girls aren't harpers." After her hand is accidentally injured and then deliberately

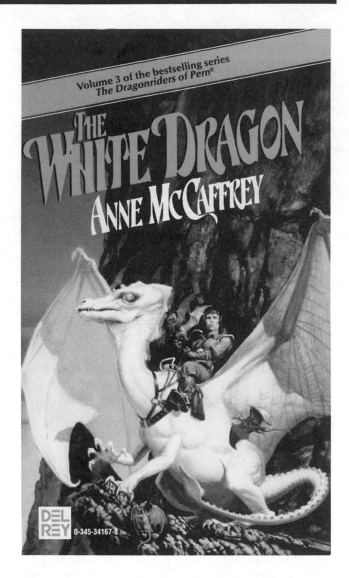

When Jaxom breaks the rules by training his dragon to fly, he finds himself facing an extraordinary challenge in this 1978 work.

mistreated to prevent proper healing that would allow her to play again, Menolly runs away. Outside of the Hold, she faces the dangers of Thread and the challenges of survival by herself—but she is not alone, as she befriends and cares for a set of young fire lizards, small cousins to Pern's mighty dragons. The book concludes as Menolly is rescued from Threadfall and her talent is discovered by the Harper Guild. Reviewing this first title in the YA trilogy, Joan Barbour concluded in *School Library Journal*, "The author explores the ideas of alienation, rebellion, love of beauty, the role of women and the role of the individual in society with some sensitivity in a generally well-structured plot with sound characterizations."

Menolly encounters a new set of problems in *Dragonsinger,* the second book in the trilogy. Although she has arrived at the Harper Hall and has started training to be a harper, she still must face the prejudice of some teachers and the resentment of students jealous of her talent and her fire lizards. With her usual determination, and the aid of new friends such as the apprentice Piemur, Menolly overcomes these troubles to achieve happiness. Piemur takes center stage in the third "Harper Hall" book, *Dragondrums,* and together the trilogy contains "strong characters" as well as "a nice balance between problems that are present in any civilized society and a sense of humor that

Killashandra risks losing everything she knows in order to begin her life as a musician on the planet Ballybran.

lightens both exposition and dialogue," Zena Sutherland wrote in the *Bulletin of the Center for Children's Books.*

Although Pern is inhabited by flying dragons and dominated by a near-feudal society—elements typical of fantasy worlds—McCaffrey's creation is based on solid scientific principles. The author frequently consults with scientific experts in order to make her ideas fully-fleshed and believable; 1988's *Dragonsdawn,* in fact, reveals the story of how the original colonists of Pern used genetic manipulation to develop Pern's dragons. The book features two of Pern's first dragonriders, young lovers Sean and Sorka, as they participate in the grand experiment and take up the battle against Threadfall. "Pernophiles, rejoice!" announced *Booklist*'s Sally Estes in a review of this addition to the Pern series. "At last McCaffrey unfolds her early vision of the colonizing of the beautiful, Earthlike, uninhabited planet of Pern. . . . [T]his will delight Pern fans while satisfying their curiosity about how it all began."

McCaffrey has continued her saga with books published throughout the 1990s, building the entire series to fifteen books in all. With her 1994 *The Dolphins of Pern,* McCaffrey emphasized dolphins over dragons—the third most intelligent species on Pern. *Kirkus Reviews* commented of this title, "McCaffrey's solid characterizations and lush descriptions counterbalance the feathery plot, making this latest trip to Pern a pleasant, sentimental respite among old and familiar friends." With the 1997 novel *The Masterharper of Pern,* McCaffrey brings front and center the harpist Robinton, who had walk-on roles in many of the earlier books. "McCaffrey is amazing," remarked *Booklist*'s Estes in a review of the book. "She is so steeped in the lore, history, and environment of her brilliantly created planet Pern and its people that she doesn't have to write her tales about it in sequence." Estes went on to describe *The Masterharper of Pern* as "[t]autly plotted and featuring good characterization." McCaffrey's most popular series, originally planned as one short story, shows no signs of faltering or ending, after over three decades of life.

A Writer of Many Parts

As has been noted, the emotional focus of the Dragonrider series—and other McCaffrey works such as the "Crystal Singer" and "Raven Women" novels—puts the technology in the background, unlike many science fiction novels. This emphasis on people and feelings has led some critics to christen the Pern books "science fantasy." McCaffrey, however, believes the use of emotion is appropriate to science fiction. As she related in her *SAAS* entry, one of her first (and most popular) stories, "The Ship Who Sang," was born of her grief over her father's death: "'Ship' taught me to use emotion as a writing tool. And I do, with neither apology nor shame, even though I am writing science fiction, a *genre* not often noted, in those days, for any emotions, only intellectual exercise and scientific curiosities."

This moving short story spawned another popular McCaffrey series, all of which—except for the first in the series—are co-written with various other authors. The books in this series follow the lives of men and women who have been physically crippled and give up their physical form to use their brains to operate various spaceships. Often such tales end in a quirky resolution of love between brain and brawn. Reviewing the first in the series, *The Ship Who Sang,* a reviewer for *Publishers Weekly* noted that the book was "a sure-fire love story for man or machine." Helva has been separated from her malformed body since the time of her birth. Now her physical being is manifested in a spaceship which has intelligence and emotions. She manages to find love with human "brawn" such as Jennan who help operate the ship, eventually coming so in tune with his musical talents that she becomes known throughout the galaxies as the Singing Ship. Reviewing the third book in the series, *The Ship Who Searched,* co-written with Mercedes Lackey, *Kliatt*'s Linda Tashbook concluded, "A perfect combination of SF, adventure, and romance, this is sure to please a wide variety of readers."

Other popular McCaffrey series include the "Rowan" books that deal with an advanced society which uses telepathy and telekinetics to support its technology. The books also tell the story of a mother and daughter's search for love, a typical McCaffrey motif. In her "Crystal Singer" series, McCaffrey once again as in her "Harper Hall" series uses music as a metaphor for individual growth and personal freedom. Music is in fact a passion of McCaffrey's, who studied voice for nine years. In the lead title in the series, *Crystal Singer,* Killashandra Ree is rejected as vocal soloist, but then joins a band of Crystal Singers, who use voice to mine precious crystal on the planet Ballybran. Gerald Jonas, reviewing the novel in the *New York Times Book Review,* noted the "exotic and meticulously detailed" locale, and the "young, beautiful, intelligent, sexy, and courageous" heroine. But for Jonas, the real heart of the book was McCaffrey's "preoccupation with obsession. Obsession on a Melvillean scale is Miss McCaffrey's subject, and her method as well." Jonas concluded that "Killashandra's obsession [for crystal singing] comes alive, and readers who get past the first 50 pages will find themselves sharing it."

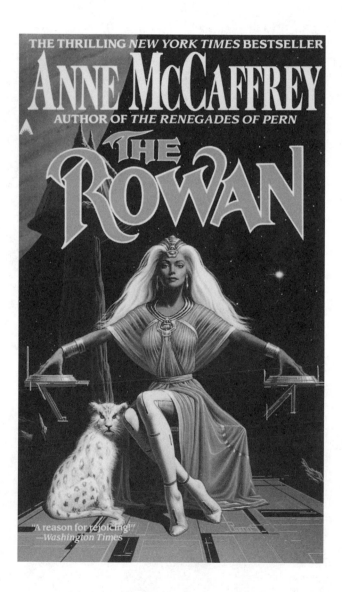

A lonely but powerful telepath receives a distress call from someone whose abilities rival her own in McCaffrey's 1990 work.

Independence and survival are the subjects of McCaffrey's "Freedom" series, launched in 1995 with *Freedom's Landing*. The Catteni conquerors of Earth take human slaves with them to a potentially habitable new planet they have just discovered. These humans become pawns in this new universe in a war between galactic powers after they are abandoned on the planet Botany. Here the former slaves initiate a Robinson Crusoe style adventure of survival. There is also a love story thrown in, between a human and one of the former Catteni masters, as well as the discovery of a mysterious civilization which is using the planet in bizarre ways. Reviewing this first title in the series, *Publishers Weekly* remarked, "McCaffrey has created another set of winning protagonists and a carefully detailed, exotic background on which to develop a new series." With the 1998 work *Freedom's Challenge*, the third and perhaps final installment in the story, the planet Botany is now under attack by the Eosi and the original human colonists must repulse this new onslaught, using technology they have stolen from their former masters. *Booklist*'s Estes called the book a "very satisfying tale," and also remarked that "McCaffrey continues to amaze with her ability to create disparate, well-realized worlds and to portray believable humans, convincing aliens of varied sorts, and credible interactions between them all."

A further group of related novels deals with the infant Acorna who has amazing powers of intellect, curing, and analysis. Written with Margaret Ball, *Acorna: The Unicorn Princess* introduces the precocious infant with a unicorn-like strange protuberance growing out of her forehead. Another collaborative effort are the books in the "Power" series written with Elizabeth Ann Scarborough, *Powers That Be, Power Lines,* and the 1995 *Power Play,* all of which feature the strong female protagonist, Yanaba Maddock, and her adventures on the icy planet Petaybee.

The multi-faceted McCaffrey has also tried her hand at historical fiction for young readers, with her Arthurian tale *Black Horses for the King*. Another stand-alone title is the 1999 *Nimisha's Ship,* in which the title character shows an early proclivity for things mechanical. Nimisha becomes heir to her father's starship factory and develops into a starship designer of no meager talents herself. When her father dies, she is beset with enemies who want her out of the way; on a test

---

If you enjoy the works of Anne McCaffrey, you may also want to check out the following books:

Margaret Wander Bonanno, *The Others,* 1990.
Susan Cooper, *Over Sea, under Stone,* 1966.
Joan D. Vinge, *Psion,* 1982.

---

flight of one of her ships, Nimisha is sucked into a wormhole and lands on a distant planet. According to Estes in *Booklist,* "this is a page-turner all the way."

McCaffrey, who moved to Ireland in 1970 following her divorce, maintains a rigorous work schedule. In addition to her writing, she also owns a livery stable and equitation center at her home in Country Wicklow, Dragonhold-Underhill, an outgrowth of her long-held love of horses and riding. McCaffrey denies that horses were her inspiration for dragons of Pern, however. "Horses are stupid," she told *Booklist*'s Monaghan. "Dragons are smart. But cats are fire lizards. So they're derived from cats." McCaffrey is pragmatic when it comes to describing her work. "Do not ascribe to me any deep philosophical messages," she wrote in her *SAAS* entry. "I don't have any, merely examples of what people can do when pushed to perform at their limits. Most of my books are love stories, too. . . . Generally I write for a purely commercial reason: I've signed a contract and received an advance. I find 'inspiration' when working with the elements of the story I'm already writing: I don't wait around for Inspiration to strike me. . . . I shall continue to write—I can't NOT write anyhow—until I am too frail to touch the keys of my word processor."

■ Works Cited

Barbour, Joan, review of *Dragonsong, School Library Journal,* April 1, 1976, p. 91.

Bogle, Edra C., "Anne McCaffrey," *Dictionary of Literary Biography,* Volume 8: *Twentieth-Century American Science Fiction Writers,* Gale, 1981.

Cart, Michael, "Miss M the Divine," *School Library Journal,* June, 1999, pp. 23-26.

Review of *The Dolphins of Pern, Kirkus Reviews,* August 14, 1994, p. 1031.

Review of *Dragonflight, Junior Bookshelf,* August, 1969, p. 259.

Review of *Dragonflight, Publishers Weekly,* July 8, 1968, p. 166.

Estes, Sally, review of *Dragonsdawn, Booklist,* September 1, 1988, p. 4.

Estes, Sally, review of *The Masterharper of Pern, Booklist,* October 15, 1997, p. 363.

Estes, Sally, review of *Freedom's Challenge, Booklist,* March 1, 1998, p. 1044.

Estes, Sally, review of *Nimisha's Ship, Booklist,* January 1, 1999.

Review of *Freedom's Landing, Publishers Weekly,* April 24, 1995, p. 64.

Jonas, Gerald, "Imaginary People," *New York Times Book Review,* August, 29, 1982, pp. 10-11.

McCaffrey, Anne, entry in *Something about the Author Autobiography Series,* Volume 11, Gale, 1991, pp. 241-56.

McCaffrey, Anne, "The 1999 Margaret A. Edwards Award Acceptance Speech," *JOYS,* Summer, 1999, pp. 19-21.

Monaghan, Pat, "The Booklist Interview: Anne McCaffrey," *Booklist,* March 15, 1994, pp. 1300-1.

Review of *Restoree, Publishers Weekly,* August 21, 1967, p. 76.

Reynolds, Gary K., *Science Fiction and Fantasy Book Review,* July, 1979.

Review of *The Ship Who Sang, Publishers Weekly,* September 15, 1969, p. 61.

Sloan, James, and Eugene Sloan, *Chicago Tribune Book World,* July 13, 1986.

Sutherland, Zena, review of *Dragondrums, Bulletin of the Center for Children's Books,* July-August, 1979, p. 195.

Tashbook, Linda, review of *The Ship Who Searched, Kliatt,* November, 1992, p. 16.

■ For More Information See

BOOKS

Children's Books and Their Creators, edited by Anita Silvey, Houghton Mifflin, 1995.

Children's Literature Review, Volume 49, Gale, 1997.

Contemporary Literary Criticism, Volume 17, Gale, 1981.

St. James Guide to Young Adult Writers, St. James Press, 1999.

Walker, Paul, *Speaking of Science Fiction: The Paul Walker Interviews,* Luna, 1978.

PERIODICALS

Booklist, May 15, 1995, p. 1611; December 15, 1996, p. 692; March 15, 1999, p. 1260.

Library Journal, June 15, 1995, p. 98; May 15, 1997, pp. 106, 165; June 15, 1997, p. 101; May 15, 1998, p. 119; February 15, 1999, p. 187.

New York Times Book Review, August 29, 1982; January 8, 1984; January 8, 1989; June 22, 1997, pp. 22, 24.

Publishers Weekly, January 20, 1997, p. 398; May 26, 1997, p. 71; November 24, 1997, p. 363; April 26, 1999, p. 60.

School Library Journal, July, 1997, p. 116; April, 1998, p. 161; August, 1998, p. 196.

Wilson Library Bulletin, February, 1989; November 1993, pp. 90-91; May, 1995.*

—Sketch by J. Sydney Jones

Todd McFarlane

Spawn, HBO, 1998—; coproduced and directed animated video for Pearl Jam's "Do the Evolution," 1998, and co-directed video for Korn's "Freak on a Leash."

■ Personal

Born March 16, 1961, in Calgary, Alberta, Canada; son of a printer and a homemaker; married July 27, 1985; wife's name, Wanda (a business executive); children: daughters Cyan and Kate. *Education:* Eastern Washington State University, B.A. in general studies, 1984.

■ Addresses

Office—Todd McFarlane Productions, Inc., 40 W. Baseline Rd., Ste. E-105, Tempe, AZ 85283.

■ Career

Comic artist for Marvel and DC, 1984-92, drew titles such as *Scorpio Rose, The Incredible Hulk, Batman, Detective, Batman: Year Two, Invasion, Amazing Spider-Man,* and *Spider-Man;* cofounded Image Comics, 1992; founded McFarlane Toys, 1994; founder of Todd McFarlane Productions, Todd McFarlane Entertainment, and McFarlane Design Group; executive producer of *Todd McFarlane's*

■ Awards, Honors

Two Emmy Awards for animation, for *Todd McFarlane's Spawn,* HBO; Grammy Award nomination, Best Short Form music video, 1999, for Pearl Jam's "Do the Evolution"; Grammy Award, Best Short Form music video, 2000, for Korn's "Freak on a Leash."

■ Writings

(Illustrator) David Michelinie, *Stan Lee Presents Spider-Man Vs. Venom,* Marvel, 1990.

(With others) *Batman: Year Two,* Warner Books, 1990.

Stan Lee Presents Spider-Man: Torment, Marvel, 1992.

(With Rob Liefeld and Fabian Nicieza) *Stan Lee Presents X-Force and Spider-Man in Sabotage,* Marvel, 1992.

(Illustrator with Sal Buscema) Gerry Conway and David Michelinie, *Spider-Man: The Cosmic Adventures,* Marvel, 1993.

(With Steve Ditko, John Romita, and Mark Bernardo) *Spider-Man Unmasked,* Marvel, 1997.

Spawn Book 1, TSR, 1997.

Spawn Book 2, TSR, 1997.

Spawn Book 3, TSR, 1997.

Spawn Book 4, TSR, 1997.

Spawn Book 5: Death and Rebirth, illustrated by Greg Capullo, Image Comics, 1998.

Spawn Book 6: Pathway to Judgement, illustrated by Greg Capullo, Image Comics, 1998.

Spawn Book 7: Deadman's Touch, illustrated by Greg Capullo, Image Comics, 1998.

(With Frank Miller) *Spawn-Batman,* Image Comics, 1998.

(Editor) Brian Holguin, *Todd McFarlane Presents: Kiss Psycho Circus,* illustrated by Angel Medina and Kevin Conrad, Image Comics, 1998.

Spawn Book 8: Betrayal of Blood, illustrated by Greg Capullo, Image Comics, 1999.

Spawn Book 9: Urban Jungle, Image Comics, 1999.

Spawn Book 10: Vengeance of the Dead, illustrated by Danny Miki and Ashley Wood, Image Comics, 2000.

Spawn Book 11: Crossroads, illustrated by Danny Miki and Kevin Conrad, Image Comics, 2000.

■ Sidelights

Comic fans feel fortunate that Todd McFarlane's dreams of playing professional sports never came to fruition. Instead, the Canadian-born baseball nut began drawing comics, first pencilling for Marvel and DC, the big two of the industry, then injecting the long-running and popular series the *Amazing Spider-Man* with some new blood by stylizing the artwork and adding a new villain to the tale. Thanks to some indignation at the way comic artists were treated in the business, he soon ventured out to form his own company and decided right away to showcase an original character he had devised as a college student. Thus, *Spawn* was born. McFarlane's creation was a runaway success, becoming the top-selling comic in the United States and in several European countries and leading to animated television episodes, a live-action film, and a line of hot-selling action figures. The comic's popularity entrenched McFarlane's fledgling firm, Image Comics, as one of the top three. And in early 1999, even those not fond of comics caught news of McFarlane with his eye-popping $3 million purchase of Mark McGwire's record-setting baseball that marked his seventieth home run during the 1998 season.

McFarlane was born on March 16, 1961, in Calgary, Alberta, Canada, but when he was a baby, his family moved to Southern California. His father was a printer, and his mother was a homemaker; they divorced when McFarlane was in college. Early on, he harbored a love of and talent for baseball and held dreams of turning professional. His family moved back to Calgary when he was fourteen, and McFarlane became an athlete at William Aberhart High School. However, he was also "the best doodler in the class," as he recalled in a *People* article. Although he never held an interest in comic books as a child, at age seventeen, McFarlane discovered the genre and eventually began collecting works and copying his favorites.

Remaining committed to his goal of playing baseball, McFarlane accepted an athletic scholarship in 1981 from Eastern Washington State University in Cheney, Washington, after attending community college. He studied art and printing in school and was sketching his own comic creations. Despite his talent, he did not pursue drawing as his livelihood until he broke his ankle sliding into home plate during a college game, dashing his hopes for a solid career on the baseball field. Subsequently, he began sending out drawings to almost all of the comic publishing companies in the United States and Canada, reaping more than 700 rejection letters.

Lands Work at Marvel Comics

In March of 1984, McFarlane graduated from college with a bachelor of arts in general studies with an emphasis in communications, fine arts, and graphic design. Shortly before graduation, after mailing his portfolio out for fourteen months, he finally received an offer from the comic giant Marvel to pencil a minor story called *Scorpio Rose,* which ran as an eleven-page back-up in the more well-known comic *Coyote.* McFarlane once remarked in a *People* article that his persistence apparently paid off. "Editors knew my package was coming in every month. After a while, they said, 'Just give him some work and shut him up.'"

Although the position lasted only a short time, McFarlane went on to provide drawings for a

(Facing page) McFarlane received two Emmy Awards as executive producer of the HBO film "Spawn," starring Michael Jai White.

number of issues of the popular series *The Incredible Hulk* in 1987. Soon he also began doing freelance pencilling for Detective Comics (DC), the other bigwig in the industry, on titles like *Batman, Detective,* and *Batman: Year Two.* Also, when the two rival companies agreed to produce a book combining some of their top characters, called *Invasion,* they hired McFarlane to pencil favorites like Superman, Wonder Woman, and the Green Lantern.

Creates New Look for Spider-Man

In 1989 McFarlane began drawing and providing covers for Marvel's longstanding *Amazing Spider-Man,* jazzing up the veteran title with a new look, replacing the web with a more rubbery-looking substance, and enlarging Spider-Man's eyes to look more insect-like. The almost surreal appearance bowled over fans, boosting the book's ranking from number nine to number one and making McFarlane one of the hottest properties on the comic circuit. He then asked Marvel if he could also write the strip, and although they turned him down, they did offer the temperamental artist an offshoot title in order to keep him happy. The first issue of his creation, *Spider-Man,* was released in September of 1990 and set a record for the best-selling comic book of all time, eventually surpassing 2.5 million copies.

As the most recognized name in the comic artist field, anything carrying McFarlane's name flew off the shelves. Although he commanded nearly a $2 million annual salary, he did not own the rights to his work and knew that past artists had often experienced exploitation by publishers. In August of 1991, he began plotting how to form his own publishing firm where artists could retain the rights to their works. One day, in February of 1992, McFarlane felt especially perturbed when he was ordered to re-do some panels that the Comics Code Authority had rejected, so he walked out. Moreover, as he remarked to Joe Chidley in *Maclean's,* "It was just the constant grind." Leading six other prominent artists, McFarlane marched into the office of Marvel's president, Terry Stewart, and declared that they were all quitting. Unconcerned Marvel executives wished them well and let them know they were welcome to return. "They thought we couldn't do the printing and that we were dumb," McFarlane noted in an article for *Success.* "I said, 'These guys are going to

Todd McFarlane holding Mark McGwire's seventieth home run baseball.

sit back and do nothing because they think we'll be back in three months,' and that's what happened."

McFarlane and his cronies Erik Larsen, Jim Lee, Rob Liefeld, Whilce Portacio, Marc Silvestri, and Jim Valentino set up their own business, Image Comics, which allowed artists creative control over their characters and let them savor all the rewards of their success. McFarlane's first endeavor was *Spawn,* the concept for which had been occupying his imagination since high school. "Of all the characters I created," McFarlane told Chidley, "Spawn was the guy. On some levels, his existence is pried from mine. He's got a bit of a bad attitude, and I'd say the same for me."

Spawn Takes Off

After the first issue of *Spawn* shipped in May of 1992, the comic rose to become the best-selling independent comic of all time, moving 1.7 million copies. McFarlane would eventually print it in seventeen languages and sell it in more than 100 nations. The macabre story centers on the character of Spawn, also known as Al Simmons, the real-life name of McFarlane's former college roommate and baseball teammate, who now works for McFarlane's outfit. A grotesque and flawed protagonist, Spawn was formerly a top-notch government assassin who is killed and makes a pact with the devil in order to regain life and return to see his beloved wife. However, she does not recognize his burned physique and has already remarried, to his best friend, and Spawn discovers too late that part of the deal is that he must lead the army of Armageddon to destroy humankind.

Spawn's artwork, while appealing mainly to preteen and teenage males, is exceptionally grisly. Scenes depict beating hearts ripped from victims' chests, impalings with various blunt instruments, and a dismembered arm used as a writing utensil. However, the sophisticated themes and other intriguing elements added a fresh zest to the gory genre. For instance, the protagonist, even though his flesh is severely mangled, is definitely an African American man. "I got tired of Clark Kent and Superman and everyone all being good-looking white guys," noted McFarlane to David Wild in *Rolling Stone*.

Soon after *Spawn* came out, McFarlane was swamped with offers from toy companies like Mattel, Hasbro, and Playmates seeking to license his characters. However, none would give him creative control over the production, so he forged his own business, McFarlane Toys, in January of 1994 in order to ensure that the quality of the goods met his standards. The large corporations scoffed at his plan, but he showed them up. The exactingly detailed, if somewhat disturbing, action figures sold millions of units, amassed several industry awards, and consistently rank in the top ten in sales. McFarlane Toys soared to become the fifth-largest action-figure maker in the United States.

Next came a short television run, with McFarlane executive producing six half-hour animated segments of *Todd McFarlane's Spawn* for the HBO network, which aired in May of 1997 and won an Emmy award. Six more were shown in May of 1998, with another six scheduled in May of 1999. The first season was collected on video and became HBO's top-selling original video release of

If you enjoy the works of Todd McFarlane, you may also want to check out the following:

The works of Neil Gaiman, including the "Sandman" series of graphic novels.
The graphic novels of Alan Moore, who created the popular "Watchmen" series.
The work of Frank Miller, including the tenth anniversary edition of his groundbreaking *Batman: The Dark Night Returns*, 1997.

all time. Other *Spawn* spin-offs include CD-ROM and video games, a board game, trading cards, and a number of other comic titles based on other *Spawn* characters. It was not long before Hollywood took note, fresh off the success of comics-turned-movies like *The Crow* and *The Mask*.

McFarlane agreed to work on a live-action version of *Spawn*, starring Michael Jai White as Spawn and John Leguizamo as Clown (Satan), with New Line Cinema because they allowed him to retain most of the merchandising rights as well as have a hand in the creative side. The film debuted in August of 1997 with a respectable showing at the box office, reaping $50 million within a few weeks. The movie soundtrack debuted on the *Billboard* chart at number seven. Despite his flirtation with Hollywood, McFarlane prefers to steer clear of the limelight, and spoke harsh words for the city in his interview with Wild in *Rolling Stone*. He related, "Hollywood is for the most part in the 310 area code, and I honestly believe 310 is the real mark of the beast. The whole 666 thing is just a cover story—there are real devils in the flesh walking that place."

Branching Out

By mid-1997, McFarlane was worth an estimated $100 million. His long-term goal was to make his Spawn character as recognizable as Walt Disney's iconic Mickey Mouse. Branching out beyond *Spawn*, McFarlane was granted a license to produce action toys for the blockbuster 1998 summer movie *The X-Files* and later won the contract to produce figures for 1999's *Austin Powers: The Spy Who Shagged Me*, a sequel to the cult hit starring

Mike Meyers. He also announced that he was creating a comic book and action figure based on veteran rocker Ozzy Osbourne, as well as a line of psychedelic Beatles figures to commemorate the twenty-fifth anniversary re-release of their film *Yellow Submarine*. In another realm, in 1998 he teamed with Pearl Jam lead singer Eddie Vedder to create an animated video for their song "Do the Evolution" from the *Yield* album. It collected more than forty international awards and was nominated for a 1999 Grammy.

Although he was known as a superstar to the comic subculture marked by its fervent fans, McFarlane was not as well known outside of his field. That changed when he garnered much news attention by announcing that he was the purchaser of the baseball that hitting phenomenon Mark McGwire slammed to reach his record-setting seventieth home run in September of 1998. He bought the ball for just over $3 million in an anonymous telephone bid in January of 1999 and the following month, went public with his identity. He added it to his growing collection of historic baseballs, which included other home run balls from McGwire and Sammy Sosa.

McFarlane married his college sweetheart, Wanda, on July 27, 1985, in Calgary. She has a degree from Eastern Washington State and taught high school biology before leaving that career to become an executive in her husband's business. They lived on Vancouver Island in British Columbia for a time, then moved to an upper-middle class enclave of Phoenix, Arizona, and now live in Tempe, a Phoenix suburb. McFarlane has two daughters, Cyan and Kate, both born in the 1990s. A self-described "sports geek," he also is apart owner of the Edmonton Oilers hockey team and continues to play baseball in an amateur league at Tempe's Diablo Stadium in Arizona.

■ Works Cited

Chidley, Joe, "Dawn of Spawn," *Maclean's*, August 11, 1997, p. 52.

Lipton, Michael A., "Spawn Meister: Todd McFarlane Draws a Superhero from beyond the Grave," *People*, August 18, 1997, p. 99.

"Renegades," *Success*, February, 1996, p. 32.

"Spidey's Man," *People*, May 6, 1991, p. 105.

Wild, David, "Satanic Majesty," *Rolling Stone*, June 12, 1997, p. 126.

■ For More Information See

PERIODICALS

Advertising Age, February 16, 1998, p. 41.

Arizona Republic, October 19, 1997, p. EV5.

Columbian, February 9, 1999.

Entertainment Weekly, February 21, 1997, p. 86; December 19, 1997, p. 81.

Newsweek, August 4, 1997, p. 68.

People, May 26, 1997, p. 16.

USA Today, February 9, 1999, p. 8C.

Washington Times, February 27, 1999, p. B4.

ON-LINE

Spawn Web site, located at http://www.spawn.com (April 1, 1999).

Jacquelyn Mitchard

■ Personal

Born in 1952; married Dan Allegretti (a journalist; died, 1993); children: five.

■ Addresses

Home—Madison, WI. *Agent*—Jane Gelfman, Gelfman, Schneider Literary Agents Inc., 250 West 57th St., New York, NY 10107.

■ Career

Newspaper reporter; newspaper columnist, *Milwaukee Journal Sentinel*, beginning in 1985; author of nonfiction and fiction.

■ Writings

Mother Less Child: The Love Story of a Family, Norton, 1985.
Jane Addams: Pioneer in Social Reform and Activist for World Peace, Gareth Stevens, 1991.

(With Barbara Behm) *Jane Addams: Peace Activist*, Gareth Stevens, 1992.
The Deep End of the Ocean, Viking, 1996.
The Rest of Us: Dispatches from the Mother Ship, Viking, 1997.
The Most Wanted, Viking, 1998.

Also author (with Amy Paulsen) of the screenplays *The Serpent's Egg* and *Typhoid Mary*. Author of essays, including "Mother to Mother,"anthologized in *The Adoption Reader*, Seal Press (Seattle, WA), 1995.

■ Adaptations

The Deep End of the Ocean was adapted for a film starring Michelle Pfeiffer, Columbia, 1999.

■ Sidelights

Heralded as a first-rate storyteller, Jacquelyn Mitchard of Madison, Wisconsin, sold her 1996 book *The Deep End of the Ocean* after writing a mere one hundred pages of it. The book concerns a Midwestern family, the Cappadoras, that collapses in on itself after three-year-old Ben Cappadora is kidnapped from a hotel lobby in Chicago.

Before Mitchard's success as a novelist, she worked as a newspaper columnist for the *Milwau-*

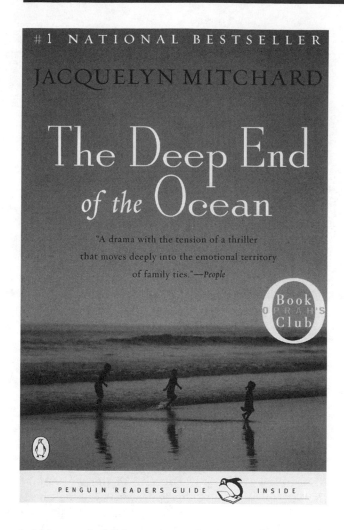

A kidnapped child reappears many years later in this 1996 story of how the family is affected by these events.

kee Journal Sentinel. Her strong desire to have children, a nearly fatal tubal pregnancy, and her efforts to cope with her inability to conceive and overcome the emotional and psychological aspects of infertility compelled Mitchard to write an account of her ordeal in *Mother Less Child*. In *Publishers Weekly*, Genevieve Stuttaford advised, "The casual reader may feel she covers the material too thoroughly, but those faced with a similar reality will empathize with the couple's plight. Mitchard writes frankly and well of a painful subject that haunts all too many." Her frankness includes discussion of how her marriage nearly failed because of the strain created by her desire to conceive a child.

Mitchard's skill and thoroughness as a writer is evidenced in her 1991 nonfiction children's book,

Jane Addams: Pioneer in Social Reform and Activist for World Peace. In 1993, when her husband, journalist Dan Allegretti, died of cancer, Mitchard was determined to keep freelancing. She used her experience as a reporter and columnist to write "*everything* for *anybody*" to pay the bills. I wrote warning labels: 'Don't point the paint-sprayer at your face while operating.' I put up with a lot of horrible rejection, but I wouldn't give in," she told Jeff Giles in *Newsweek*.

Her persistence was rewarded when she received a sizable advance for *The Deep End of the Ocean*, secured a distribution deal with the Book of the Month Club, and sold the book's movie rights to Peter Guber's film production company, producer of *Batman*. With five children to support, financial success is especially important to Mitchard.

The 1999 film version of *The Deep End of the Ocean* starred Michelle Pfeiffer and Cory Buck.

A Family Apart

Critics noted the heart-squeezing anxiety of *The Deep End of the Ocean*, specifically remarking on the intriguing characters. Donna Seaman wrote in *Booklist*, "She describes Beth's [Ben's mother] unraveling with clinical finesse, then proceeds to chronicle every aspect of the high-profile search for the missing child, the media feeding frenzy over this ideal prime-time tragedy, and the psychological toll such a cruel and mysterious disappearance exacts."

Nine years pass in the suspenseful plot, giving adequate time to explore the various family member's feelings, especially those of teenage Vincent Cappadora, who was seven when his brother disappeared. It was Vincent who was instructed to watch Ben in the crowded hotel lobby while his mother checked in. During these years, Beth's anxiety and grief has led her to neglect Vincent, her daughter Kerry, and her husband Pat. Reviewer Sybil S. Steinberg, in *Publishers Weekly*, declared that Mitchard's plot is permeated with "disturbingly candid" revelations regarding familial relationships. Gail Collins, in the *New York Times Book Review*, described the book as "not so much a thriller as a gut wrencher." Mitchard delves into all the relationships, Giles suggested in *Newsweek*, "Don't bother predicting the end: there's a plot twist that'll spin you around no matter which way you're looking."

The novel received rave reviews long before the release of the 1999 movie adaptation. In July 1996, Susan Heeger of the *Los Angeles Times Book Review* wrote that as a parent herself, she tries to "avoid the pain of reading novels about kidnapped, abused or dying children. Once in a while, though, a book like Mitchard's rises above the obvious horrors of its subject to tell a bigger story about human connection and emotional survival. *The Deep End of the Ocean* is devastating, yes, but so well observed and perceptive it's hard to shy away from. It's also masterfully paced—beginning with a prologue set a decade after Ben's kidnapping and winding back to the event itself—and the hours, days, and years that follow." Similarly, a reviewer praised *The Deep End of the Ocean* in *Publishers Weekly*: "Readers who explore the uncharted reaches of "the deep end of the ocean" with the Cappadoras will find this compelling and heartbreaking story—sure to be compared to *The Good Mother*—impossible to put down."

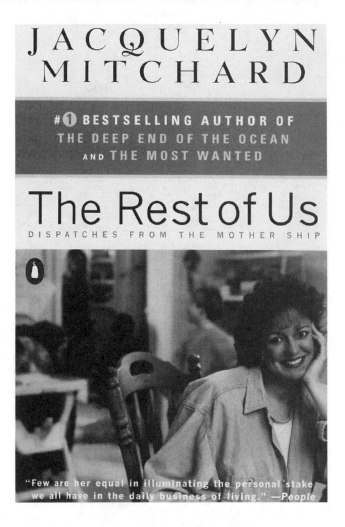

This work is a collection of the best of Mitchard's popular syndicated column about everyday life.

Better Times

With the novel's grand reception, Mitchard has been able to enjoy a more luxurious life than she had become accustomed to as a single, widowed mother of five. In *People*, Alex Tresniowski wrote that "The success of *Deep End* has enabled Mitchard, who gets help from three part-time nannies (two of whom double as editorial assistants), to build herself a private bathroom and whisk her family to Italy for two weeks this summer. She writes her column at home and keeps sane by sticking to a rigid daily plan. 'Everything is scheduled,' she explains. 'Fifteen minutes has become a substantial period of time. If I brush my hair once, if I read to my children, then that's a good day.'"

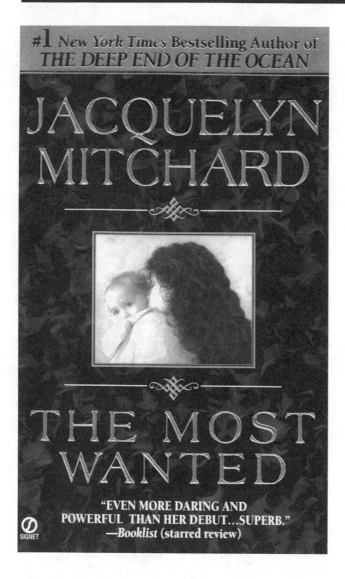

#1 *New York Times* Bestselling Author of
THE DEEP END OF THE OCEAN

JACQUELYN
MITCHARD

THE MOST
WANTED

"EVEN MORE DARING AND
POWERFUL THAN HER DEBUT...SUPERB."
—*Booklist* (starred review)

A young woman strikes up a correspondence with a prison inmate, leading to a dangerous romance, in this 1998 novel.

Good days were plentiful in the late 1990s for Mitchard. Her second novel, *The Most Wanted*, published in 1998, could easily have been a flop. After all, what could follow in the footsteps of a novel like *Deep End*? But when the reviews came in, most critics applauded Mitchard for being uncompromising of her gift; for not quickly spitting out a similar, flashy second act, but instead penning an entirely new, gripping story. About *The Most Wanted*, which concerns a young girl's infatuation with a prison inmate, Donna Seaman wrote that Mitchard's "new book is even more daring and powerful than her debut." *People's*

Emily Listfield said, "Anyone who has ever fallen for an unsuitable love will respond to Mitchard's tale of the yearning that transcends reason."

If you enjoy the works of Jacquelyn Mitchard, you may also want to check out the following books:

Bernhard Schlink, Carol Brown Janeway, *The Reader*, 1999.
Anita Shreve, *The Pilot's Wife*, 1996.
Nora Roberts, *River's End*, 1999.

Reviewers also approached her collection of columns from the *Milwaukee Journal-Sentinel, The Rest of Us: Dispatches from the Mother Ship*, with much hesitation, but in the end, applauded its honesty. Paula Chin wrote in *People*, "Mitchard first comes off as a cross between author Joyce Maynard and former *New York Times* columnist Anna Quindlen— a blandly sensible, predictably liberal sort who roots for good (courage, politeness, garage sales). . . . But something about Mitchard—one could call it grace—grows on you. She mines her children's lives without exposing or exploiting them; she writes about her husband's premature death without displaying rage or inspiring pity; she exults in a perfectly ordinary, perfectly splendid day, without mawkishness. And bully for Mitchard that she's still plugging away (her column is now nationally syndicated). Few are her equal in illuminating the personal stake we all have in the daily business of living."

■ Works Cited

Chin, Paula, "The Rest of Us: Dispatches from the Mother Ship," *People*, December 8, 1997, p. 45.
Collins, Gail, review of *The Deep End of the Ocean*, *New York Times Book Review*, August 18, 1996, p. 22.
Review of *The Deep End of the Ocean*, *Publishers Weekly*, April 1, 1996, p. 54.
Giles, Jeff, review of *The Deep End of the Ocean*, *Newsweek*, June 3, 1996, pp. 72-74.
Heegen, Susan, "Shock Waves From a Little Boy Lost," *Los Angeles Times Book Review*, July 14, 1996, pp. 4, 8.

Listfield, Emily, "The Most Wanted," *People*, June 1, 1998, p. 41.

Seaman, Donna, review of *The Deep End of the Ocean*, *Booklist*, April 1, 1996, p. 1324.

Seaman, Donna, review of *The Most Wanted*, *Booklist*, April 15, 1998, p. 1356.

Steinberg, Sybil S., review of *The Deep End of the Ocean*, *Publishers Weekly*, April 1, 1996, p. 54.

Stuttaford, Genevieve, review of *Mother Less Child: The Love Story of a Family*, *Publishers Weekly*, February 1, 1985, p. 353.

Tresniowski, Alex, "Harried . . . with children," *People*, September 23, 1996, p. 133.

■ For More Information See

PERIODICALS

Booklist, March 15, 1985, p. 1019.

Choice, October, 1991, p. 245.

Kirkus Reviews, January 15, 1985, p. 81; March 15, 1996, p. 400; April 1, 1998, p. 429.

Library Journal, March 15, 1985, p. 67; April 15, 1996, p. 123.

Publishers Weekly, February 1, 1985, p. 353.

Mike Myers

■ Personal

Born May 25, 1963, in Liverpool, England (some sources say Scarborough, Ontario, Canada or Toronto, Ontario, Canada); immigrated to Scarborough, Ontario, Canada; Canadian and British citizen; married Robin Ruzan (a screenwriter), May 22, 1993. *Hobbies and other interests:* Hockey.

■ Addresses

Home—Los Angeles, CA. *Agent*—United Talent Agency, 9560 Wilshire Blvd., Suite 500, Beverly Hills, CA 90212.

■ Career

Actor, comedian, and screenwriter. Appeared in television commercials in Canada, beginning 1970; cast member, Second City comedy troupe, Toronto, beginning 1981, and Chicago, mid-1980s-89; cast member, *Mullarkey & Myers,* 1984; actor, *110 Lombard* (pilot), CBS, 1988; cast member and writer, *Saturday Night Live,* 1989-94; *Saturday Night*

Live Goes Commercial (special), NBC, 1991; *Saturday Night Live Halloween Special* (special), NBC, 1991; *Saturday Night Live: All the Best for Mother's Day* (special), NBC, 1992. Actor in movies, including *Wayne's World,* Paramount, 1992; *So I Married An Axe Murderer,* TriStar, 1993; *Wayne's World 2,* Paramount, 1993; and (also producer) *Austin Powers: International Man of Mystery,* New Line Cinema, 1997. Guest actor and host on television programs, including *The Littlest Hobo,* syndicated, 1979; *MTV's 1990 Video Music Awards,* MTV, 1990; *MTV's 1991 Video Music Awards,* MTV, 1991; *The Forty-third Annual Primetime Emmy Awards Presentation,* Fox, 1991; *The Sixty-fourth Annual Academy Awards Presentation,* ABC, 1992; *Saturday Night Live,* NBC, 1997; *Sparkle Lounge,* 1997; *MTV Movie Awards,* MTV, 1997; and *The Russell Gilbert Show,* 1998. Interviewed Madonna for *Interview* magazine, 1993; has toured with Barbra Streisand as character "Linda Richman;" frequent guest on television talk shows.

■ Awards, Honors

Emmy Award for Outstanding Writing in a Variety or Musical Program (with others), 1989, for *Saturday Night Live;* MTV Movie Award for best on-screen duo (with Dana Carvey), 1992, for *Wayne's World;* MTV Movie Award for best dance sequence, MTV Movie Award for best villain, MTV Movie Award nominee for best comedic performance, and Blockbuster Entertainment Award nominee for favorite actor in a comedy, all 1998, all for *Austin Powers: International Man of Mystery.*

■ Writings

SCREENPLAYS

(With Bonnie Turner and Terry Turner) *Wayne's World,* Paramount, 1992.

(Uncredited) *So I Married an Axe Murderer,* TriStar, 1993.

Wayne's World 2, Paramount, 1993.

Austin Powers: International Man of Mystery (also known as *Austin Powers*), New Line Cinema, 1997.

Austin Powers: The Spy Who Shagged Me, New Line Cinema, 1999.

OTHER

(With wife, Robin Ruzan) *Wayne's World: Extreme Close-Up,* Hyperion (New York City), 1992.

Also writer for television shows and specials, including *Saturday Night Live,* NBC, 1989-94; *The Dave Thomas Comedy Show,* CBS, 1990; and *Saturday Night Live Halloween Special,* NBC, 1991.

■ Work in Progress

Acting in films, including *Meteor; McClintock's Peach,* West Wind Entertainment; *Just Like Me,* New Line Cinema; *It's A Dog's Life* (also known as *Pet People*), Warner Bros.; and *Sprockets,* Universal.

■ Sidelights

Canadian actor and comedian Mike Myers became a star in the early 1990s with his array of instantly recognizable characters such as Wayne, the television-addled, heavy-metalhead teenager whose world revolves around a quixotic search for "babes"; and Linda Richman, the bourgeois Jewish housewife (based on Myers's mother-in-law) who hosts a fictitious "Coffee Talk" show and advises viewers to "talk amongst yourselves." Beginning in 1992 with *Wayne's World,* Myers began directing his comedic talents towards screenwriting, penning scripts and adapting his characters for films in which he also stars, including *Austin Powers: International Man of Mystery.*

Wayne, undoubtedly Myers's most popular creation, is the star of a public-access talk show broadcast out of his parents' paneled basement in Aurora, Illinois, where, with his friend Garth (played by *Saturday Night Live* colleague Dana Carvey), he holds forth on beer, rock music, and a teenage vision of sexual conquest. Myers has told interviewers that Wayne is very much based on himself and his friends as they grew up in the white suburbs of Scarborough, Ontario, in the 1970s. "Wayne is me. I am Wayne," he told the *Miami Herald.* "I had a great childhood. . . . And now I hate adulthood. . . . I like adulthood to the extent that I'm more free to be a child." In a similarly self-deprecating vein, he told *Entertainment Weekly* that he was "a feral child raised by television" in "a very suburby suburb of Toronto, very flat—there are a lot of doughnut stores and factory carpet outlets." Yet Myers was obviously no average child, and he admitted to a *Rolling Stone* interviewer that among the rowdy teens he hung out with, he was the one who always got his homework done and whose moral sense caused him to advise against vandalism. He was also a student who, in high school, wrote essays on the films of Louis Malle and on a comparison between James Bond movies and author Joseph Campbell's mythic hero cycle.

Born in Liverpool, England, in 1963, Myers immigrated with his parents to Ontario at a very young age. His British roots remain important to him: he treasures a distant relationship to the Romantic poet William Wordsworth (first cousin, seven generations removed), and asserts comically that until age four, he thought John Lennon and his father were the same person because no one else in Scarborough spoke with a Liverpool accent. Myers's father, who earned his living selling encyclopedias, was a devotee of British comedy such as *Monty Python's Flying Circus,* a program he encouraged his children to watch, and of rock music such as the Talking Heads. Myers's mother, a former actress, found work for her gifted son in television commercials from the time he was eight years old.

It was from watching the *Dick Van Dyke Show,* Myers told the *Miami Herald* interviewer, that he first conceived the ambition of becoming a comedy writer. Myers idolized the original *Saturday Night Live* cast members from the time he was eleven. He was working out informal comedy routines as a youngster, too, and early versions of

Myers starred as Wayne Campbell and Dana Carvey as his sidekick, Garth, in the wildly popular 1992 film *Wayne's World*, based on characters created by Myers for *Saturday Night Live*.

Wayne appeared, as self-parodies for his peer group, during his adolescence.

From Second City to *SNL*

Although he had applied to York University in Toronto, Myers obtained an audition to the famous Second City comedy troupe on the day he graduated from high school, and was hired the same day. "My last exam was at 9 a.m. My audition for Second City was at noon. I got accepted at three," he recalled for Brian D. Johnson of *Maclean's*. He spent the early 1980s in the Toronto troupe of Second City, then moved to the Chicago troupe, honing his improvisational craft along the way. In 1989, he was summoned to New York by *Saturday Night Live* (*SNL*) producer Lorne Michaels, a fellow Canadian, on the recommendation of cast members. Awed by his first real visit to New York City, Myers stopped Michaels

at one point in mid-interview to ask whether that tall, spired building he could see through the window was really the Empire State Building. As with Second City, Myers was hired immediately and was soon successful after joining the cast.

His stint on *SNL* boosted Myers to stardom. His characters became high points of the show, and their catchphrases became widely echoed among youngsters. Particularly popular was Wayne's "Not!," which was used to deflate any overblown affirmative statement. *Esquire*'s Alex Gross appraised the character and the phrase this way: "A parody of the ubiquitous talkshow format, 'Wayne's World' is also about a world in which our last common experience is the joy of watching and deconstructing bad TV. Wayne's trademark exclamation—"Not!'—is the kind of all-obliterating riposte that TV in the cable era demands." *Washington Post* writer Todd Allan Yasui called Myers "a standout in an ensemble, no doubt due

Myers appeared with Nancy Travis in the 1993 film *So I Married an Axe Murderer.*

to his ability to create vastly different personas with a rubbery face, manic gestures and dialects. . . . Myers is a Chaplin kind-of-guy, a physical comic actor. He's a skeletal mishmash of body language."

Yet the persona of Myers himself, offstage, had remained very much that of a likable fellow, Yasui observed. Myers and Carvey took their Wayne-and-Garth routine to the big screen in 1992, unsure of its prospects but confident of its comic quality; they were rewarded with one of the major hits of the year and an even bigger cult following. *Wayne's World,* made on a thirteen million dollar budget, earned forty million dollars in its first two months and kept going from there. The sequel, *Wayne's World 2* (1993), did well but not well enough to meet the expectations that the

first installment had raised; another 1993 movie script by and starring Myers, *So I Married an Axe Murderer,* was a commercial flop although it has retained a core following on the video-rental market.

At that point in his career, Myers was feeling overwhelming by his heavy schedule, which juggled regular *Saturday Night Live* appearances with films and tours. He was also grieving over the death of his beloved father after along struggle with Alzheimer's disease and the death of his wife's brother in a car accident. When his contract expired in 1994, Myers quit *Saturday Night Live* and, on the advice of *SNL* old-timer Bill Murray, took some time off to assess his life and to do what he wanted, which in his case was to take skating lessons and play recreational hockey.

The year off, which translated into three years away from the big screen, was "great," as Myers told the online interviewer for the *Mr. Showbiz* website. He visited relatives in Canada and England, spent time with his wife Robin, whom he had married in 1993, and recharged his creative batteries.

The Origin of Austin Powers

It was while driving home from hockey practice that Myers heard Dusty Springfield singing the Burt Bacharach song "The Look of Love" on the car radio, which provided him with the inspiration for a new character, Austin Powers, a 1960s mod British fashion photographer who doubles as a secret agent. Developing the character informally, Myers would ask his wife campy questions such as, "Hey baby, you wanna swing?" That creative setting was perfect for Myers, who told Mr. Showbiz, "Everything I've ever done has been to try to make girls laugh at parties. Now that I'm married, Robin is my one girl that I make laugh." He also developed the Powers character as front man for a mock rock group, Austin Powers and Ming Tea, which played in Los Angeles clubs for a while and featured real-life rock stars Susanna Hoffs of the Bangles on guitar and Matthew Sweet on keyboards.

After a time, his wife urged Myers to write down the Powers routine. He did so in the form of a screenplay, which he wrote in three weeks and sold to New Line Cinema. He talked his producers into hiring his friend Jay Roach as director, and Roach allowed his star a great deal of improvisational freedom on camera. "He is a brilliant improv artist," Roach told *Maclean's* Johnson. "He loved to play to the crew, and I rolled a lot of film after the place where the cut would be. Sometimes, he was literally writing like a lucid dreamer, generating images without pause or the slightest hesitation."

The film *Austin Powers: International Man of Mystery* is an energetic spoof of British spy movies of the 1960s with intense overtones of Beatles movies, "Swinging London," and such 1960s touchstones as the television show *Rowan and Martin's Laugh-In.* Myers plays both Austin Powers and his nemesis, Dr. Evil, a bald, scarfaced man in a gray Nehru jacket who pets a white-furred cat while pressing buttons that send his henchmen to fiery

If you enjoy the works of Mike Myers, you may also want to check out the following:

Jim Carrey's "Ace Ventura" films, as well as *The Mask,* 1994, and *Liar, Liar,* 1997.

The movies of Peter and Bobby Farrelly, including *Kingpin,* 1996, and *There's Something about Mary,* 1998.

Adam Sandler's comedies, including *Happy Gilmore,* 1996, and *The Wedding Singer,* 1998.

deaths. Although not a major big-screen hit, the film received good reviews and became quite popular as a rental; its affectionate parodies of British culture made it especially popular in that country. One very enthusiastic reviewer was Marianne Goh of *Inkpot Movie Reviews,* who declared it "a great movie," partly because of its many celebrity cameos and its chemistry between Myers and costar Elizabeth Hurley. "*Austin Powers: International Man of Mystery* will take you on a psychedelic walk down memory lane," Goh assured even those viewers who were too young to remember the Sixties. Similarly adapting Myers' own vocabulary to his review, Jeff Shannon, in *seattle.sidewalk,* proclaimed, "If you know all the targets that Myers is aiming at, you'll have a bloody groovy time, baby."

This new cult following left Myers in a position to muse philosophical for Johnson in his *Maclean's* interview. "You go through phases in life," he told Johnson, reflecting on the stages of adulthood. "You get a futon. You get a futon on a frame. You get a grown-up bed. You get married. You get dogs. You have kids. We're in our dog phase now."

A Phenomenal Response

Months after its release, *Austin Powers* was praised by the public and media as something never before done or seen in film, "a new kind of phenomenon: a national cult megahit," Owen Gleiberman wrote in *Entertainment Weekly.* Gleiberman admitted in that article that himself couldn't help jumping on the bandwagon: "I was wandering through a video store, and I saw

A spoof of 1960s British spy movies, *Austin Powers: International Man of Mystery* catapulted Myers (shown here with costar Elizabeth Hurley) to superstardom.

half a dozen people staring up at TV monitor, idiot grins plastered on their faces, as they watched Austin vanquish the Fembots with his arse-thrusting, nipple-diddling dance to 'I Touch Myself.' I joined the gawkers, and was soon beaming idiotically too. It was obvious that we'd all seen the movie before (some more than once). Yet Meyers' shameless exuberance was addictive; you had to keep watching him. . . . The glory of Myers as Austin Powers is that he was willing to be majestically uncool, transcendently embarrassing. What, in the end, could be more extreme than that?"

Following hype like that, it's no wonder that 1999's *Austin Powers: The Spy Who Shagged Me*, "awaited by legions of panting devotees," as

Kendall Hamilton put it in *Newsweek*, descended one notch lower on the cult-o-meter. "There is just enough joy in *The Spy Who Shagged Me* to make you wish there had been more of it. Myers and his collaborators, cowriters Michael McCullers and director Jay Roach, don't do anything terribly wrong, yet the new movie, I'm afraid, is a mixed bag, baby," critiqued Gleiberman. Movie reviewer Janet Maslin of the *New York Times* agreed that the new Austin Powers movie was "several love beads short of its predecessor, but some of that was bound to happen once Austin's novelty dimmed." *The Spy Who Shagged Me*, which picks up where the first left off and introduces Dr. Evil's new best friend, a pint-sized clone dubbed Mini-Me, was nevertheless applauded by several critics for its clean writing, crafty double entendres, and absolute absurdity. "'The Spy Who Shagged Me' is mostly the goofy, jubilant fun it ought to be," wrote Hamilton in *Newsweek*. "[It] mostly does a good job of paring down and improving the first film's minor characters," mused Janet Maslin in the *New York Times*. At the box office, the movie did better than its predecessor. It played during the prestigious French festival, and pulled in $20 million on the Friday of its North American opening. *Austin Powers: International Man of Mystery*, by comparison, only earned $9.5 million in its entire first weekend. Things couldn't be going any groovier for Myers.

But is his life behind-the-scenes as sweet? Surprisingly, Myers has been rumoured to be an uptight

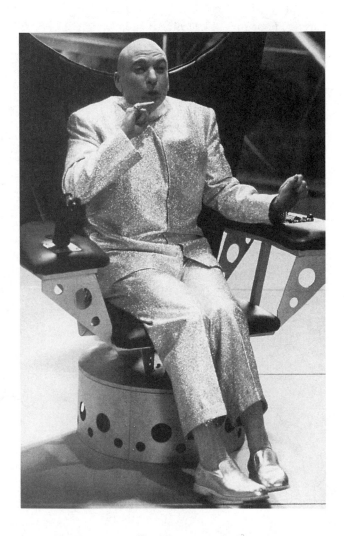

In *Austin Powers: The Spy Who Shagged Me*, Myers reprised his dual roles as the lovable British secret agent and his nemisis, Dr. Evil.

ogre on the set. He insists this is an untruth that "spreads virally each time it is repeated." In a *Rolling Stone* interview, he told Chris Heath that the rumour comes from two difficult days on the set of *So I Married an Axe Murderer*, the 1993 film he made following his father's death from Alzheimer's Disease. "I was heartbroken, and just not a happy person at the time. I didn't get along with the director, but just for two days. It was sixty great days and two bad days. It was an old-fashioned disagreement that got personal, and it became the story of that movie."

On set of *The Spy Who Shagged Me*, it seems Mike Myers decided to take his character's own advice: "Oh, behave!" During breaks, he was the goofy child-turned-comic everyone knows and loves. "Between takes, Myers drives a trolley around the set himself, like a kid," wrote Heath in *Rolling Stone*. "He wanders over to the camera crane and carefully examines the words printed large on its side: SWISS CRANE. "I think it's sick," he says. "Are there no American cranes?"

■ Works Cited

Gleiberman, Owen, "Wood vs. Evil," *Entertainment Weekly*, June 18, 1999, p. 51.

Goh, Marianne, review of *Austin Powers: International Man of Mystery*, Inkpot Movie Reviews Web site, located at http://www.inkpot.com/film/austinpowers.html (1998).

Gross, Alex, "It's a Wayne's, Wayne's, Wayne's, Wayne's World," *Esquire*, March, 1992, p. 69.

Hamilton, Kendall, "Mr. Mojo Rising," *Newsweek*, January 21, 1999.

Heath, Chris, "Yeah, Baby, It's Mike's World," *Rolling Stone*, June 10, 1999, p. 66.

Johnson, Brian D., "Mike's English Mayhem," *Maclean's*, May 5, 1997, pp. 66-67.

Maslin, Janet, "*Austin Powers: The Spy Who Shagged Me*—The Girls All Go for His Euphemism," *New York Times*, June 11, 1999, pp. 1-4.

Myers, Mike, interview in *Miami Herald*, February 12, 1992.

Myers, Mike, interview on *Mr. Showbiz* Web site, located at http://www.mrshowbiz.com (1998).

Shannon, Jeff, review of *Austin Powers: International Man of Mystery*, *Seattle.sidewalk* Web site, located at http://seattle.sidewalk.com (1997).

Yasui, Todd Allen, "Say Hello to SNL's Latest Star," *Washington Post*, April 22, 1990, p. 7.

■ For More Information See

BOOKS

Contemporary Theatre, Film, and Television, Volume 11, Gale, 1994.
Newsmakers 1992, Gale, 1992.

PERIODICALS

Booklist, February 1, 1992, pp. 1001, 1015.
Cosmopolitan, May, 1993, p. 86.
Entertainment Weekly, May 17, 1991; February 21, 1992, pp. 32, 51; February 28, 1992, p. 16; March 6, 1992, p. 65; August 14, 1992, p. 64; October 9, 1992, p. 9; December 25, 1992, p. 7; February 19, 1993, p. 8; August 6, 1993, p. 34; March 4, 1994, p. 68; February 10, 1995, p. 77; May 9, 1997, p. 84.
Interview, August, 1993, p. 76.
Los Angeles Times, November 3, 1991.
Maclean's, February 24, 1992, p. 58; July 26, 1993, p. 40.
New Statesman & Society, May 22, 1992, p. 36.

Newsweek, May 19, 1997, p. 84.
New York, February 24, 1992, p. 118.
New Yorker, December 13, 1993, p. 126.
New York Times, May 2, 1997, p. B7; May 4, 1997, p. SM24.
People, February 24, 1992, p. 15; August 9, 1993, p. 19; December 20, 1993, p. 20; April 4, 1994, p. 84; February 27, 1995, p. 34; May 5, 1997, p. 22.
Premiere, March, 1992, pp. 19, 70; August, 1992, p. 93.
Publishers Weekly, January 20, 1992, p. 59.
Rolling Stone, November 16, 1989; March 19, 1992, p. 34; September 3, 1992, p. 64; August 19, 1993, p. 82.
Seventeen, January, 1994, p. 64.
Time, March 2, 1992, p. 68; December 20, 1993, p. 63; March 31, 1997, p. 89; June 21, 1999, pp. 70-71.
Variety, February 17, 1992, p. 69; March 23, 1992, p. 1; August 2, 1993, p. 44; December 20, 1993, p. 31.
Washington Post, February 14, 1992; February 16, 1992; July 30, 1993; December 10, 1993.

Kristen D. Randle

■ Personal

Born May 8, 1952, in Kansas City, MO; daughter of Jack Delmont (an engineer) and Jackie (maiden name, Sneed) Downey; married Guy Lawrence Randle (a music producer), April 17, 1978; children: Virginia, Cammon, Charlotte, Jackson. *Education:* Brigham Young University, B.A., 1973, additional study, 1975-76. *Politics:* "Moderately Conservative." *Religion:* Latter Day Saints ("Mormon").

■ Addresses

Agent—c/o William Morrow & Company, 1350 Avenue of the Americas, New York, NY, 10019.

■ Career

Teacher at Brigham Young University and at high schools in Utah; secretary and treasurer of Rosewood Recording Company; partner in Moonstone Media (music production company); has recorded several albums of children's songs. Has also worked as a studio manager, bookkeeper, singer, genealogist, dental assistant, and photographer.

■ Awards, Honors

Best Books, American Library Association (ALA), 1995; New York City Public Libraries, 1996; Dorothy Canfield Fischer (Vermont), 1996; Utah Association of Literature, 1996; and Book of the Year for Young Adults, Michigan Library Association, 1996, all for *The Only Alien on the Planet*.

■ Writings

YOUNG ADULT NOVELS

Home Again, Embryo, 1981.
One Song for Two, Bookcraft (Salt Lake City, UT), 1984.
The Morning Comes Singing, Bookcraft, 1986.
On the Side of the Angels, Bookcraft, 1989.
The Only Alien on the Planet, Scholastic, 1995.
Breaking Rank, Morrow, 1999.

CHILDREN'S PICTURE BOOKS

Why Did Grandma Have to Die?, illustrated by Shauna Mooney, Bookcraft, 1988.

■ Work in Progress

Young adult, science fiction, and fantasy books.

■ Sidelights

Author Kristin D. Randle has an uncanny knack for pinpointing and dealing with the kinds of concerns and emotional turmoil that her young

Kristen D. Randle with her family.

adult (YA) readers are struggling to deal with. This no doubt accounts for the growing popularity of her books, the first of which was published by small regional publisher in her home state of Utah. However, in 1995 Randle reached a national audience for the first time with her acclaimed novel *The Only Alien on the Planet*. That book, which has won seven literary awards and been widely praised by reviewers, is her best-known and most successful effort to date.

Despite her success, Randle still does not consider writing her "career." That has meant that unlike most successful authors, she is not represented by a literary agent. What is more, she prefers spending time with her husband and children or working at the family's recording studio to sitting at a keyboard tapping out stories. Randle works at her

writing only sporadically—mostly when "she feels a story coming to her that needs to be told," as she explained in a 1997 entry in *Something About the Author Autobiography Series*. "If I could give up writing, I would. Like a shot. Achieving a book is just too darned much work. But I don't seem to be able to give it up," she added.

While Randle's haphazard approach may be somewhat unorthodox, it seems to suit her well. She has written several novels, all of which deal with young people struggling to come to grips with such universal concerns as friends, school, and the search for self-identity. That the need for truth and meaning in one's life is a recurring themes in Randle's fiction is no accident; being a member of the Church of the Latter Day Saints (commonly known as LDS or Mormons), she imbues her writing with the same strong sense of moral values. "For the record, I believe in right and wrong," Randle explained in an autobiographical sketch that appears on her Internet homepage. "I believe the right choices are often tough ones, that personal comfort isn't as important as service to other people, that truth isn't a matter of personal perception, I believe in weighing consequences. I don't believe in whining, or in an effort to sidestep responsibility. This doesn't mean that I don't make mistakes; I just believe that they are *my* mistakes when I make them. And I believe that Believing, itself, is terribly important—for people and for communities."

Randle was born in Independence, a suburb of Kansas City, Missouri. She was the eldest of the three children of Jack and Jackie Downey. Both were college graduates; Randle's father was an engineer, while her mother earned a Bachelor's degree in chemistry. Jack Downey lost his job on the same day his daughter Kristin was born, but he found another one building new terminals for Trans World Airlines (TWA). He was frequently transferred around by the company. As a result, the family was highly mobile and lived all over the country. Despite these many moves, Randle recalls her childhood as a happy one filled with fond memories. "I had a great time as a child," she wrote in *SAAS*. "My family was strong and happy and healthy."

Drawn to Books

Young Kristen spent the first four years of her life in Kansas City, and then the Randles moved to Los Angeles. Other stops on their travels included a return stay in Kansas City; Harsdale, New York; and Arlington,Texas. As a result of her family's peripatetic lifestyle and their conversion to the Mormon faith during their time in Los Angeles, Randle often found it difficult to make lasting friendships at the schools she attended or in the communities where she lived. Instead, she found solace in music—she has always loved to sing— and in the world of books. All the members of the Downey family were avid readers; Jack Downey loved science fiction, and Jackie historical nonfiction. "It was in L.A. that I discovered the library. And horse books," Randle wrote in *SAAS*. "I love the feel of them in my hand, I love the way they look, lined up on shelves and piled in corners." Given her fascination with the printed

word, it was inevitable that Randle would begin to dream of writing (as her father also had). However, it was another ten years before she actually began trying to do so.

Upon her graduation from high school in the spring of 1969, Randle enrolled at Brigham Young University (BYU) in Provo, Utah. There she earned a Bachelor of Arts degree in 1973, and developed an interest in photography and poetry. Although she had earned a teaching certificate, Randle had no desire to return to the classroom. Instead, she worked at a succession of low-paying jobs, as a receptionist and a clerk in a retail store. She began writing as an outlet for the frustrations she was feeling. "The stories were pretty terrible— fairy-tale melodramas," she wrote in *SAAS*. "I'd

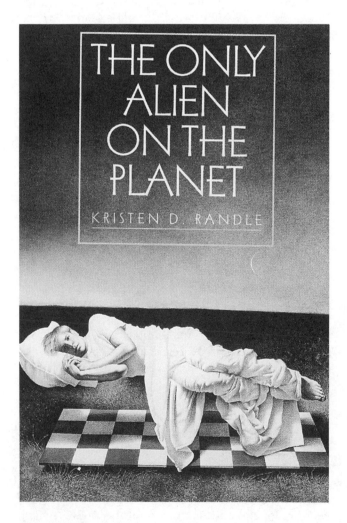

Ginny discovers that her new friend Smitty is harboring a terrible secret in this 1995 novel.

sit for hours at my old, clunky typewriter, mildly annoyed at my roommates when they trooped through and shattered the mood."

Finally, in the fall of 1975 Randle decided to go to graduate school at BYU, and she took a job there as a teaching assistant—"pushing around helpless freshmen, more like," she quipped in the blurb that appears on her Web site. It was also around this time that Randle met her husband-to-be: Guy Randle is a fellow Mormon who earns his living as a musician. The couple dated for two years before marrying in 1978. "We built a house on the river, added a recording studio (our means of support), and had a baby," Randle recalled in her *SAAS* sketch. She began working as an editor for a small publishing house, and in the course of her duties she rewrote a book for her employer. Doing so convinced her that she could write her own book. The result was a YA novel entitled *Home Again*, which was published in 1981 by Bookcraft, a Mormon publisher in Salt Lake City.

Gains Attention for *Alien*

Randle educated all four of her children at home, working at her writing when time and circumstances allowed. She produced three more novels for Bookcraft over the next eight years: *One Song For Two* (1984), *The Morning Comes Singing* (1986), and *On the Side of the Angels* (1989), as well as a children's story book called *Why Did Grandma Have to Die?* (1988). Being without a literary agent, Randle had lots to learn about the ways of the publishing industry beyond Utah. However, after a couple of false starts, in 1989 she found a national publisher for her YA novel *The Only Alien on the Planet*. That book reached a wide audience both in North America and overseas, where it was translated into Norwegian and Italian. The novel also won widespread critical praise, being included on the American Library Association Best Books list for 1995 and winning the Michigan Library Association's Best Book of the Year award, among other honors.

The Only Alien on the Planet is the story of Ginny Christianson, whose happy life is disrupted when her family moves during Ginny's senior year at high school and her brother leaves for college. Feeling lonely and confused at her new school, Ginny befriends an enigmatic young man named Smitty Tibbs, a bright, but silent student whom

---

If you enjoy the works of Kristen D. Randle, you may also want to check out the following books:

James W. Bennett, *I Can Hear the Mourning Dove*, 1990.
Joanne Greenberg, *I Never Promised You a Rose Garden*, 1964.
Tres Seymour, *Life in the Desert*, 1992.

---

the other kids derisively refer to as "the Alien." When Ginny and a girlfriend attempt to draw Tibbs out of his shell, they inadvertently uncover a terrible secret that he has been hiding. Eventually, the boy overcomes his problems, and he and Ginny begin a romance.

Critical reactions to *The Only Alien on the Planet* were generally favorable. Reviewer Anne O'Malley of *Booklist* wrote the "overall impact of this psychological novel is . . . powerful." Susan L. Rogers of *School Library Journal* described the novel as "utterly compelling," even though she felt the story's ending "fall[s] into place a little too easily and neatly"; nonetheless, she concluded that the novel is "a fast-moving, unusual contemporary romance that should have great appeal." Judy Sasges of the *Voice of Youth Advocates* praised *The Only Alien on the Planet* as "an earnest novel with good intentions." She noted that the "dialogue is stiff,and at times too mature for the character." According to Sasges, *The Only Alien on the Planet* does not offer a true-to-life depiction of mental illness, but concluded that "Despite these weaknesses, the novel is involving, has a hopeful ending, and will appeal to older YAs."

Successful Follow-up

Randle's next YA novel built on the critical and commercial success of *The Only Alien on the Planet*. *Breaking Rank* is another tale of a young woman who reaches out to someone who is a social outcast. Seventeen-year-old high school student Casey Willardson's family and friends are concerned when she begins tutoring Thomas Fairbairn, a member of a secretive male gang called the. The story is told from the alternating viewpoints of the two principal characters. Inevitably, social labels and preconceptions crumble as Casey and

Thomas get to know one another and gradually fall in love.

Like *The Only Alien on the Planet*, *Breaking Rank* was well received by reviewers, and *Booklist* cited the novel as one of its Top Ten Books of 1999. *Booklist* reviewer Shelle Rosenfeld praised the novel as "[g]ritty, smart, and realistic." "This modern, insightful Romeo and Juliet story is a rare and notable contribution to the teen fiction genre," wrote Rosenfeld. of *Horn Book* reviewer Kitty Flynn faulted "a plot . . . [that] bogs down in details," but judged *Breaking Rank* "a sensitively told story that resonates with loss and, in the end, hope."

The theme of hope—and of the essential goodness of people—is a recurring one in Randle's fiction, which is strongly moral without being preachy. That this is the case is very much a reflection of the author's view of the world and the strong convictions that form a framework for her own life. "I think my characters tend to be composites of all sorts of people and ideas. My stories seem to come out of a mosaic of memories and observations, pictures mixed with meaning," Randle explained in the sketch that appears on her Web site.

The author has also said that while some stories beg to be told, she feels that writers should choose carefully what they write. "The arts we share should strengthen, enlarge heart and mind, give hope, have at least a suggestion of meaning. . . ." she once stated. "Art should comfort us, bring us hope, ennoble us, shore up our courage, put higher prices on us, allow us to see ourselves as people with choices, even in the midst of seemingly impossible circumstances. Selling a book means nothing. Offering a gift of self means everything. . . . You search for light—you head for it and you take as many as you can along. You give your best."

■ Works Cited

Flynn, Kitty, review of *Breaking Rank*, *Horn Book Magazine*, March, 1999, p. 212.
O'Malley, Anne, review of *The Only Alien on the Planet*, *Booklist*, January 15, 1995, p. 913.
Randle, Kristen D., autobiographical sketch, Kristen Randle Internet Web site, located at http://www.kristen.randle.com.
Randle, Kristen D., entry for *Something About the Author Autobiography Series*, Volume 24, Gale, 1997, pp. 197-215.
Rogers, Susan L., review of *The Only Alien on the Planet*, *School Library Journal*, March, 1995, p. 225.
Rosenfeld, Shell, review of *Breaking Rank*, *Booklist*, May 1, 1999, p. 1590.
Sasges, Judy, review of *The Only Alien on the Planet*, *Voice of Youth Advocates*, April, 1995, p. 26.

■ For More Information See

PERIODICALS

ALAN Review, Fall, 1999, p. 36.
Kirkus Reviews, March 15, 1995, p. 392.
Kliatt, January, 1997, p. 10.
Publishers Weekly, January 23, 1995, p. 71; May 17, 1999, p. 80.
School Library Journal, May, 1999, p. 130.
Voice of Youth Advocates, April, 1995, p. 26; December, 1999, p. 338.

—Sketch by Ken Cuthbertson

J. K. Rowling

▪ Personal

Born c. 1965, in Chipping Sodbury, England; children: Jessica. *Education:* Attended Exeter University.

▪ Addresses

Home—Edinburgh, Scotland. *Agent*—c/o Scholastic, Inc., 555 Broadway, New York, NY 10012.

▪ Career

Amnesty International, secretary; teacher of English as a Foreign Language, Portugal. Writer, 1996—.

▪ Awards, Honors

Scottish Arts Council Grant, 1996; Children's Book of the Year, British Book Awards, and Gold Winner, Smarties Book Prize, both 1997, Birmingham Cable Children's Book Award, the Young Telegraph Paperback of the Year, Sheffield Children's

Book Award, and short-listed for The Guardian Fiction Award and the Carnegie Medal, all for *Harry Potter and the Philosopher's Stone;* Gold Winner, Smarties Book Prize, 1998, and shortlist, Whitbread Children's Book of the Year Award, both for *Harry Potter and the Chamber of Secrets;* Anne Spencer Lindbergh Prize in Children's Literature, 1997-98, and ABBY Award, American Booksellers Association, 1999, both for *Harry Potter and the Sorcerer's Stone.*

▪ Writings

Harry Potter and the Philosopher's Stone, Bloomsbury, 1997, published in the U.S. as *Harry Potter and the Sorcerer's Stone,* Scholastic, 1998.

Harry Potter and the Chamber of Secrets, Bloomsbury, 1998, Scholastic, 1999.

Harry Potter and the Prisoner of Azkaban, Bloomsbury, 1999.

Harry Potter and the Doomspell Tournament, Arthur A. Levine, 2000.

▪ Adaptations

Harry Potter and the Sorcerer's Stone and *Harry Potter and the Chamber of Secrets* have been optioned for motion pictures by Warner Bros.

Rowling's "Harry Potter" books have been translated into several languages, including French,

German, Italian, Dutch, Greek, Finnish, Danish, Spanish, and Swedish.

■ Work in Progress

More novels about the school career of Harry Potter (to a total of seven).

■ Sidelights

J. K. Rowling is a British author of novels for young people who caused an overnight sensation with her first book, *Harry Potter and the Philosopher's Stone*, which sold out of its first edition quickly and has been reprinted many times. Even before publication, publishers in the United States were vying for rights to the book, with top bidding going to Scholastic, which paid $100,000, the most ever for a first novel by a children's book author. *Harry Potter and the Philosopher's Stone* rose to the top of the children's best-seller lists in 1998, and was optioned by Warner Brothers for a movie. Its sequel, *Harry Potter and the Chamber of Secrets,* went to the top of the adult best-seller lists in England shortly after its 1998 release, and consumer demand in the U.S. for the book brokered a new era in Internet sales of books internationally, fueling concern over publishing rights.

Rowling plans to continue her Harry Potter saga for seven books, spinning a magical blend of wit and fantasy—a surreal melange of "the dark juvenile novels of Roald Dahl and C. S. Lewis," according to Carla Power, writing on the "Harry Potter" phenomenon in *Newsweek*. Rowling is good copy: a busy mom who wrote much of her first "Harry Potter" adventure while sitting in coffeehouses as her little daughter napped beside her, she presents a Cinderella story every bit as fanciful as the one she concocted in her book. But Rowling herself, winner of numerous awards and now employed full-time in her life's ambition as a writer, has taken her success in stride, changing her old one-bedroom flat in Edinburgh for a comfortable house, but still continuing her habit of writing in cafes.

A British Upbringing

Born near Bristol, England, Rowling grew up with a younger sister and a distinct inclination toward storytelling. Rabbits played a large part in her early tales, for Rowling and her sister badly wanted a rabbit. Her first story, at age five or six, involved a rabbit dubbed, quite logically, Rabbit, who got the measles and visited his friend, a giant bee named Miss Bee. As Rowling commented, "Ever since Rabbit and Miss Bee, I have wanted to be a writer, though I rarely told anyone so. I was afraid they'd tell me I didn't have a hope."

Two moves took the Rowling family eventually to the town of Tutshill near Chepstow in the Forest of Dean along the border of England and Wales. This brought a long-time country-living dream to fruition for Rowling's parents, both Londoners, and the nine-year-old Rowling learned to love the countryside in this new abode. She and her sister could wander unsupervised amid the fields and play along the River Wye. "The only fly in the ointment was the fact that I hated my new school," Rowling once noted. It was an old-fashioned school with roll-top desks and a teacher who frightened Rowling.

From Tutshill Primary, Rowling went to Wyedean Comprehensive School. "I was quiet, freckly, short-sighted and rubbish at sports," she commented of these years. Rowling confided to Roxanne Feldman in an interview in *School Library Journal* that the character of Harry's friend Hermione is loosely based on herself at age eleven. English was her favorite subject and she created serial stories for her friends at lunchtime, tales involving heroic deeds. Contact lenses soon sorted out any feelings of inferiority in the young Rowling; writing became more a compulsion and less of a hobby in her teenage years. Attending Exeter University, Rowling studied French, something she later found to be a big mistake. Her parents had advised her that bilingualism would lead to a successful career as a secretary. "Unfortunately I am one of the most disorganised people in the world," she related, which obviously posed a significant problem to a budding secretary.

Working at Amnesty International, Rowling discovered one thing to like about life as a secretary: she could use the computer to type up her own stories during quiet times. At age twenty-six, Rowling gave up her office job to teach English in Portugal. It was there that she began yet another story that might become a book, about a boy who is sent off to wizard school. All during the time she spent in Portugal, Rowling took notes on this story and added bits and pieces to the life of her protagonist, Harry Potter. In Portugal she also met the man who became her husband, had a daughter, and got divorced. She does not believe in doing things by half measures.

Of Naps and Harry Potter

Back in England, she decided to settle in Edinburgh and set about raising her daughter as a single mother. Accepting a job as a French teacher, she set herself a goal: to finish her novel before her teaching job began. This was no easy task with an active toddler in hand. Rowling confined her writing to her daughter's nap time, much of it spent in coffeehouses where the un-

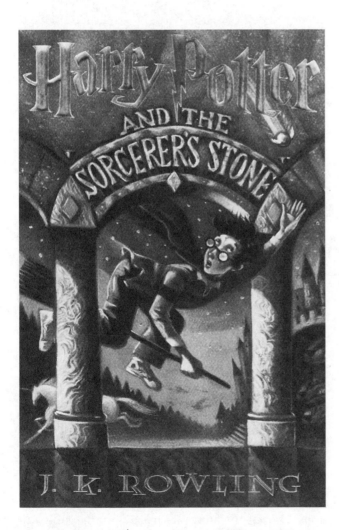

When he attends wizard school, Harry Potter enters a world of magic and struggles against dark forces to protect the Sorceror's Stone.

derstanding management allowed her space for her papers. In her interview with Feldman, Rowling commented that she had no idea what sort of reception the book would get, if she was even able to get it published. "I knew how difficult it would be just to get a book published. I was a completely unknown writer. I certainly could never have expected what's happened. It's been a real shock." She was able to send off her typed manuscript to two publishers before beginning her teaching post, but it was not until several months later that the happy news arrived that her long-time intimate, Harry Potter, would appear between the covers of a book in England. And then a few months later, the American rights were bought for a stupendous price and Rowling said good-bye to teaching.

"Think Luke Skywalker," opined an Associated Press writer in a profile of the suddenly successful author which appeared in *Hoosier Times.* "Then add a broom, a bunch of oddball buddies like the Goonies, and an athletic contest where wizards great and small desperately try to fix the outcome." This is only a rough approximation of the world to which Rowling's first novel, *Harry Potter and the Sorcerer's Stone* (published as *Harry Potter and the Philosopher's Stone* in England) introduces the reader.

Harry Potter, an orphan, has led a miserable life with the Dursley family, his maternal aunt and uncle. Ever since Harry arrived unannounced at their doorstep the Dursleys have been put out, as has their vile son, Dudley. Harry has taken up residence in a broom closet under the stairs, bullied at school and mistreated by the Dursleys. Small, skinny, and bespectacled, Harry is an unlikely hero. The only thing physically interesting about Harry is the lightning-shaped scar on his forehead.

"Harry had a thin face, knobbly knees, black hair and bright green eyes," Rowling wrote in the novel. "He wore round glasses held together with a lot of Scotch tape because of all the times Dudley had punched him in the nose." That quote goes a long way to demonstrating not only Rowling's tongue-in-cheek humor, but also her sensitivity in portraying the difficulties of being a child.

When Harry turns eleven, he receives a letter. Of course the Dursleys keep it from him, but finally another letter gets through to Harry telling him that he has been admitted to Hogwarts School of Witchcraft and Wizardry. This is the first that Harry has known about his parents being wizards, or that they were killed by the evil sorcerer, Voldemort, or that he himself is something of a legend in wizard circles for having survived Voldemort's attack, which, by the way, left the scar on his forehead. Before he knows what is happening, he is swept off by the giant Hagrid, keeper of the keys at the school, on a flying motorcycle. Thus begins what Rayma Turton in *Magpies* called "a ripping yarn," and a "school story with a twist." Instead of boring math and geography, Harry takes lessons in the History of Magic and in Charms, or Defenses against the Dark Arts. He becomes something of a star at the school athletic contest, quidditch, an aerial sort of soccer match played on broomsticks. He forms friendships with Ron and Hermione and encounters students not quite so pleasant, such as the sly Draco Malfoy. He investigates the secrets of the forbidden third floor at Hogwarts, battles evil in the form of professor Snape whom Harry fears means to steal the sorcerer's stone which promises eternal life, and discovers the secret behind his scar. In short, Harry learns to be his own person.

"The language is witty, the plotting tight, the imagination soars," Turton commented. "It's fun." A writer for the Associated Press observed that "Rowling has an unerring sense of what it means to be 11, and her arresting, brick-by-brick construction of Harry's world has turned a rather traditional plot into a delight." Hogwarts is a composite of the typical English public school (which is actually private in America), yet turned on its head. Harry is lodged in Gryffindor house, rivals of another house, Slytherin; his school supplies include a message-bearing owl and a magic wand. "The light-hearted caper travels through the territory owned by the late Roald Dahl," observed a reviewer for *Horn Book,* who concluded that *Harry Potter and the Sorcerer's Stone* is a "charming and readable romp with a most sympathetic hero and filled with delightful magic details." A *Booklist* commentator called the book "brilliantly imagined and written," while a critic for *Publishers Weekly* noted that there "is enchantment, suspense and danger galore. . . ."

A classic tale of good versus evil, as well as a coming-of-age novel with a unique flavor, *Harry Potter and the Sorcerer's Stone* is not simply a novel

In this, the third work in Rowling's enormously successful "Harry Potter" series, the young wizard is endangered when the prisoner Sirius Black escapes from the fortress of Azkaban.

about magic and wizardry. As Michael Winerip commented in the *New York Times Book Review,* "the magic in the book is not the real magic of the book." For Winerip, and countless other readers, it is the "human scale" of the novel that makes it work. "Throughout most of the book, the characters are impressively three-dimensional," Winerip noted, concluding that Rowling "had wizardry inside," achieving "something quite special" with her first novel. "Rowling's secret," wrote Paul Gray in *Time* magazine, "is as simple and mysterious as her uncanny ability to nourish the human hunger for enchantment: she knows how to feed the desire not just to hear or read a story but to live it as well."

Sequels Prove Equally Popular

Even as enthusiastic reviews were pouring in from America, Rowling's second installment of the "Harry Potter" saga was published in England. *Harry Potter and the Chamber of Secrets* takes up where the first novel stopped. Harry returns to second term at Hogwarts in a flying car, and deals with old and new characters alike. One of these newcomers is Nearly Headless Nick, a poor creature upon whom an executioner made a messy cut; another is a ghost who inhabits the girls' bathrooms, Moaning Myrtle. Valerie Bierman, writing in *Carousel*, noted that "this plot is brilliantly scary with horrible happenings, mysterious petrifyings and a terrifying conclusion." A reviewer in *Publishers Weekly* asserted that, if possible, the story is even more inventive than *Harry Potter and the Sorcerer's Stone* and Rowling's "ability to create such an engaging, imaginative, funny and, above all, heartpoundingly suspenseful yarn is nothing short of magical."

The third installment in the "Potter" series, *Harry Potter and the Prisoner of Azkaban,* begins when Harry is thirteen and starting his third year at Hogwarts School for Witchcraft and Wizardry. A notorious mass murderer who is a henchman of the evil Lord Voldemort has escaped from Azkaban Prison and comes looking for Harry. Despite the danger, Harry is quite preoccupied with an upcoming match of quidditch where he plays the most important position, that of the Seeker. Perhaps therein lies part of the secret to the success of the Potter books opined Gregory Maguire in *New York Times Book Review*: "J. K. Rowling's fantasies celebrate a boy's relish in physical prowess as well as the more bookish values of moral and intellectual accomplishment." And even while the adventures are thrilling, a reviewer in *Publishers Weekly* felt that they appear to be laying the groundwork for even more breathless excitement. "The beauty here lies in the genius of Rowling's plotting. Seemingly minor details established in books one and two unfold to take on unforeseen significance, and the finale, while not airtight in its internal logic, is utterly thrilling."

Harry's life-threatening adventures in *The Prisoner of Azkaban* indicated a subtle but distinct shift away from the lightheartedness that characterizes the first two novels, but such a shift was "inevitable," Rowling admitted in the *School Library Jour-*

If you enjoy the works of J. K. Rowling, you may also want to check out the following books:

Joan Aiken, *Is Underground,* 1993.
Diane Duane, *So You Want to Be a Wizard,* 1983.
Roald Dahl, *Dannny the Champion of the World,* 1975.

nal interview. "If you are writing about Good and Evil, there comes a point where you have to get serious." Commenting on the darker tone of the novel, Gray wrote that it "demonstrates Rowling's considerable emotional range. She can be both genuinely scary and consistently funny, adept at both broad slapstick and allusive puns and wordplay."

Harry Potter and the Chamber of Secrets and *Harry Potter and the Prisoner of Azkaban* leapt to number one on the adult best-seller lists in England, prompting a feeding frenzy for them in America. But eager readers have reason for solace as well. Rowling has sketched out plots for seven "Harry Potter" novels in all, taking him through his years at Hogwarts, to age seventeen and graduation. Maguire conjectured: "Maybe by then J. K. Rowling will have achieved what people who love the best children's books have labored after: breaking the spell of adult condescension that brands as merely cute, insignificant, second rate the heartiest and best of children's literature."

■ Works Cited

Bierman, Valerie, "Working from Home," *Carousel*, summer, 1998, p. 23.

"British Author Rides up Charts on a Wizard's Tale," *Hoosier Times*, http://www.hoosiertimes.com/stories/1998/11/29/lifestyle.981129_D7_JJP10151.sto (November 29, 1998).

Feldman, Roxanne, "The Truth about Harry," *School Library Journal*, September, 1999, pp. 137-39.

Gray, Paul, "Wild About Harry," *Time*, September 20, 1999, pp. 67-72.

Review of *Harry Potter and the Chamber of Secrets, Publishers Weekly*, May 31, 1999, p. 94.

Review of *Harry Potter and the Prisoner of Azkaban, Publishers Weekly*, July 19, 1999, p. 195.

Review of *Harry Potter and the Sorcerer's Stone*, *Booklist*, January 1, 1999, p. 783.

Review of *Harry Potter and the Sorcerer's Stone*, *Horn Book*, January, 1999, p. 71.

Review of *Harry Potter and the Sorcerer's Stone*, *Publishers Weekly*, July 20, 1998, p. 220.

Maguire, Gregory, "Lord of the Golden Snitch," *New York Times Book Review*, September 5, 1999, p. 12

Power, Carla, "A Literary Sorceress," *Newsweek*, December 7, 1998, p. 79.

Rowling, J. K., *Harry Potter and the Sorcerer's Stone*, Levine/Scholastic, 1998.

Turton, Rayma, review of *Harry Potter and the Philosopher's Stone*, *Magpies*, March, 1999.

Winerip, Michael, review of *Harry Potter and the Sorcerer's Stone*, *New York Times Book Review*, February 14, 1999, p. 26.

■ **For More Information See**

PERIODICALS

ALAN Review, Fall, 1999.

Bulletin of the Center for Children's Books, September, 1999, p. 28.

Books for Keeps, September, 1997, p. 27; July, 1999, pp. 6-7.

Kirkus Reviews, June 1, 1999, p. 888.

Publishers Weekly, February 15, 1999, pp. 33-34.

Reading Time, February, 1999, p. 43.

School Librarian, August, 1997, p. 147; spring, 1999, p. 35.

School Library Journal, October, 1998, pp. 145-46; July, 1999, pp. 99-100.

—Sketch by J. Sydney Jones

Rich Wallace

■ Personal

Born January 29, 1957, in Hackensack, NJ; divorced in 1996; children: two sons. *Education*: Montclair State College (now University), B.A., 1980.

■ Addresses

Home—P.O. Box 698, Honesdale PA 18431. *Office*—*Highlights for Children*, 803 Church St., Hones-dale, PA 18431.

■ Career

Herald News, Passaic, NJ, editorial assistant, 1978-79; sports reporter, 1979-82; *Daily Advance*, Dover, NJ, sports editor, 1982-84, news editor, 1984-85; *Trenton Times*, Trenton, NJ, copy editor, 1985-86, assistant city editor, 1986-87; *Highlights for Children* magazine, copy editor, 1988-90, assistant editor, 1990-92, coordinating editor, 1992—.

■ Awards, Honors

American Library Association Best Books for Young Adults selection, and American Library Association Recommended Book for Reluctant Young Adult Readers, both 1996, both for *Wrestling Sturbridge*.

■ Writings

Wrestling Sturbridge, Knopf, 1996.
Shots on Goal, Knopf, 1997.

■ Adaptations

Wrestling Sturbridge was recorded on audio cassette, Recorded Books, 1996; *Shots on Goal* was recorded on audio cassette, Recorded Books, 1998.

■ Work in Progress

Playing Without the Ball: A Novel in Four Quarters, expected spring, 2001.

■ Sidelights

In his novels *Wrestling Sturbridge* and *Shots on Goal*, young adult novelist Richard Wallace has used "the metaphors of sports to explore universal themes of emerging adulthood and self-definition," according to *Horn Book* reviewer Maeve Visser Knoth. "Like other good writers," stated Ken Donelson in the *St. James Guide to Young Adult Writers,* "Wallace recognizes the importance of telling a story that involves readers—mostly boys, but also girls and women—who recognize that the book is about sports and much, much more."

Wallace was born January 29, 1957, in Hackensack, New Jersey. Raised by his college-educated parents along with six brothers and sisters, Wallace, as he told *Authors and Artists for Young Adults* (*AAYA*), started writing "little stories" in the first grade. But academics were not Wallace's strong suit. As he remembered, "I found school generally a bit boring, and I stopped reading much of anything I didn't have to from about sixth grade until well after college." What did capture Wallace's interest? "My ambitions as a teenager," he told *AAYA*, "were focused on being the best runner I could possibly be. I was heavily into sports and devoted myself to trackand cross country running."

In high school, however, Wallace "began to write extensively … just diaries in which I sorted out my life and purged a lot of emotion." He also gained valuable experience by working on his school's newspaper. Wallace's evolution as a writer continued at New Jersey's Montclair State College. He took creative writing classes, including one that required him to pen a novel, one chapter per week. He also interned at the Passaic *Herald-News,* where he was later offered a paid writing and reporting position. Sports once again captured the majority of Wallace's attention, though. "I spent most of my energy on the track and cross country teams," he told *AAYA*. In fact, Wallace left college just two credits short of a degree. A couple of years later, he returned and completed "two one-credit, half-semester physical education courses (bowling and soccer) so I could get my degree and stop lying on my resume."

After graduating from Montclair State in 1980 with a bachelor of arts degree, Wallace told *AAYA* that he "played around with that novel [from creative writing class] for quite a few years." He finished the work and sent it to publishers, but "none took it because it's a disjointed, poorly planned book." Wallace did receive a "nice rejection letter" from Patricia Gauch, an editor at Philomel. Gauch also shared some positive comments from the in-house

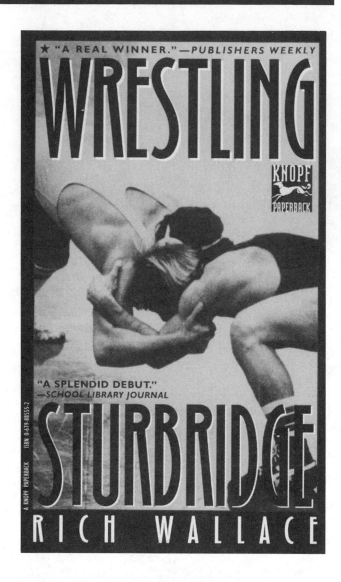

In this 1996 work, Wallace's debut novel, a young wrestler with little else to hope for is determined to become state champion.

staff, including several from Tracy Gates. Gates would later play a pivotal role in the publication of *Wrestling Sturbridge.*

Over the next eight years, Wallace continued his newspaper career, working variously as a sports reporter, news editor, and assistant city editor at a variety of New Jersey newspapers. He also married and became a father to two boys. In 1988, Wallace began working for *Highlights for Children* as a copy editor. Today, he is a senior editor at the magazine, and publishing well-written stories has become Wallace's passion. "I love the field," he told *AAYA*. "I've met virtually no one who works editorially in this field—children's publishing—whose first and overwhelming priority isn't to bring out great books and magazines."

Wrestling with Teenage Emotions

Wallace had continued his own writing efforts during this period. In 1996, after working on a number of novels that "showed promise but didn't go anywhere," as he told *Publishers Weekly* contributor Heather Vogel Frederick, Wallace finally had a story that was different. "This one gelled right from the beginning," Wallace continued, "I knew where it was going." Wallace sent the manuscript to Gates, who years earlier had complimented his first, failed effort. Gates, now an editor at Knopf, suggested changes to the new work, including a few additional scenes and chapters that fleshed out the story. "*Wrestling Sturbridge* wouldn't be what it is without Tracy, not by a long shot," Wallace remarked to Frederick.

Wrestling Sturbridge is the story of Ben, a high school senior and varsity wrestler who tires of being practice fodder for Al, his teammate and close friend. Faced with a bleak future in a dead-end town, Ben decides to challenge for Al's spot on the squad, despite the fact that Al is a top contender for the state title. Ben also begins a romance with the intelligent, tough-minded Kim, who believes in Ben more than he believes in himself. But "Wallace isn't writing a sports fairy story," a *Publishers Weekly* contributor declared. Instead, *Wrestling Sturbridge* offers a "strong portrait of a smothering small town," *Horn Book* reviewer Maeve Visser Knoth remarked, "and the hopelessness that it engenders in an adolescent." "Anyone even remotely curious about small-town America need look no further than this exemplary first novel," stated the *Publishers Weekly* critic.

Reviewers also praised the author's narrative voice. Wallace, "like Ben, whose voice is so strong and clear here," wrote Debbie Carton in *Booklist*, "weighs his words carefully, making every one count." "He [Ben] tells the story in a spare way appropriate to his undemonstrative, nonverbal nature," a *Kirkus Reviews* critic stated, "recording fast and furious wrestling action, the steady burn of his own anger and frustration, and brief but telling glimpses of the people around him." *Wrestling Sturbridge,* Donelson concluded, "is about young people who care about life and about keep-

ing promises they've made to themselves and others. It is a rare sports story because there is no super-hero and no villain."

Another Troubled Friendship

The setting for *Shots on Goal*, Wallace's next book, remains in Sturbridge but moves to the soccer field. A critic in *Kirkus Reviews* declared, "Wallace flattens the sophomore jinx in this taut, present-tense tale of an underdog high-school soccer team battling internal dissension." The instigators of this

This coming-of-age novel centers on a young man, his changing relationships with friends and family, and his passion for soccer.

internal dissension are Barry "Bones" Austin and his best friend, Joey. Bones realizes that he is stuck in "second place," not only on the soccer field, where he is the team's second-best player (after Joey), but also at home, where his older brother, Tommy, is the favored son of their parents.

Tension arises when Bones' object of desire, Shannon, begins dating Joey. Bones also grows of resentful of Joey's increasingly selfish play on the field. As the soccer season rolls on, "a face-off [begins] between the two teens," *Booklist* critic Frances Bradburn stated, "each striving to find his own identity without the other, in spite of the other." The face-off finally comes to an end after "the two friends square off in a fight which makes both aware how important their soccer team and their friendship are," according to Donelson.

Like *Wrestling Sturbridge*, *Shots on Goal* earned praise for its fully-developed characters and exciting action. Dina Sherman, writing in *School Library Journal*, felt that the "situations and emotions that Bones experiences are all very real, and young people will relate to them." A critic in the *Bulletin of the Center for Children's Books* added that "the soccer matches are fast, the interaction with girls unromantically realistic, and the voice is engaging, as Bones tells his story as a rueful eyewitness account."

In his forthcoming book, *Playing Without the Ball: A Novel in Four Quarters*, Wallace again invites readers to enter the world of high school sports in Sturbridge. The main character is Jay, a high school basketball player who supports himself by working part-time in a bar, while also living by himself above the bar. Jay meets Spit, a singer in a band that often performs at the bar. Wallace told *AAYA* that "you could say the book is about sex drugs and rock and roll, but it's as much about basketball as anything."

Writing Metaphors For Life

The writing process is a lengthy one for Wallace, and patience is key. The author "starts with a character and a situation. Plotting comes after I've gotten well under way, if at all." These characters or situations often have originated from Wallace's old journals, his children, or "from experiences I have as an adult that I can twist a little bit and think I can picture happening to me

If you enjoy the works of Rich Wallace, you may also want to check out the following books:

Terry Davis, *Vision Quest*, 1979.
Chris Crutcher, *Running Loose*, 1983.
Theodore Weesner, *Winning the City*, 1990.

when I was a teenager." The next step is research, "but not in any traditional way," Wallace declares. His books are set in "contemporary small-town Pennsylvania, which is where I live. So I pay attention to the world I live in." Details are important, Wallace added, "like the arrangement of soda bottles in the Turkey Hill convenience store or the way the streets look at dusk on an October evening from the cliff overlooking the town." Finally, Wallace will "write intensely for a few months" until the book is finished. The author also stated that he doesn't "fight writer's block. I expect long dry periods in which something may be incubating in my head, but I'm not really working on it."

Why does Wallace write about sports? As the author told *AAYA*, he simply doesn't "know any other way to approach what I do. Sports has been my mindset since a very young age, and I'd have trouble getting inside a head that didn't function that way." Furthermore, the author sees "sports as a metaphor for life." But Wallace adds that he "didn't set out directly to draw a parallel between the growth and stresses of a friendship and the internal strife of a soccer team [in *Shots on Goal*]." Nor did Wallace see "wrestling as a metaphor for self-awareness [in *Wrestling Sturbridge*] or basketball playing as potentially akin to addiction [in *Playing Without the Ball: A Novel in Four Quarters*]. They just came out that way."

Wallace has but one goal for his writing: "I really just want to be honest," he told *AAYA*, honest in the representation of how teenage boys struggle to find themselves while "striving to the best that they can be, making continual mistakes, and eventually seeing the light." Wallace also hopes that, after reading his books, "some kids will realize their potential. I have kids tell me all the time, for example, that *Wrestling Sturbridge* changed their lives. They can't articulate why, but they don't have to." Critics agree that Wallace's novels have touched young adults; as Donelson stated, "It's safe to say that many readers . . . await whatever Wallace has to offer."

■ Works Cited

Bradburn, Frances, review of *Shots on Goal*, *Booklist*, September 15, 1997, p. 224.

Carton, Debbie, review of *Wrestling Sturbridge*, *Booklist*, September 1, 1996, p. 128.

Donelson, Ken, *St. James Guide to Young Adult Writers*, St. James Press, 1999, pp. 860-61.

Frederick, Heather Vogel, "Flying Starts: Six Children's Book Newcomers Share Thoughts on Their Debut Projects," *Publishers Weekly*, July 1, 1996, pp. 34-37.

Knoth, Maeve Visser, review of *Wrestling Sturbridge*, *Horn Book*, November-December, 1996, p. 747.

Sherman, Dina, review of *Shots on Goal*, *School Library Journal*, November, 1997, pp. 124-25.

Review of *Shots on Goal*, *Bulletin of the Center for Children's Books*, December, 1997, pp. 143-44.

Review of *Shots on Goal*, *Kirkus Reviews*, July 15, 1997, p. 1118.

Wallace, Richard, e-mail interview with *Authors and Artists for Young Adults*, November, 1999.

Review of *Wrestling Sturbridge*, *Kirkus Reviews*, May 15, 1996, p. 752.

Review of *Wrestling Sturbridge*, *Publishers Weekly*, June 3, 1996, p. 84.

■ For More Information See

PERIODICALS

Horn Book, November, 1997, p. 687.

Kliatt, August, 1997, p. 53; September, 1997, p. 15.

Los Angeles Times Book Review, September 15, 1996, p. 11.

Tribune Books (Chicago), April 14, 1996, p. 7.

Voice of Youth Advocates, June, 1997, p. 114.

—*Sketch by Ann Schwalboski*

Tim Winton

Personal

Born in 1960, in Western Australia; children: three. *Education:* Attended Curtin University, Perth.

Career

Writer.

Awards, Honors

Vogel Award, Allen & Unwin Australia, 1981, for *An Open Swimmer;* Miles Franklin Award, Arts Management Party Limited (Australia), 1984, for *Shallows,* and 1992, for *Cloudstreet;* Deo Gloria Prize for religious writing, 1991, for *Cloudstreet;* Best Books for Young Adults, American Library Association, 1992, for *Lockie Leonard, Human Torpedo; The Riders* was shortlisted for the Booker Prize, 1995; Commonwealth Writers Prize best novel award, South East Asia and South Pacific section, 1995, for *The Riders.*

Writings

FOR YOUNG PEOPLE

Jesse, illustrated by Maureen Prichard, McPhee Gribble (Melbourne, Victoria, Australia), 1988.

Lockie Leonard, Human Torpedo, McPhee Gribble (South Yarra, Victoria, Australia), 1990, Little, Brown (Boston), 1991.

The Bugalugs Bum Thief, illustrated by Carol Pelham-Thorman, Puffin (Ringwood, Victoria, Australia), 1991.

Lockie Leonard, Scumbuster, Piper (Chippendale, New South Wales), 1993, Macmillan, 1993.

Lockie Leonard, Legend, Pan (Chippendale, New South Wales), 1997.

Blueback: A Fable for All Ages, Macmillan (South Melbourne), 1997.

NOVELS

An Open Swimmer, Allen & Unwin (Sydney, Australia), 1982.

Shallows, Graywolf Press (St. Paul, MN), 1984.

That Eye, the Sky, McPhee Gribble (Fitzroy, Victoria, Australia), 1986, Atheneum (New York City), 1987.

In the Winter Dark, McPhee Gribble (Melbourne, Australia), 1988.

Cloudstreet, McPhee Gribble (Melbourne, Victoria), 1991, Graywolf Press, 1992.

The Riders, Macmillan (Chippendale, New South Wales), 1994, Scribner (New York City), 1995.

The Collected Shorter Novels of Tim Winton (includes *Open Swimmer, That Eye, the Sky,* and *In the Winter Dark*), Picador (London), 1995.

SHORT STORY COLLECTIONS

Scission and Other Stories, McPhee Gribble (Fitzroy, Australia), 1985.
Minimum of Two, McPhee Gribble, 1987, Atheneum, 1988.
Blood and Water: Stories (contains "Minimum of Two" and "Scission"), Picador (London), 1993.

OTHER

(With Trish Ainslie and Roger Garwood) *Land's Edge,* Pan Macmillan with Plantagenet Press (Chippendale, New South Wales), 1993.
(With Bill Bachman) *Local Color: Travels in the Other Australia,* The Guidebook Company (Hong Kong), 1994.

Contributor to books, including "My Father's Axe," *The Oxford Book of Australian Short Stories.* Also the author of film scripts.

■ Adaptations

Lockie Leonard, Human Torpedo was adapted by Paige Gibbs for the stage, and performed by Perth Theatre Company; *That Eye, the Sky* was adapted for stage by Justin Monjo and Richard Roxburgh, 1994, and released as a movie in 1995, starring Peter Coyote. *The Riders* was optioned for filming by Jan Chapman in 1995.

■ Sidelights

Australian writer Tim Winton has won critical acclaim for novels featuring richly evoked settings and roundly drawn characters that embark on journeys of self-discovery. An avowed Christian, Winton also incorporates religious themes and imagery into his adult novels and shortstories, and some critics have remarked that universal questions of good and evil, humanity and brutality lie beneath his characters' dilemmas. *Los Angeles Times Book Review* writer Carolyn See described Winton as "a novelist, a great one, because against all evidence and odds, he reminds us of what it is

to be human, and reminds us to be proud of our humanity."

Winton has written several novels, film scripts, short stories, and books for young people. *Shallows* was the first of his novels to find its way into American bookstores, appearing in 1984—the same year it won Australia's esteemed Miles Franklin Award for literature. Set in a small Australian seaside town, the novel focuses on a community still clinging to its more prosperous past as an important whaling center. "Have a Whale of a Time in Angelus," the civic billboards proclaim, while the town suffers economic decline engendered by the growing obsolescence of the whaling industry; whales stranded in shallow coastal waters provide a metaphor for the charac-

Winton's 1984 novel concerns a whaling town experiencing economic hardship.

ters' moral strandedness. Queenie Coupar, a descendant of the town's first family, and her urban-transplant husband Cleve are central to the story, as is her wealthy grandfather and the story of the whaling industry itself with its salty, sometimes violent personnel and the blood and gore that accompany the hunt and slaughter. Winton's novel describes the disintegration of the town's status quo when Greenpeace activists arrive to protest the remnants of the whaling industry.

Shallows was praised by reviewers for its evocation of the whale and the activities aboard a whaling ship, with *Los Angeles Times* reviewer Carolyn See comparing the novel to Herman Melville's classic *Moby Dick.* The critic contended that Winton's use of the whale leitmotif, "so definitively used by Melville, is here new and startling." Other reviewers were equally laudatory, although Elizabeth Ward, writing in the *Washington Post Book World,* faulted Winton for "some excesses. He typically writes in a dense, economical, heavily physical style . . . but he also likes to feature snot, nose-pickings, vomit and so forth to an extent which can be distasteful." Yet Ward also noted that "*Shallows* is that rare thing, not historical fiction, but fiction which brings the history of a place to life." Stuart Evans of the London *Times* praised Winton's creation of the cast of characters and the novel's portrayal of "pride, loneliness, longing for love, and the struggle between nostalgic heroics and the heroism of compassion."

Looks at Australian Life

That Eye, the Sky is the first of Winton's works to overtly explore religion. Mary Ellen Quinn of *Booklist* lauded the "original style that reflects the exuberance of the ten-year-old narrator" and labeled the book "enormously appealing." The story is set in rural Western Australia and is narrated by a young boy named Morton Flack, whom everyone refers to as Ort. *Washington Post* reviewer Ward called the designation of Ort as the novel's storyteller and spiritual center "a cunning stroke, since the naïveté of the child's mind allows for, or renders artistically possible, the visionary and miraculous elements that in the end redeem the family's suffering." The suffering in question has been brought on by a number of incidents: Ort's parents are former free-spirits of the 1960s, pining for their past, and his father has recently suffered a disabling car accident that has left him

A surfer and a "metal head" join forces to rid their town's harbor of industrial waste in this humorous work.

incapacitated. Ort's grandmother lives with the family and is also bedridden and possibly afflicted with senile dementia. His teenage sister Tegwyn longs to leave the family home, which is surrounded by dying trees and a mysterious glowing cloud that hovers above at night.

As *That Eye, the Sky* begins, another ex-hippie enters the Flack household in the person of evangelical preacher Henry Warburton. He soon becomes an integral, if not destructive, part of their lives: baptizing Ort and his mother, helping take care of Ort's invalid father, and having his way with Tegwyn. Ort confides in Warburton of his strange visions of the sky, which seems to be keeping watch on him in the form of a giant eye, and of the other apparitions that plague the boy.

However, Warburton is not a typical cleric, and eventually his hypocrisy sets a series of events in motion that conclude the novel.

Writing again about Winton for the *Washington Post*, Ward found some technical flaws with *That Eye, the Sky*, namely in young Ort's ability to recall very long passages of adult conversation. Yet the critic granted that Winton's "use of natural imagery—of moon and cloud, sky and water and dying trees—to suggest Ort's experience of the ineffable is as graceful as a poet's." In the *New York Times*, Garrett Epps described the book as "a thoroughly engaging story of childhood, tragedy and faith," that should not be dismissed because of unfamiliar Australian slang terms, while a *Publishers Weekly* reviewer concluded that "unforeseen effects end the wrenching story that proves love like Ort's can prevail against hell itself."

Cloudstreet, set just after World War II in Australia, is about an unlucky gambler, Sam Pickles, who has inherited a large house in Perth. Since he and his wife prefer not to work, they rent half of the house to the Lamb family. The Lambs are radically different from the Pickles, and the clashes and bond between the two over the years in their coexistence form the basis of the novel. *Voice Literary Supplement* contributor Joy Press called Winton's style in *Cloudstreet* "mellifluous yet veined with pathos . . . it grabs you with its stream of words, and then gradually slows down to the pace of life." Noting that the author's verbiage is "sometimes overripe," Press maintained: "that only adds to its charm, and Winton balances the ballast with his wonderful silences, those mesmeric moments listening to the house breathe or the terrible pauses before bad luck strikes."

Earns Booker Prize Nomination

In *The Riders*, Winton chronicles the destruction of a young Australian family who has moved to Ireland. Scully is building a home for his wife, Jennifer, and their seven-year-old daughter when Jennifer leaves the pair. Distraught, the father and daughter search for her throughout western Europe, and in some ways the novel becomes a chase mystery, rife with clues and frantic travels, but the dilemma is never resolved. The "riders" of the title are a quartet of phantom horsemen who appear to Scully in his darkest moments. He becomes more obsessed with finding his wife, but

A wise fish advises Abel throughout his life in this simple tale of kinship and the sea.

the trauma suffered by his daughter because of the breakup is only exacerbated by his behavior and eventually brings him back from the edge.

The Riders, published in 1995, was Winton's 13th book in 13 years. But in a *Publishers Weekly* interview that same year, he confessed that he never planned to write a novel a year. "I just plan to stay at the desk. Books take their own time. I run to a pretty loose schedule, but I guess I've been lucky that books just come along," he laughed, and admitted that he at times writes two books simultaneously. "If you have a very long-term project, you need alternative work to freshen you up. Anything gets boring."

Critics are in awe of Winton's decision to become a writer at the tender age of 10, and that when he was 17, he was earning as much as $800 for stories he submitted to magazines in Australia. But no matter how much he was earning, people mocked his chosen profession. "Writing in one's spare time is the more acceptable, British thing to do, and deep down, Mom and Dad would have preferred if I'd become an English teacher. But I never wanted another job," he told Michele Field in the *Publishers Weekly* interview, "I had stumbled on one idea, and was too timid to go any further. It was a vocation."

The Riders is the "pole-opposite" to Winton's own experiences. The novel's main character, Scully, frustrates him as much as he must frustrate the reader," Winton told Field. "Scully is one of those people who builds himself around the shape of another thing—in Scully's life, it's his wife, but for another person, it could be a political position, or another ideal. They become an idea of themselves rather than themselves. I think some readers will bear with him out of identification, and others out of cold curiosity."

But readers and critics alike didn't simply "bear with" this protagonist and narrative, they found it "irresistible", in the words of one reviewer. They lavished praise on Winton for his lyrical prose and, as a *Publishers Weekly* reviewer put it, Winton "conjures up settings with a magician's hand. . . . His terse, lyrical descriptions, the throbbing energy of his prose, can illuminate a scene like a lightning bolt, cut like a knife or wring the heart. *Publishers Weekly* concluded that "Readers . . . will find his talent fiercely honed." *The Riders* earned Winton a Booker Prize nomination in 1995.

Pens Works for Young Adults

Along with his other works, Winton has also written several popularbooks for young adults, including *Lockie Leonard, Human Torpedo,* and *Lockie Leonard, Scumbuster.* In his first *Lockie Leonard* story, Lockie and his family have just moved to a small town in time for him to begin high school. Lockie finds it a bit difficult fitting in: he lives on the wrong side of the tracks, his father is a cop, and he's obviously a city boy. His talent for surfing, however, wins him leadership in the surfing club and the attention of the most popular girl in school. Maeve Visser Knoth, writing in *Horn Book,* observed that although the situation is not new

---

If you enjoy the works of Tim Winton, you may also want to check out the following books:

Judith Clarke, *The Heroic Life of Al Capsella,* 1988.
Jack Driscoll, *Skylight,* 1991.
Ray Maloney, *The Impact Zone,* 1986.

---

to young-adult fiction, "the dialogue and characters . . . are fresh and original." She concluded that Winton has introduced a "lovable, vulnerable adolescent" who deals with his coming-of-age "with humor if not grace." A *Publishers Weekly* critic predicted that the author's "dry, typically Down Under wit" and his use of unfamiliar, somewhat daunting Australian slang "should charm young readers on this side of the equator."

In *Lockie Leonard, Scumbuster,* Lockie becomes involved with trying to do something about the industrial pollution problem, while going through his usual falling in and out of love, and having his share of ups and downs in school. *School Librarian* contributor Patricia Peacock noted that Winton's ending "is typically off-beat and funny." She also maintained that young readers will enjoy the stories "without noticing the underlying wisdom of Tim Winton's observations."

In the 1995 *Publishers Weekly* interview, Field commented that "It is often that landscape in Winton's books which come across as the really strong, and reassuring element in the characters' lives. 'I guess it is a non-European notion of mine,' Winton responded. 'A European grows up surrounded by both landscape and human doings; but my experience is that "human doings" seem pretty paltry in the Australian landscape.'"

Winton again makes use of landscape as a reasuring element for his characters in his 1998 novel, *Blueback.* In this case, it's the sea and the blue grouper who lives there that calms Winton's protagonist, 10-year-old Abel. Abel names the grouper Blueback, a fish known for its intelligence and courage. Through his friendship with the magnificent fish, Abel learns about human greed and the world's ecological problems, and eventually becomes a marine biologist, devoting his life to the coastal paradise where Blueback continues to swim.

Blueback received mixed reviews; while many critics enjoyed the values inherent in this fable, most believed it was more suitable for adolescent readers than for adults. A 1998 *Publishers Weekly* review stated, "Though the language is lyrical, Winton pares it down, deliberately simplifying his prose in the service of a clearly articulated call for ecological responsibility." Reviewer Donna Seaman, writing in *Booklist*, called the work "a memorable and redemptive fable of our maddening times."

■ **Works Cited**

Review of *Blueback, Publishers Weekly,* January 5, 1998, p. 57.

Epps, Garrett, review of *That Eye, the Sky, New York Times,* May 17, 1987, p. 50.

Evans, Stuart, review of *Shallows, Times* (London), August 7, 1986.

Field, Michele, "Tim Winton: I Got a Jump on My Generation," *Publishers Weekly,* May 29, 1995, pp. 62-63.

Knoth, Maeve Visser, review of *Lockie Leonard, Human Torpedo, Horn Book,* March-April, 1992, pp. 212-13.

Review of *Lockie Leonard, Human Torpedo, Publishers Weekly,* November 22, 1991, p. 57.

Peacock, Patricia, review of *Lockie Leonard, Scumbuster, School Librarian,* May, 1996, p. 77.

Press, Joy, review of *Cloudstreet, Voice Literary Supplement,* April, 1992, p. 5.

Quinn, Mary Ellen, review of *That Eye, the Sky, Booklist,* March 15, 1987, p. 1095.

Review of *The Riders, Publishers Weekly,* April 3, 1995, p. 44.

Seaman, Donna. "Blueback," *Booklist,* February 15, 1998, p. 986.

See, Carolyn, review of *Shallows, Los Angeles Times Book Review,* July 7, 1986.

See, Carolyn, review of *Minimum of Two, Los Angeles Times Book Review,* May 23, 1988.

Review of *That Eye, the Sky, Publishers Weekly,* January 23, 1987, p. 63.

Ward, Elizabeth, review of *Shallows, Washington Post Book World,* August 10, 1986, p. 5.

Ward, Elizabeth, review of *That Eye, the Sky, Washington Post,* April 3, 1987.

■ **For More Information See**

PERIODICALS

ALAN Review, Fall, 1999, p. 39.

Booklist, December 15, 1991, p. 761.

Books for Keeps, March, 1996, p. 12.

Kirkus Reviews, January 1, 1987, p. 20.

Magpies, July, 1991, p. 29; November, 1993, p. 23.

Publishers Weekly, March 6, 1995, p. 23.

Times Literary Supplement, June 13, 1986, p. 645; October 10, 1986, p. 1130; September 3, 1993, p. 23; February 17, 1995, p. 20.

Acknowledgments

Acknowledgments

Grateful acknowledgment is made to the following publishers, authors,
and artists for their kind permission to reproduce copyrighted material.

KEVIN J. ANDERSON. Alvin, John, illustrator. From a cover of *Star Wars: Jedi Search* by Kevin J. Anderson. Bantam Books, 1994. Cover art copyright © 1994 by John Alvin and Lucasfilm Ltd. Reproduced by permission. / From a cover of *Star Wars: Shadow Academy* by Kevin J. Anderson and Rebecca Moesta. Berkley Jam Books, 1995. TM & © 1995 Lucasfilm Ltd. All Rights Reserved. Used Under Authorization. / Howe, John, illustrator. From a cover of *Born of Elven Blood* by Kevin J. Anderson and John Gregory Betancourt. Atheneum Books for Young Readers, 1995. Jacket design © 1995 Byron Preiss Visual Publications, Inc. Jacket illustration © 1995 by John Howe. Reproduced by permission. / Struzan, Drew, illustrator. From a cover of *Star Wars: Darksaber* by Kevin J. Anderson. Spectra, 1996. (R), TM, and © 1996 Lucasfilm Ltd. All rights reserved. Used under authorization. / Lauffray, Mathieu, illustrator. From a cover of *Star Wars: Tales of the Jedi: The Sith War* by Kevin J. Anderson. Dark Horse Comics, 1996. Star Wars (R) & © 1996 Lucasfilm Ltd. All rights reserved. Used under authorization. / Anderson, Kevin J. (artwork on wall), photograph. Reproduced by permission.

POUL ANDERSON. Whelan, Michael, illustrator. From a cover of *The Enemy Stars* by Poul Anderson. Reproduced by permission. / Sweet, Darrell K. From a cover of *Three Hearts and Three Lions* by Poul Anderson. Baen Books, 1993. Reproduced by permission. / Alexander, Paul. From a cover of *Orion Shall Rise* by Poul Anderson. Baen Books, 1991. Reproduced by permission. / Anderson, Poul. From a cover of *The Boat of a Million Years* by Poul Anderson. TOR, 1991. Reproduced by permission. / Elmore, Larry. From a cover of *Operation Chaos* by Poul Anderson. Baen Books, 1992. Reproduced by permission. / Di Fate, Vincent. From a cover of *Harvest of Stars* by Poul Anderson. Copyright © 1993 Poul Anderson. Reproduced by permission of Tor Books. / Anderson, Poul, photograph. Reproduced by permission.

JAMES BALDWIN. From a cover of *Go Tell It On The Mountain* by James Baldwin. Laurel, 1952. Copyright © 1952, 1953 by James Baldwin. Copyright renewed 1980, 1981 by James Baldwin. Reproduced by permission of Dell Publishing, a division of Random House, Inc. / Glinn, Burt, illustrator. From a cover of *Notes Of A Native Son* by James Baldwin. Beacon Press, 1955. Copyright © 1955, renewed 1983, by James Baldwin. Reproduced by permission. / Gross, Stuart, illustrator. From a cover of *If Beale Street Could Talk* by James Baldwin. Laurel, 1974. Copyright © 1974 by James Baldwin. Reproduced by permission of Dell Publishing, a division of Random House, Inc. / Horn, Paula, illustrator. From a cover of *The Fire Next Time* by James Baldwin. Vintage Books, 1962. Copyright © 1962, 1963 by James Baldwin. Copyright renewed 1990, 1991 by Gloria Baldwin Karefa-Smart. Reproduced by permission of Random House, Inc. / Baldwin, James (seated, hands crossed in lap), photograph by Carl Van Vechten. The Estate of Carl Van Vechten. Reproduced by permission.

JOAN BAUER. From a cover of *Squashed* by Joan Bauer. Laurel-Leaf Books, 1992. Copyright © 1992 by Joan Bauer. Reproduced by permission of Dell Publishing, a division of Random House, Inc. / Ramhorst, John, illustrator. From a cover of *Sticks* by Joan Bauer. Yearling, 1996. Copyright © 1996 by Joan Bauer. Reproduced by permission of Dell Publishing, a division of Random House, Inc. / Minor, Wendell, illustrator. From a cover of *Rules of the Road* by Joan Bauer. G. P. Putnam's Sons, 1998. Jacket art and design © 1998 by Wendell Minor. Reproduced by permission of the illustrator. / Minor, Wendell, illustrator. From a cover of *Backwater* by Joan Bauer. G. P. Putnam's Sons, 1999. Jacket art © 1999 by Wendell Minor. Reproduced by permission of the illustrator.

FRANCESCA LIA BLOCK. Block, Francesca Lia, photograph by Claudia Kunin. Reproduced by permission of Francesca Lia Block.

JUDITH CLARKE. From a cover of *The Heroic Life of Al Capsella* by J. Clarke. Henry Holt and Company, 1990. Jacket photograph copyright © 1990 by Greg Goebel. Jacket design copyright, © 1990 by Abby Kagan. Reprinted by permission of Henry Holt and Company, LLC. / Lill, Debra, illustrator. From a cover of *The Lost Day* by Judith Clarke. Henry Holt and Company, 1997. Jacket illustration copyright © 1999 by Debra Lill. Reprinted by permission of Henry Holt and Company, LLC. / Chesworth, Michael, illustrator. From a cover of *Al Capsella and the Watchdogs* by Judith Clarke. Henry Holt and Company, 1990. Jacket design and illustration copyright © 1991 by Michael Chesworth. Reprinted by permission of Henry Holt and Company, LLC.

DOUGLAS COUPLAND. From a cover of *Generation X: Tales For An Accelerated Culture* by Douglas Coupland. St. Martin's Press, 1991. Copyright © 1991 by Douglas Campbell Coupland. Reproduced by permission. / Estrada, Sigrid, photographer. From a cover of *Shampoo Planet* by Douglas Coupland. Pocket Books, 1992. Copyright © 1992 by Douglas Campbell Coupland. Front cover photo © Sigrid Estrada. Reproduced by permission of the illustrator. / Earnest, Robert, illustrator. From a cover of *Life After God* by Douglas Coupland. Pocket Books, 1994.

HENRI MATISSE. *Harmony in Red,* painting by Henri Matisse. Art Resource. Reproduced by permission. / *The Snail,* 1953, painting by Henri Matisse (1869-1954). © Succession H. Matisse, Paris / ARS, NY. Tate Gallery, London, Great Britain. / *La danse,* drawing by Henri Matisse. AP/Wide World Photos. Reproduced by permission. / Matisse, Henri, photograph by Carl Van Vechten. Reproduced by permission of the Carl Van Vechten Trust.

ANNE MCCAFFREY. Sweet, Darrell K., illustrator. From a cover of *To Ride Pegasus* by Anne McCaffrey. Ballantine Books, 1973. Copyright © 1973 by Anne McCaffrey. Reproduced by permission of Random House, Inc. / Marcellino, Fred, illustrator. From a cover of *Dragonsong* by Anne McCaffrey. Atheneum, 1976. Cover illustration © 1976 by Fred Marcellino. Reproduced by permission of the illustrator. / Whelan, Michael, illustrator. From a cover of *The White Dragon* by Anne McCaffrey. Ballantine Books, 1978. Copyright © 1978 by Anne McCaffrey. Reproduced by permission of Random House, Inc. / Whelan, Michael, illustrator. From a cover of *Crystal Singer* by Anne McCaffrey. Ballantine Books, 1982. Copyright © 1982 by Anne McCaffrey. Reproduced by permission of Random House, Inc. / Romas, illustrator. From a cover of *The Rowan* by Anne McCaffrey. Ace Books, 1990. Copyright © 1990 by Anne McCaffrey. Reproduced by permission of Ace Books, a division of Penguin Putnam Inc. / McCaffrey, Anne (wearing gold chain and pearls), photograph by Edmund Ross. Reproduced by permission.

TODD MCFARLANE. White, Michael Jai, in the movie *Spawn,* 1997, photograph. Peter Iovino/New Line Cinema. © 1997 New Line Cinema. The Kobal Collection. Reproduced by permission. / McFarlane, Todd (holding Mark McGwire baseball), photograph by Marty Lederhandler. AP/Wide World Photos. Reproduced by permission. / McFarlane, Todd, photograph. AP/Wide World Photos. Reproduced by permission.

JACQUELYN MITCHARD. Wilson, Brad, photographer. From a cover of *The Deep End of the Ocean* by Jacquelyn Mitchard. Penguin Books, 1996. Copyright © Jacquelyn Mitchard, 1996. Reproduced by permission of Penguin Books, a division of Penguin Putnam Inc. / Horan, Kevin, photographer. From a cover of *The Rest of Us: Dispatches From the Mother Ship* by Jacquelyn Mitchard. Penguin Books, 1997. Copyright © Jacquelyn Mitchard, 1997. Reproduced by permission of Penguin Books, a division of Penguin Putnam Inc. / From a cover of *The Most Wanted* by Jacquelyn Mitchard. A Signet Book, 1998. Copyright © JacquelynMitchard, 1998. Reproduced by permission of Signet Books, a division of Penguin Putnam Inc. / Pfeiffer, Michelle with Cory Buck, in the movie *The Deep End of the Ocean,* 1999, photograph. The Kobal Collection. Reproduced by permission. / Mitchard, Jacquelyn, photograph by Jerry Bauer. © by Jerry Bauer. Reproduced by permission.

MIKE MYERS. Myers, Mike and Dana Carvey (holding a photo of Guess Girl Claudia Schiffer), in the movie *Waynes's World,* photograph by Suzanne Tenner. Suzanne Tenner/Fotos International/Archive Photos, Inc. Reproduced by permission. / Myers, Mike with Nancy Travis, in the movie *So I Married An Axe Murderer,* 1993, photograph. The Kobal Collection. Reproduced by permission. / Hurley, Elizabeth, Mike Myers, in the movie *Austin Powers,* 1997, photograph K. Wright. The Kobal Collection. Reproduced by permission. / Myers, Mike, at Los Angeles premiere of *54,* August 24, 1998, photograph by E. J. Flynn. AP/Wide World Photos. Reproduced by permission. / Myers, Mike, in the movie *Austin Powers: The Spy Who Shagged Me,* 1999, photograph. The Kobal Collection. Reproduced by permission.

KRISTEN D. RANDLE. Palencar, John Jude, illustrator. From a jacket of *The Only Alien on the Planet* by Kristen D. Randle. Scholastic Inc., 1995. Jacket painting © 1995 by John Jude Palencar. Reproduced by permission. / Randle, Kristen (with family), photograph. Reproduced by permission.

J. K. ROWLING. GrandPre, Mary, illustrator. From a jacket of *Harry Potter and the Sorcerer's Stone* by J. K. Rowling. Arthur A. Levine Books, 1998. Jacket illustration © 1998 by Mary GrandPre. All rights reserved. Reproduced by permission of Arthur Al Levine Books, an imprint of Scholastic Press, a division of Scholastic Inc. / GrandPre, Mary, illustrator. From a cover of *Harry Potter and the Prisoner of Azkaban* by J. K. Rowling. Arthur A. Levine Books, an imprint of Scholastic Press, 1999. Jacket art © 1999 by Mary GrandPre. Reproduced by permission. / Rowling, J. K., 1998, photograph. AP/Wide World Photos. Reproduced by permission.

RICH WALLACE. Valeri, Mike, illustrator. From a cover of *Wrestling Sturbridge* by Rich Wallace. Alfred A. Knopf, 1997. Cover photo © 1997 Mike Valeri/FPG International. Reproduced by permission of Alfred A. Knopf, Inc. / Erickson, Jim, illustrator. From a cover of *Shots on Goal* by Rich Wallace. Alfred A. Knopf, 1998. Cover photo © 1998 TSM/Jim Erickson. Reproduced by permission of Alfred A. Knopf, Inc. / Wallace, Rich, photograph. Reproduced by permission.

TIM WINTON. Garvey, Robert, photographer. From a cover of *Shallows* by Tim Winton. Graywolf Press, 1993. Reproduced by permission of Robert Garvey. / Rothfeld, Steven, illustrator. From a cover of *Blueback: A Contemporary Fable* by Tim Winton. Scribner, 1997. Copyright © 1997 by Tim Winton. Reproduced by permission of Scribner, an imprint of Simon & Schuster Macmillan. / Kroninger, Stephen, illustrator. From a cover of *Lockie Leonard, Scumbuster* by Tim Winton. Margaret K. McElderry Books, 1999. Jacket illustration copyright © 1999 by Stephen Kroninger. Reproduced by permission of the illustrator. / Winton, Tim, photograph by Trish Ainslie and Roger Garwood. Reproduced by permission.

Cumulative Index

Author/Artist Index

The following index gives the number of the volume in which an author/artist's biographical sketch appears.